Bayern

New Highlight 5

Cornelsen

New Highlight Bayern, Band 5

Im Auftrage des Verlages erarbeitet von
Raymond Williams, York

Auf Grundlage der ursprünglichen Ausgabe ENGLISH H • Highlight, Band 5
(herausgegeben und erarbeitet von Roderick Cox, Aachen • Raymond Williams, York)

Verlagsredaktion
Susanne Döpper (Projektleitung) • Grit Ellen Sellin (verantwortliche Redakteurin)
Eva Baumgart • Stefanie Dalhoff • Natasha Doerrie • Oliver Gascoigne

Anhang
Ingrid Raspe, Düsseldorf

Beratende Mitwirkung
Petra Fiedler, Forchheim • Kunigunde Fraas, Würzburg • Martina Goßler, Bayreuth
Roman Kofler, Gaißach • Sonja Sonnauer, Postau • Hella Tinis-Faur, Bad Kissingen
Petra Würschinger, Regensburg

Illustration
Carlos Borrell, Berlin • Moritz Friedrich, Berlin • Jeongsook Lee, Köln • Andy Peters, Norfolk

Umschlaggestaltung
Klein & Halm Grafikdesign, Berlin, unter Verwendung eines Fotos von Avenue Images / Fancy

Layoutkonzept
Christoph Schall

Layout und technische Umsetzung
Heike Freund, Hameln

Begleitende Tonträger zu diesem Band
Text-CDs zum Schülerbuch
ISBN 978-3-464-34444-6

www.cornelsen.de

1. Auflage, 3. Druck 2013

Alle Drucke dieser Auflage sind inhaltlich unverändert
und können im Unterricht nebeneinander verwendet werden.

Druck: Stürtz GmbH, Würzburg

ISBN 978-3-464-34443-9

Inhalt gedruckt auf säurefreiem Papier aus nachhaltiger Forstwirtschaft.

INHALT

[] 1. Vorkommen von Strukturen, die nur verstanden werden sollen (rezeptive Strukturen)
* wahlfreie Bestandteile des Lehrwerks (fakultativ)

[] 1. Vorkommen von Strukturen, die nur verstanden werden sollen (rezeptive Strukturen)

* wahlfreie Bestandteile des Lehrwerks (fakultativ)

Unit 5 A better life

ANHANG

(Ohr-Symbol)	Als Hörtext oder Song auf der CD vorhanden
1 2	= CD 1, Track 2.
▸ W 1	Workbook, Übung 1 der Unit
●	schwierige Aufgabe

[] 1. Vorkommen von Strukturen, die nur verstanden werden sollen (rezeptive Strukturen)
* wahlfreie Bestandteile des Lehrwerks (fakultativ)

What's in book 5?

5 UNITS

English around the world; life in South Africa, Canada and Australia

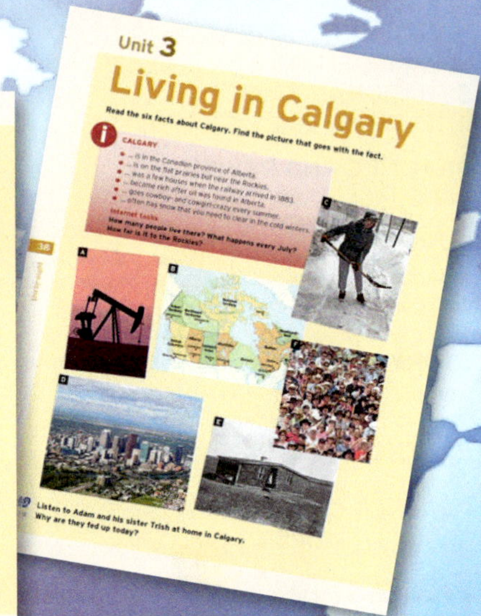

+ 5 STORIES

About the past, present ... and the future

+ 2 MAGAZINES

Fun and facts about Canada and Australia

How will it help you?

SPEAKING

- situations
- useful words and phrases
- helping people, partner work
- giving a talk

LISTENING

- dialogues and songs
- podcasts
- radio programmes
- information

READING

- magazines
- stories
- Internet pages
- adverts

WRITING

- emails
- letters
- picture stories
- making notes

Welcome to New Highlight 5!

Unit 1

English around the world

Look at the pictures from a video podcast for travellers. What country did the British tourists in the podcast visit?

1 ◉ 2 **Look at the photos and listen to the podcast about the visit. How did the tourists travel in the city?**

AND YOU?

Do you sometimes download podcasts?
How/When do you listen to them?
What kinds of podcasts do you think are most interesting?

1 3 When Hannah and Jerry were in South Africa last year they stayed at backpacker hostels. They took these photos at one hostel.

The other backpackers came from all over the world, but they all spoke English together. Can you work out which countries they come from?

Canada **South Africa** **Israel** **Australia**

We're a big country but English is our only official language. It sounds different to British or American English. Its nickname is *Strine*.

Back home we have two big official languages – French and English. Signs are sometimes in both languages.

We have eleven official languages in our country! English is one of them. About half of the white people have it as their first language.

English isn't an official language in our country, but we learn it at school. A lot of people speak it with foreigners.

What's in the photos? What's happening?

- Make notes about a picture.
- Use your notes and talk about a picture.

Four young backpackers are sitting at a table. They're eating and ...

– 4 backpackers
– sitting
– table
– eating

▸ W 1

ENGLISH IS SPOKEN AROUND THE WORLD

- Some people speak it as their first language.
- In some countries it's an official language – sometimes with other languages.
- In many other countries English is understood, and English is often needed at work.
- English is often useful when you are on holiday in countries all over the world.

Can you think of countries where English is spoken by most people?
Where have you heard English in Germany? When? Who used it?

PRESENTATION

A–B
1 ◎ 4, 5

A Delani lives in the south of Johannesburg.
It's a South African township. It's called Soweto. He's 15.
He doesn't go to school. He finished a few months ago.
His language is Zulu, but he speaks some English.

DELANI
Lots of cool things happen in Joburg. Kwaito music comes from here. It's the beat of the street.
People call it the South African hip hop. My friends and I all love Kwaito music. We listen to it on YFM radio.
And we sometimes go to Kwaito concerts, with thousands of other kids. My cousin, Funani, is a fan too.
She also lives with our family now.

FUNANI
I still go to school. I like Joburg, but people don't always find life easy here. They have a lot of crime and other problems like drugs and street violence.
I was born in a village. Our village was very quiet.
I came here a few months ago. My mother died of AIDS last year. A lot of young people here suffer from AIDS. They're born with the illness.

CHECKPOINT

***simple present:* was immer der Fall ist oder immer wieder (nicht) geschieht:**
Delani **lives** in South Africa. He **doesn't go** to school.
▸ Summary, p.18

Exercise 1: Choose the right form of the *simple present*.

1 People in Soweto (speak/speaks) different languages.
2 Delani (don't speak / doesn't speak) English at home.
3 Funani (don't come / doesn't come) from Joburg.
4 A lot of poor people (live/lives) in Soweto.
5 But now some rich people (live/lives) there too.
6 Most tourists (don't stay / doesn't stay) in Soweto.
7 Nelson Mandela's old house (stand/stands) in Soweto.

Exercise 2: Write about YFM radio – a popular radio station in South Africa.

1 YFM radio often plays	about drugs and problems in the cities.
2 Kwaito describes	some African languages, not only English.
3 You hear	to its programmes at http://www.yworld.co.za.
4 The songs tell	Kwaito music.
5 Teenagers also buy	magazines about Kwaito music and fashions.
6 Some fans listen	the life of young people.

Y™ FM99.2 YONA KE YONA

▸ W 2, 3

B

Amy Davis has put some new photos on her homepage.
Click here to view her homepage and blog.

Welcome to Amy's homepage!

This is Saturday at our lovely new home in the north of Johannesburg.
Here we're spending an afternoon in the garden.
Some friends are visiting us.
We're having a *braai*.
That's what a barbecue is called in South Africa.
It's an Afrikaans word.

We're cooking ostrich steaks today.
We're eating salad and other things too.
Two of the boys are making some drinks for us.

This December is so hot in Joburg. Tom is cooling off in the pool.
(He's drinking lemonade, by the way. He isn't drinking a cocktail!)

Dad isn't enjoying the braai with us.
He's working today. So he isn't in the pictures.
He's fitting a security fence for a neighbour.
His new firm is doing OK. The work is keeping Dad really busy.
Lots of people in this part of Joburg are buying security fences at the moment.
This is one of his cars.

CHECKPOINT

present progressive: **was gerade (z.B. auf einem Foto) geschieht:**

The family **is spending** this afternoon in the garden. We**'re drinking** lemonade.

▸ Summary, p.18

Exercise 3: Write information for Amy's homepage. What's happening in the photos?

1 My brothers	is cooking	themselves in the garden.
2 Some friends	are lying	the afternoon with us.
3 Mum	isn't spending	ostrich steaks for us.
4 A few boys	are eating	ostrich steaks with salad.
5 Some of us	are enjoying	in the sun.
6 Dad	are spending	the afternoon with us.

Exercise 4: Answer the questions about Amy's photos.

1 What's the family doing on Saturday?
2 What are they eating?
3 What's Tom drinking?
4 Why isn't Amy's dad in the photos?
5 What's he fitting?
6 Why is his firm so busy?

▸ W 4, 5

LISTENING – English around the world

1 6–8

1 Song: The lion sleeps tonight

1 Before you listen: Look at the name of the song. What continent do you think it's from?
2 Read the questions. Then listen to the song for the answers.
a) Is the song about life in the country or the city?
b) Is the song for a child at night or for men who are looking for wild animals?
c) Is all the song in English?

2 Carl and Linda are buying things for a weekend camping trip in Canada.

1 Before you listen: Can you think what things Carl and Linda will perhaps need?
2 Read the sentences. Then listen to the scene and decide: true or false?
a) They're looking for a tent.
b) Linda isn't sure about camping.
c) They're planning a trip to the north.

3 This weather report is on the radio.

1 Before you listen: Which four words do you think will be in this report?

→ sunny • nurse • temperature • crisps • fine • degrees

2 Read the sentences. Then listen to the report for the right details.
a) The report is for Sydney/Cape Town.
b) Today it'll be 10/15/25 degrees.
c) Sunday will be sunny/wet.

▸W 6–8

READING – Notices in a hostel

1 Read the notices on page 13. Find the right ending from the texts.

1 You can make breakfast ... a) in your room. b) in the kitchen.
2 The assistant will ... a) do lots of different jobs. b) cook breakfasts.
3 With *Baz Bus* you need only one ... a) backpack. b) ticket.

2 Write the sentence in the text that tells you ...

1 ... how you book a bus to the airport.
2 ... how much it costs to go online.
3 ... how long the assistant's job is for.

3 True, false or not in the text?

1 You can buy a souvenir at the hostel.
2 The hostel sells tickets for a bus service.
3 The barbecue on Saturdays is free.
4 Stay one night for the free airport bus.

4 Dictionary work

Look up these words in your dictionary. What do they mean in the text here?

1 swap 2 pick up 3 access 4 convenient 5 flyers

▸W 9

Lion House Hostel

Your fun place in Cape Town

Welcome to Lion House

- ***Breakfast*** From 8 to 11 a.m. Or make your own in the guest kitchen.
- ***Internet*** Access is no problem. Internet rates are only R8 an hour.
- ***Money*** We can swap your US dollars, pounds and euros for rand.
- ***Braai*** We have a barbecue every Saturday near the swimming pool.
- ***Airport*** If you stay three nights here, we pick you up or take you to the airport for free. Ask at the desk the night before.
- ***Trips*** Ask at the desk for ideas: shark cage diving, township tours, adventure tours, safaris. Or see the flyers in the TV lounge.

Need some extra pocket money?

Assistant wanted
You'll help around the hostel with jobs like cleaning, working in the garden, serving breakfasts. Minimum time is two weeks, but we prefer longer. Pay by the hour. Interested? See Gary at the desk.

Why not get a Lion House T-shirt ?

Sizes L and XL.
Different colours.
In the pool shop.

Great souvenir!

BAZ BUS
HOP-ON HOP-OFF SOUTH AFRICA DOOR-TO-DOOR!

- Baz Bus offers independent travellers and backpackers a flexible and safe way to explore South Africa.
- With your Baz Bus ticket in hand, you can hop on and off as often as you like along the route.
- You are picked up and dropped off at the door of your backpacker hostel.
- There are over 180 hostels to select from and more than 40 cities, towns and villages to visit en route!

Check out our website: www.bazbus.com

Ask at the desk for tickets and more information.

Lost
Small World guide book "South Africa".
If you find it, please leave it at the desk.
Cheers, Carol

SPEAKING – Talking to people

Einen Fremden ansprechen
Excuse me.
Can you help me, please?
Perhaps I can help you?

Verständnisschwierigkeiten
Pardon?
I'm sorry. I don't understand.
I don't understand that word.
Can you say that again, please?
Can you speak more slowly, please?

Rückfragen
Walk down Grove Street?

Wortprobleme
I'm sorry. I don't know the English word for it.
I mean a ticket there and back /
something with the times of the trains / ...
I mean this/these here.
One/Some of these, please.

I'd like a hot dog. But without those ...
– *Without onions?*
That's right.
– *Would you like mustard?*
Sorry. I don't understand that word.
– *This?*
Oh yes, please.

We're looking for the museum with the famous pictures.
– *Oh, you mean the art gallery? Walk down Grove Street.*
Walk down Grove Street? Thank you.

SITUATIONS

1 Wie sagst du das auf Englisch?

1 Können Sie mir bitte behilflich sein?
2 Können Sie das bitte noch einmal sagen?
3 Ich kenne das englische Wort leider nicht.
4 Eins von diesen, bitte.

2 Was würdest du sagen, wenn ...

1 ... ein südafrikanischer Kellner sehr schnell spricht?
2 ... ein israelischer Tourist im Zeitungsgeschäft kein Deutsch kann?
3 ... du nicht verstanden hast, ob der Bus um 4.15 oder 4.50 abfährt?
4 ... du nachfragen willst, ob es Schülerkarten zu ermäßigten Preisen gibt?

● 3 Du kennst das englische Wort nicht. Versuche, es zu umschreiben.

Example: Stadtführer – *a book with information about the city / something about this city / ...*

1 Ein Netzteil für dein Handy
2 Tabletten gegen Kopfschmerzen
3 Eine Umhängetasche
4 Ein Satz Spielkarten
5 Dir ist schlecht.
6 Eine Umkleidekabine

▸ W 10

SCENE

1 **What can you do at the reception in a hotel or hostel?**

2 **Talk about the photo at a hostel in Cape Town. These questions will help.**

- Who's in the photo?
- What are the people wearing?
- Who are they talking to?
- What are they carrying?
- Where are the people standing?

1 9

3 **What things are the couple asking about?**

MAN Hi there, guys.
PIERRE Hi. Say, can we use the Internet? We need to check our emails.
MAN Fine. You'll find computers over there.
PIERRE How much is it?
MAN R8 an hour.
RINA Are there some good day trips here?
MAN How about watching elephants? Or a township tour? Or the beach?
PIERRE The beach sounds boring.
MAN Not with sharks! You can go shark cage diving. Here's a leaflet.

PARTNER WORK

Interpreting practice: Work with two other partners. Then change your roles.

Partner A: You don't speak English. Look at page 84.
Partner B: You must help A and C. Look at this page.
Partner C: You don't speak German. Look at page 87.

Dialogue 1: At a reception in a hostel

PARTNER A ⇨ YOU

PARTNER C ⇨ YOU

...

● **Dialogue 2: At a snack bar**

PARTNER A ⇨ YOU

PARTNER C ⇨ YOU

...

Tipp:
Achte darauf, dass die Pronomen geändert werden müssen:
I'd like ...
Sie/Er möchte ....

► W 11

LANGUAGE

1 Radio YFM is at a Kwaito concert. What's Chubi saying about the concert?

isn't singing • is coming • are playing • is happening • is going
are helping • aren't getting • are dancing • are having

1 Welcome to the *One Nation* concert. The concert ... at Johannesburg Stadium.
2 Today the bands ... any money. The stars ... to help children who have AIDS.
3 At the moment a lot of teenagers ... to the music.
4 The money from their tickets ... to important AIDS projects.
5 So the fans ... fun and they ... children too.
6 But one star ... his latest hit now. – Because E'Smile ... to us!

2 On safari: Choose the right form: *simple present* or *present progressive*.

1 *(visit / are visiting)* The tourists in this photo ... South Africa. Thousands of tourists ... South Africa every year. Tourists often ... Kruger Park.
2 *(travel / are travelling)* Many tourists ... on safaris. These tourists ... to a national park.
3 *(look for / are looking for)* The tourists in the photo ... wild animals. Tourists always ... animals. They usually ... lions.
4 *(drives / is driving)* Jim ... every day. Today Jim ... to a lake.
5 *(meet / are meeting)* Elephants often ... at the lake. Perhaps they ... there today.

• 3 Finish the article. Put in the *simple present* verb.

call • hate • know • play • record • say • sing (2x) • sound

Kwaito – real South African Music
People sometimes ... that Kwaito is the voice of black youth. It ... like an African form of American House music. First the bands ... the music in a studio. Then at concerts they ... the recording and only ... the words. In South Africa a white person sometimes ... a black person *kaffir*. Black people ... that. On an early album Arthur Mafokate ... *Don't call me kaffir*. Most young black South Africans ... the words of that song.

► W 12, 13

4 Word pool: Put the tourism words in three groups.

apartment • caravan • climb • fly • guide book • hike • hostel
hotel • house • map • pay • postcard • ride • skate • snack
swim • souvenir • tent • ticket • travel • wait • walk

Find words for ...

- what tourists do:
  climb, ...
- where tourists stay:
  apartment, ...
- what tourists buy at kiosks:
  guide book, ...

► W 14

WRITING

- Wenn man etwas erzählen will, verwendet man meist *simple past*-Formen.
- Oftmals fangen Sätze mit Zeitangaben an, z. B: *Last week ..., One day ..., Later ..., After that ...*

1 Look at the picture. Choose the right sentences and tell the story.

Südafrika
- Last year Heike and Alex went to South Africa.
- Next year Heike and Alex will visit South Africa.

Reisemittel
- They had a car to travel round the country.
- They travelled around the country by bus.

Unterkunft
- They stayed at backpacker hostels.
- They stayed at expensive hotels with other tourists.

2 Look at the picture. Can you write the story?

Kaufhaus
Tina / was / a / Last week / department store / in / in Germany

Tourist
English / tourist / An / spoke / to / the / assistant

Verkäufer
tourist / The / didn't understand / assistant / the / foreign

Hilfe
them / Tina / spoke / English / so / helped / she

3 Look at the picture. Can you write the story?

Urlaub Last week Dave ...

Flughafen He travelled to ... and waited ...

An Bord gehen Then the passengers began ...

Pässe und Bordkarten They showed ...

Kein Pass But Dave ...

● 4 Look at the picture in Exercise 3. Write the rest of the story.

Daves Gefühle **Pass finden** **Boden** **Schalter** **Ausgang**

Dave felt ... Then a passenger ...

► W 15, 16

SUMMARY

Die Gegenwartsformen (Wiederholung)

Es gibt zwei Möglichkeiten, über Handlungen in der Gegenwart zu sprechen:

Lisa **plays** football.

Hier erfährst du nur, dass sie Fußball spielt, nicht ob sie im Moment spielt. Diese Form nennt man *simple present* (die einfache Gegenwartsform).

Lisa **is playing** football.

Hier spielt sie gerade, in diesem Augenblick. Diese Form nennt man *present progressive* (die Verlaufsform der Gegenwart).

Bildung

So sehen die beiden Gegenwartsformen aus:

simple present

- Aussagen
  Tom **reads** *Teen* magazine.
  I **eat** cornflakes for breakfast.
- Fragen
  Does Tom **read** *Teen* magazine?
  Do you **eat** cornflakes for breakfast?
- Verneinungen
  Tom **doesn't read** *Teen* magazine.
  I **don't eat** cornflakes for breakfast.

present progressive

Tom **is reading** *Teen* magazine.
I'm eating cornflakes.

Is Tom **reading** *Teen* magazine?
Are you **eating** cornflakes?

Tom **isn't reading** *Teen* magazine.
I'm not eating cornflakes.

Gebrauchsbeispiele

Du gebrauchst die Gegenwartsformen in solchen Fällen:

simple present

- Über Gewohnheiten sprechen:
  I go to town on Saturdays.
- Über ein Hobby sprechen:
  I ride a mountain bike.
- Fragen, ob jemand etwas (oft) macht:
  Do you read comics?
- Über das Klima sprechen:
  It rains a lot in Manchester.
- Einen Tagesablauf beschreiben:
  I have a wash at 7 a.m.

present progressive

- Sagen, was du gerade tust, etwa am Handy:
  I'm just going to town.
- Ein Bild oder Foto beschreiben:
  Dad is riding a mountain bike.
- Fragen, was jemand gerade tut:
  Are you reading a new book?
- Sagen, wie das Wetter jetzt ist:
  I'm so wet! **It's raining** cats and dogs!
- Sagen, was jemand gerade tut:
  Where's Tom? – **He's having** a wash.

Typische Zeitangaben

simple present

every day/week/...
on Mondays/Tuesdays/...
often • usually • sometimes
never • always

present progressive

at the moment • just • now

IN DIESER UNIT HAST DU WIEDERHOLT, WIE ...

... du sagst, was oft oder manchmal geschieht.	▸ We sometimes go to Kwaito concerts.
... du sagst, was normalerweise der Fall ist.	▸ Del lives in Johannesburg. Cool things happen in Joburg.
... du sagst, was gerade geschieht.	▸ Dad is working today. Tom is drinking lemonade.
... du etwas erzählst.	▸ I went on holiday. I went to Spain. We travelled by bus. The hostel was great.

DU KANNST AUCH VERSTEHEN, ...

... was gesprochen wird.	▸ English is spoken in Australia.
... wie etwas genannt wird.	▸ It's called Kwaito.
... wo jemand geboren ist.	▸ I was born in a village.

▸ EXAM PRACTICE p. 90

▸ W Test yourself 1–4

STORY 1

What's a hero for you?

My hero – Nelson Mandela

Competition

Who's your hero and why?

Write and tell us about your hero.
Win 1000 US dollars!
Texts can be about a famous person (David Beckham, Hillary Clinton) or you can write about somebody who isn't famous – your teacher, your mum, for example.
Send your text to …

Robert saw a competition in a magazine for young people.
"A thousand dollars!" he thought.
"I'd like to travel when I finish school!"
So he searched on the Internet and decided to write a text about Nelson Mandela.

Before 1994 black people in South Africa weren't allowed to do the same things as white people. They lived in different areas, went to different schools and they couldn't vote! This system was called "apartheid". Nelson Mandela wanted a better life for black people. He fought the unfair system. He has had a very interesting and difficult life. This is his story:

The boy from the village

Mandela was born in a small village in South Africa in 1918. After school he went to university to study law but he left at the end of the first year. Mandela moved to Johannesburg and got a job there. Later he started working in a law firm. He helped poor black people with their problems and finished his studies at the same time.

The political fighter

From 1952 he also began to help the African National Congress (ANC) – a political organisation against apartheid. First they organised protests to try to stop the unfair system. But Nelson Mandela thought that protests were not enough. The ANC started a campaign against the government that was not peaceful and many people died. In 1962 Mandela was sent to prison on Robben Island for life.

Mandela in prison

Life in prison was very hard. Mandela could only have one visitor and one letter every six months. Mandela was strong. He read books and wrote his biography.

More and more South Africans didn't want the apartheid system any more and many black people joined the ANC protests. People all over the world said the system in South Africa should change and Mandela must be freed. There were big concerts and protests in many countries. In 1989 South Africa got a new president, F.W. de Klerk, who believed that apartheid was wrong. In 1990 Mandela was freed after 27 years in prison!

The first black President

In 1994 everybody in South Africa, black and white, voted together for the first time. Mandela became the first black President of South Africa. He worked to bring all South Africans together. In 1993 Nelson Mandela and F.W. de Klerk won the Nobel Peace Prize for their work. Mandela is very popular. There are many films, songs and books about him. He has helped people to understand that skin colour is not important. He's my hero because he has shown that one person can change the world.

Robert took his article to the post office and began to dream of his journey to South Africa ...

By Donald Maxwell

▸ W 17, 18

Unit 2

We aren't Americans!

Look at the pictures about a country. What country is it? What do the pictures show?

Vancouver

The Canadian flag

The Rockies

The Prairies

The Mounties

Ice hockey

Quebec

Inuit people

Polar bears

Choose a picture and talk to the class about it. The notes will help you.

Vancouver	exciting, modern • on the west coast • near the Rockies
The Canadian flag	red and white • maple leaf • became flag in 1965
The Rockies	full name "The Rocky Mountains" • west • Canada to Mexico
The Prairies	grassland • very flat • very big farms • also oil
The Mounties	"Royal Canadian Mounted Police" • red uniform • sometimes ride horses
Ice hockey	very popular • national sport • is usually just called "hockey"
Quebec	biggest province • in the east of Canada • French is spoken
Inuit people	aboriginal people • the Arctic • own territory "Nunavut"
Polar bears	white bears • the Arctic • sometimes near towns in the north

Listen to the dialogue in a Canadian family. Why has Matt put a flag on his backpack?

1 11

How much do you know about Canada? Try this quiz. Then check your answers.

Canada – USA quiz

A True or false?

1. The USA has almost ten times more people than Canada.
2. Canada uses US dollars.
3. Canada is a younger country than the USA.
4. Canada has more time zones than the continental USA.
5. Both countries have a president.
6. Canada celebrates the Fourth of July.

B Which country – Canada or the USA?

1. It's the bigger country.
2. It uses kilometres, not miles.
3. It has the world's biggest shopping mall.
4. It has the highest immigration rate in the world.
5. It celebrated the first Thanksgiving Day, in 1578.
6. These stars were born there:

Nelly Furtado

Bryan Adams

Keanu Reeves

Celine Dion

Check your answers on page 93.

CANADA

- ... is the second biggest country in the world.
- ... sells oil, gas, uranium and electricity to the USA.
- ... has 34 ethnic groups.
- ... has three groups of aboriginal people: First Nations, Métis and Inuit (in the Arctic).
- ... welcomes immigrants from all over the world.
  The biggest groups today come from China and India.

Internet tasks

What's the capital of Canada?
What's the population of Canada?
What's the largest city in Canada?
Find out the distance from Toronto to Vancouver.

▸W 1–3

A–B
1 12, 13

A

We live in Canada

Megan Handke

My grandfather came here from Germany in 1955. He wanted a better life, I guess. He has lived in Calgary for years. Mom's family came here from Scotland a long time ago. They've lived in Canada for over 150 years.

Jake Androssof

My folks came here from Russia in 1899. They came because they wanted religious freedom. We've been here for over a hundred years now.

Jill Wei

We're new Canadians. We've lived in Vancouver for two years. My parents and I came here from China. I've worked here as a scientist for a year.

Jassim Ali

I've been in Canada for some months. I left Iraq because of war in my country. I went to other countries first, but now I've lived in Toronto for almost a year.

Carmen Popescu

I came here from Romania. I live in Toronto. I've lived here for five years. I'm a web designer at a computer company now. I've worked here for a year. I came here to get a better job.

CHECKPOINT

Mit dem *present perfect* und *for* kannst du sagen, wie lange etwas geschieht:
Dan **has lived** in Canada **for** a long time. The Weis **have been** here **for** two years.
▸ Summary, p. 32

Exercise 1: How long have they been in Canada?

1 Megan's grandfather			five years.
2 Jill and her parents	has lived in Canada		over 50 years.
3 The Androssofs	have lived in Canada	for	two years.
4 Carmen			some months.
5 Jassim			over a hundred years.

Exercise 2: How long have you done these things? Write about yourself.

1 I've been at this school for ... years.
2 My family has lived in ... for ...
3 I've learned English for ...
4 My favourite singer is ... I've liked him/her for ...
5 I'm wearing a ... I've had it for about ...

▸ W 4

B

The first Canadians

People have lived in Canada for thousands of years.

First Nation Canadians

At first Europeans called these people "Indians". Now they are called "First Nations". People have called them this since the 1980s.
About 600,000 of them live in Canada today.
European settlers came to Canada in the 17th century.
The settlers brought new illnesses. They killed the animals that the native people hunted. In 1763 special reserves were made for the First Nations. Today about half of them still live on these reserves.

The Métis

The children of the foreign settlers and native people were called the Métis.
There have been Métis since the 17th century.
About 300,000 Métis live in modern Canada.
Their culture is a mixture of First Nation and French Canadian.

Inuit

The Inuit people live in the Arctic parts of Canada.
They've lived there since about the year 1000. They first came to Canada from Alaska around a thousand years ago.
Now only 45,000 Inuit live in Canada. A new Inuit territory, Nunavut, was created in 1999. In the 1960s some schools were started for the children.
The traditional life of the Inuit people was one of hunting and fishing. Now they have other jobs too, though some also still hunt.
They travel by boat, by dog sled or by skidoo – a kind of snowmobile.

For centuries, life for the Inuit and First Nations stayed the same. But since other people have arrived in Canada, life has become different. Over the last two hundred years, contact with other people, technology – and now climate change – have changed the way of life. They now have many social and medical problems.

CHECKPOINT

Mit dem *present perfect* und *since* kannst du sagen, seit wann etwas geschieht:
Nunavut **has been** a territory **since** 1999. There **have been** Inuit schools **since** the 1960s.

▸ Summary, p.32

Exercise 3: The first Canadian people. Finish the information with the right time phrase.

→ about the year 1000 • 1999 • the 17th century • 1763 • the 1960s • the 1980s

1 Inuit people have been in Canada since *about the year 1000.*
2 European settlers have lived in Canada since ...
3 There have been reserves since ...
4 Canada has used the name "First Nations" since ...
5 Nunavut has been a Canadian territory since ...
6 There have been Inuit schools since ...

▸ W 5

LISTENING – At a Canadian museum

1 ◉ 14, 15

1 Outside the museum

1 Before you listen: What do you think Simon and Beth must buy at the museum?

2 Read the questions. Then listen to the dialogue for the answers.

- **a)** What's the museum about? (Calgary. / The Gold Rush. / First Nation people.)
- **b)** How much are their tickets? ($1. / $1.50. / $3.)
- **c)** What costs $1? (A guide book. / An audio guide. / A postcard.)

2 The museum audio guide

1 Before you listen: Look at the pictures and the sentences. What's the guide about?

2 Listen to the three parts of the museum audio guide. Find out: true or false?

Part one:

a) The Yukon is very big.
b) The Yukon had big cities.

Part two:

a) 100,000 men found gold.
b) Dawson City was soon big.

Part three:

a) The Yukon had no police.
b) Mounties are police.

▸ W 6, 7

READING – From a teenage magazine

1 Read the article on page 27. Then give short answers.

1 When did Steve go on the trip?

2 How many students went on the trip?

3 How many trips are there in a year?

2 Find the sentence in the article that tells you this.

1 The trip wasn't a quiet holiday.

2 How long they've had Arctic trips.

3 The trips are expensive.

3 Find the right ending for each sentence.

1 The magazine wrote an article because ...
- **a)** it sells holidays.
- **b)** it was a reader's idea.

2 Trips start in Ottawa because ...
- **a)** it's near Churchill.
- **b)** that's where the company is.

3 The Arctic is changing because ...
- **a)** the climate is changing.
- **b)** more people live there now.

4 Dictionary work

Look up these words in your dictionary. What do they mean here? Give the German word.

1 backyard **2** bridge **3** corporation **4** ecosystem **5** wheelchair

▸ W 8

COOL CANADA *readers' page* – where you tell us what we should write about

STUDENTS ON ICE
·expeditions·
ANTARCTICA · ARCTIC
www.studentsonice.com

In our own backyard

Exploring the wilderness – a Canadian tradition

Hi guys,

I'd like you to write about **Students on Ice**. I went on one of their expeditions last year and it was fantastic. We travelled round Hudson Bay on a real ice-breaker, saw polar bears, seals and whales. We met and talked to some Inuit and they told us about their lives. We learned so much about life in the Arctic.

I had lots of fun on the ship, played Inuit games, swam in one-degree water, visited the bridge at night ...

We also worked hard. It wasn't a lazy vacation. But it was a real adventure. And I made some great friends.

Sincerely,

Steve Duncan (16)

PS Great mag! I look forward to it every month!

How about visiting the Arctic this summer? Yes, you read right – the Arctic! That's what our reader Steve Duncan from Toronto did last year. And guess what – it was a *cool* trip! (Yeah, enough of the bad jokes ...) His letter reminded us of the adventures of earlier Canadians, so we thought we should find out more ...

Steve travelled with *Students on Ice*, a company based near Ottawa that has organised trips by ship for around ten years now. The expeditions were started by two young Canadians – Geoff Green and Angela Holmes. They wanted to help people to understand our planet better and to have more respect for it.

On board

Steve spent 15 days on the ship with 70 students from different countries between 14–19, as well as thirty scientists. Their trip began at the company's home in Ottawa and then the group flew the 2000km to Churchill. By ship from there they travelled around Hudson Bay.
Each year there's a trip, but to different places in the far north.

The money

The trips aren't cheap of course. They cost over $7000. Students usually find sponsors to help pay for the trip. They write to large corporations, local firms, to newspapers and radio stations. They also do part-time jobs or buy and sell things.

Expect ice

During the expedition they do activities and learn from experts about life in the Arctic. You won't see much snow in an Arctic summer except in the far north. But you can expect lots of rocks, mud and ice. So many things are changing in the Arctic because of global warming. There's less snow now. You get to see the impact of climate change on the ecosystem and the people and animals that live there. – And it's all in our own backyard!

Next week: Life with an illness for a teenager who uses a wheelchair.

COOL CANADA magazine

SPEAKING – Talking about activities in the past

Einen Bericht einleiten:
I'd like to tell you about a holiday/school trip/party/bike trip/ ...

Sagen, wann etwas geschah:
It was in June / last year / ...
It was two days ago / two years ago.
We went last month / two years ago / ...

Sagen, wo etwas geschah:
We went/flew/travelled/drove/rode to ...
We stayed at ...

Sagen, was geschehen ist:
We played/swam/hiked/met/visited/ate/looked at ...
Then ... / After that ...

Sagen, wie etwas war:
It was a quiet/lively/interesting/boring/cool place.
I thought it was too hot/wet/quiet/...
I thought it was great.
I really enjoyed myself. / I didn't really enjoy myself.

Fragen, die man dir stellt:
When did you go?
Where did you go?
What did you do?
What did you think about it?
Did you enjoy it?

I'd like to tell you about my holiday. I went to a great hotel in Italy. On the first night I found a great restaurant. I ate pizza and ...

I saw Orlando Bloom at the weekend!
– Where did you see him?
– When did you see him?
– What did you do?
– Did you speak to him?

SITUATIONS

1 Wie sagst du das auf Englisch?

1 Hat es dir gefallen?
2 Es war vor zwei Jahren.
3 Wir sind nach Spanien geflogen.
4 Mir hat es wirklich gut gefallen.

2 Was würdest du sagen?

1 Du willst jemanden fragen, wann sie/er in den Urlaub gefahren ist.
2 Du willst jemandem über eine Radtour berichten.
3 Du willst sagen, dass du mit deiner Familie nach Österreich gefahren bist.
4 Du willst jemanden fragen, ob ihr/ihm die Party letzte Woche gefallen hat.
5 Du willst sagen, dass deinen Eltern euer Urlaubsort gefallen hat, dir es aber zu ruhig war.

SCENE

Donna is planning a computer presentation to her school class about a trip.

1 16

1 Donna is practising her talk. Listen.

"I'd like to tell you about my visit to Drumheller, the Dinosaur capital of Canada ...
(slide 1) It was last month. I went there by car with my cousins.
(slide 2) We drove across the prairie. The journey from Calgary took about two hours.
(slide 3) Dinosaurs lived at Drumheller. Scientists found more than 50 animals there.
(slide 4) In the indoor museum we saw the dinosaur bones. The dinosaurs were so big.
(slide 5) Then we walked round the outdoor museum. We looked at the models of dinosaurs.
(slide 6) Later we walked round these strange rocks. They were called hoodoos.
... I hope you like the photos – my cousin Jane took them."

2 Notes on the slides will help Donna when she's giving the talk. Look at the talk. Which phrases belong to slides 3–6?

- rocks – hoodoos
- prairie – two hours
- dinosaurs – over 50 animals
- last month – by car
- outdoor museum – models
- indoor museums – big dinosaurs

► W 9

CLASS REPORT

Talk about a holiday you had or a place that you visited. Can you bring some photos?

- Bei Berichten wird *simple past* als Erzählform gebraucht.
  Last week we went to Canada. We flew to Calgary. My uncle waited for us at the airport.

Step 1	Step 2	Step 3	Step 4
Think of a holiday. ►	**Make notes.** 6–8 things. (The box on page 28 will help you). ►	**Practise your talk.** ►	**Give a talk to the class.**

LANGUAGE

1 Daniel's visit to Calgary last July. Put the verbs in the *simple past* form.

did • didn't know • didn't like • flew • had • started • stayed
took • tried • saw • walked • was • watched • went

My cousins (start) a new life in Canada last year. They (go) to Calgary, near the Rockies. Their first winter (be) very cold and they (have) a lot of snow. At first my cousins (not like) it, but then they (try) some new sports. They (walk) in snowshoes.
In July we (fly) to Calgary and (stay) with them.
My cousins (take) us to the Calgary Stampede. We (see) lots of animals and (watch) the cowboys in a rodeo. They (do) lots of exciting competitions.
I (not know) that there are cowboys in Canada!

► W 10

● 2 An ecard from Churchill. Put in *ago*, *for* or *since*.

for a week: seit (Zeitdauer)
since May: seit (Zeitpunkt)
a year **ago**: vor einem Jahr

Hello everybody,
This polar bear is near Churchill.
(We've been here … Sunday.)
There has been no ice here … June.
It has been warm here … months.
The bears arrived a few days …
They've been here … almost a week.
I took this photo an hour …
We've been on the Internet at the library … a long time.
Now we want to watch some whales!
Love, Jenny

3 It's October in Iqaluit. The winter is beginning. What things have happened this month?

1 days / become / The / colder and shorter / have
2 The tourists / Nunavut / left / have
3 on the sea / has / The ice / back / come
4 away / for / been / Some of the men / have / two weeks
5 for food / animals / have / They / hunted

4 Which flag is it?

British • Canadian • Chinese • French • German
Scottish • South African • Spanish • Welsh

Number 1 is the German flag. Number 2 is the … flag.

Do you know the names of the countries too?

1 Germany 2 …

► W 11–13

WRITING

1 Grüße aus Kanada: Finde aus der E-Mail und E-Karte heraus, wie ...

1 ... du jemandem einen wunderschönen Tag wünschen kannst.
2 ... du dich verabschieden kannst.
3 ... die Anrede in der E-Mail lautet.
4 ... du jemanden an ein Wochenende erinnern kannst.
5 ... du ein Geschenk ankündigst, das du mitgeschickt hast.
6 ... du viel Spaß beim Zuhören wünschen kannst.

Happy 16th birthday!
Hope you have a great day, Daniel.
Love from us all from Canada

From: The Stamp family
Subject: Birthday greetings
To: Daniel Haas

Dear Daniel,
We hope you like the birthday ecard that we have sent you. It was our trip up north. Do you remember that weekend? We took a photo of that big bison on the road. We're sending you a small birthday present. If you open the attachment to this email, you'll find it. You can download some music at the Internet shop. Happy listening!
Love,
The Calgary Gang

2 Daniel is answering the email from Canada. What can he write?

From: Daniel Haas
Subject: re: Birthday greetings
To: The Stamp family

Dear ...
Thank you for ...
I remember ...
Travelling up north was ...
I'm sending you ...
The music for downloading was ...
I'm listening to some of the songs ...
Love from
...

→
- all,
- meeting that big bison.
- sending the nice ecard.
- on my MP3 player now.
- two photos that I took.
- a cool present.
- a fantastic journey.
- Daniel.

● 3 Write an email to your uncle and aunt in Canada. You've been on holiday there.

- Bedanke dich für die E-Karte.
- Das Foto von dem Bären hat dir gefallen.
- Bedanke dich für die wunderbare Reise.
- Das Wochenende in den Rockies hat dir wirklich Spaß gemacht.
- Du schickst einige Fotos von den Bergen und Seen.
- Du wünschst ihnen ein wunderschönes Wochenende.
- Du verabschiedest dich.

Dear ...

► W 14

SUMMARY

present perfect mit *for/since*

- Mit *How long ...?* und der *present perfect*-Form (z. B. *have/has worked, have/has had, have/has been*) kannst du fragen, wie lange etwas geschieht.

How long **have** you **worked** here?
– Oh, about six months.

How long **have** you **had** this MP3 player?
– A week. Do you like it?

- Mit der *present perfect*-Form und *for* kannst du sagen, wie lange etwas geschieht.

Meg **has waited for** twenty minutes.

They'**ve been** on holiday **for** two days.

- Mit der *present perfect*-Form und *since* kannst du sagen, seit wann etwas geschieht.

The shop **has been** open **since** 9 o'clock.

Derek **has lived** in Toronto **since** 2005.

! Im Deutschen wird in solchen Situationen die Gegenwartsform verwendet:

How long have you lived here? Wie lange wohnen Sie hier?
I've been ill all day. Ich bin den ganzen Tag schon krank.
Mr Hill has worked here for years. Mr Hill arbeitet seit Jahren hier.

Die Unterscheidung *for/since*

- *for* verwendest du, wenn es um einen Zeitraum geht.

I've had this bike for two months. Ich habe dieses Rad seit zwei Monaten.
Megan has played hockey for years. Megan spielt seit Jahren Hockey.

Zeitraum – *for*
ten minutes • a week • a long time • years • two months • ...

- *since* verwendest du, wenn es um einen bestimmten Zeitpunkt geht.

We've lived here since 2007. Wir wohnen seit 2007 hier.
Jack has been in hospital since Tuesday. Jack ist seit Dienstag im Krankenhaus.

Zeitpunkt – *since*
2.30 p.m. • Sunday • yesterday • 2006 • October • ...

IN DIESER UNIT HAST DU WIEDERHOLT, WIE ...

... du über die Vergangenheit berichtest. ▸ *They went to Calgary.*
My cousins didn't like it.

DU HAST AUCH GELERNT, WIE ...

... du sagst, wie lange etwas andauert. ▸ *Dave has lived in Canada for ten years.*
... du sagst, seit wann etwas andauert. ▸ *We've been at the airport since 9 a.m.*
... du fragst, wie lange etwas andauert. ▸ *How long have you waited?*
How long have you been at this school?

DU KANNST AUCH VERSTEHEN, ...

... wie etwas genannt wurde. ▸ *It was called "The Gold Rush".*
... wann etwas gemacht wurde. ▸ *The first reserves were made in 1763.*
... von wem etwas getan wurde. ▸ *The company was started by two Canadians.*

▸ EXAM PRACTICE p. 90/91
▸ W Test yourself 1–3

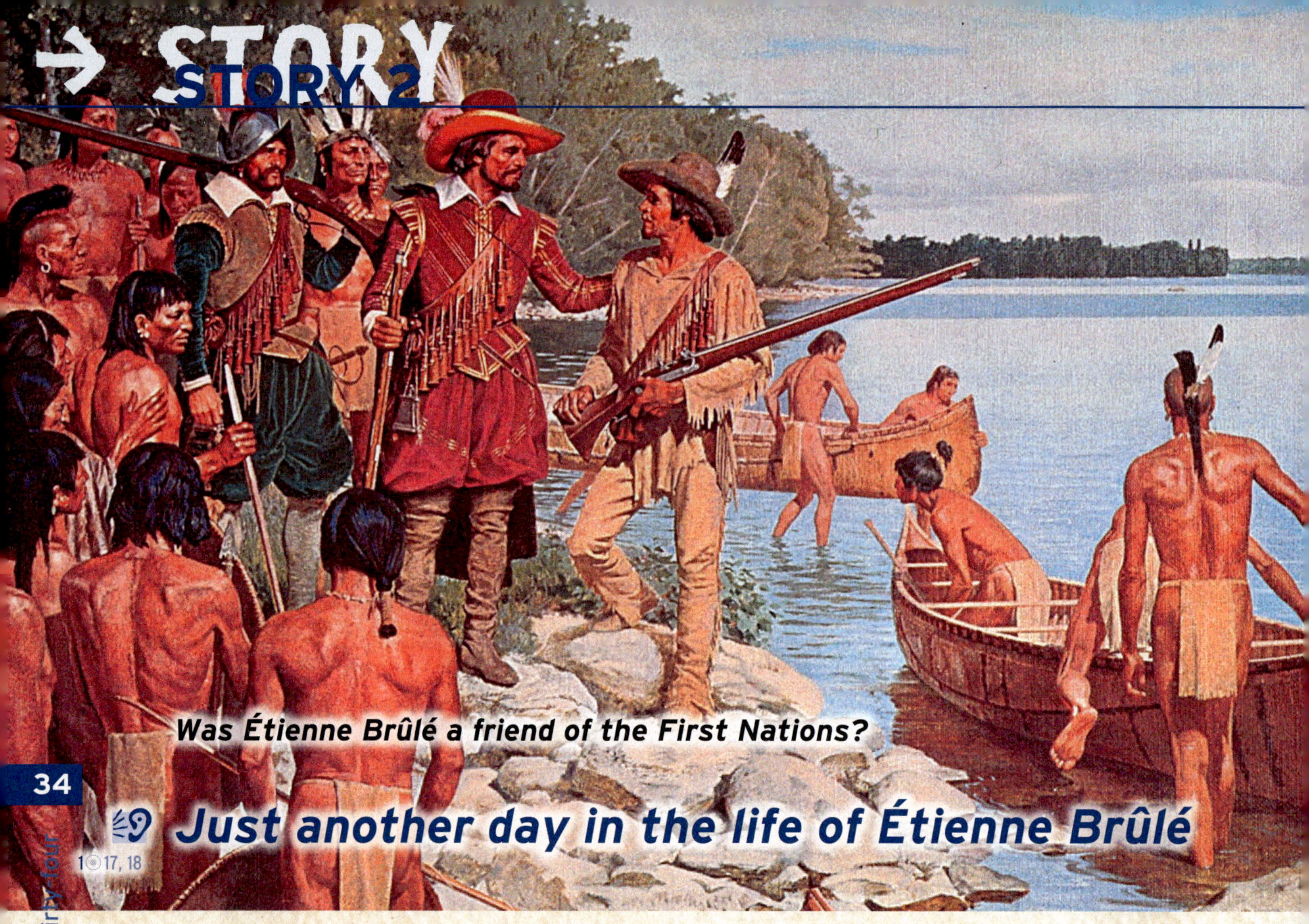

Was Étienne Brûlé a friend of the First Nations?

Just another day in the life of Étienne Brûlé

1 17, 18

Étienne Brûlé (1592–1633) was only 16 when he left his home in France and went to the new colony of Quebec. Quebec was very small, but its governor, Samuel de Champlain, had great plans for it. In 1610 he sent Brûlé to the Huron people because he wanted useful information about the land. Brûlé went on many expeditions and explored the land west of Quebec. But he liked the life with the Hurons. So he left Quebec and lived with the Huron people for over 20 years. He learned their language and way of life. He was also one of the first Europeans who saw the Great Lakes: Lake Huron, Lake Ontario, Lake Erie, and Lake Superior. Some think that Brûlé helped as a guide for the British when they captured Quebec in 1629. A few years later the Huron people killed him. Why? Nobody knows.

A part of Samuel de Champlain's map (1632)

The three Huron and Brûlé paddled their canoe without making any noise. The St. Lawrence River had a strong current. The men were on their way to Quebec and their canoe was full of pelts. They wanted to trade the pelts for guns from the French. The journey from their village to the French fortress in Quebec would take another six days.

They passed some small islands in the middle of the river. This was the most dangerous part of their journey because this was Iroquois territory. The Iroquois didn't like the Huron very much. And they hated the French!

"I don't like this place. Let's paddle faster," Brûlé said. Suddenly one of the Huron heard a noise. He said, "Shh! Be quiet!" They stopped paddling and looked around. They saw a canoe behind them. It was about 300 metres away. It came towards them very quickly and it was full of Iroquois. They looked aggressive. Brûlé and his Huron friends were strong paddlers and paddled as hard as they could. But the other canoe came closer and closer.

Suddenly they heard a gunshot. Brûlé turned around and saw five Iroquois with guns. There were more canoes behind them!

Then he heard another gunshot. The man next to Brûlé screamed. Brûlé saw that the man was injured. He was frightened.

He tried to think what they could do. Then he had an idea. He knew the river very well. He knew that they would get to the rapids of Lachine in a few minutes. That was their only chance. He told his Huron friends about his plan.

Near the rapids the water began to flow much faster. Now the distance between them and the Iroquois was only a few metres. One of the Iroquois pointed his gun at Brûlé. He wanted to shoot but the canoe moved too much. Then Brûlé gave his friends a signal. They suddenly turned the canoe to the left. Their canoe went around a big rock and through the rapids into calm water. This surprised the Iroquois. They tried to turn their canoe to the left but it was too late. There was a big rock in front of them. Their canoe hit the rock and broke. The other Iroquois tried to stop their canoes but didn't succeed. Brûlé and his men were lucky to be alive. But this was not the last time that they escaped death.

Written by Ernest Pemmann

► W 15–17

*O CANADA

1 19–25

O Canada! Our home and native land!
True patriot love in all thy sons command.
With glowing hearts we see thee rise,
With True North strong and free!
From far and wide,
O Canada, we stand on guard for thee.
God keep our land glorious and free.
O Canada, we stand on guard for thee.
O Canada, we stand on guard for thee.

Careful what you call us!

☹ We don't like …	☺ We like …
Indians	First Nations
Eskimo	Inuit
Americans (!)	Canadians

But we sometimes call ourselves – Canucks. (We're always happy when you call us that!)

© Chris McCarthy

RAP – Don't call me Eskimo

A teacher and the teenage class in Arctic Bay, Nunavut felt so strongly about this that they wrote a rap, made a video and put it on the Internet. It tells about the life of young Inuit people.

The name Eskimo came from the British
Who came here to look for gold, oil and fish.
The name means that I eat raw meat,
But we are the people – our name Inuit …

How to talk to a Canadian!

- Finish your sentences with *…, eh*?
- Say *aboot*, (not about), *coo* (not cow).
- Drive on *highways* (not *motorways* or *freeways*).
- Travel by *railway* (not *railroad*).
- Drink *pop* (not *soda*).

Just for fun, … eh! – And some people say Canadian English is like American English!

Parlez-vous français?

We don't all speak English as our first language.
Not all Canadians speak English at home. 22 % of us speak French. And about 10% – mainly immigrants – speak other languages. French is mainly spoken in Quebec – it's the official language there. And many people in Quebec think it should be an independent country.

Canadian humour

We don't take ourselves too seriously. We often make jokes about people from different parts of Canada. Canadians love bands with a sense of humour. Can you find these bands on the Internet?

Barenaked Ladies

Three Dead Trolls in a Baggie

The Arrogant Worms

Our new Canadian national anthem!

SONG – Canada's really big

When I look around me,
I can't believe what I see.
It seems as if this country
Has lost its will to live.
The economy is lousy,
We barely have an army,
But we can still stand proudly
'Cause Canada's really big!

We're the second largest country
On this planet Earth.
And if Russia
Keeps on shrinking,
Then soon we'll be first.
(As long as we keep Quebec)

The USA has tanks.
And Switzerland has banks.
They can keep them, thanks
They just don't amount.
'Cause when you get down to it,
You find out what the truth is.
It isn't what you do with it
It's the size that counts!

Most people will tell you
That France is pretty large.
But you can put fourteen Frances
Into this land of ours.
(It'd take a lotta work, it'd
take a whole lotta work)

We're larger than Malaysia,
Almost as big as Asia.
We're bigger than Australia
And it's a continent.
So big we seldom bother
To go see one another.
But we often go to other
Countries for vacation.

Our mountains are very pointy
Our prairies are not.
The rest is kinda bumpy.
But, man, do we have a lot
(We gotta lot of land, we gotta
whole lot of land.)

So stand up and be proud
And sing out very loud
We stand out from the crowd 'cause
Canada's really ***big!***

Unit 3

Living in Calgary

Read the six facts about Calgary. Find the picture that goes with the fact.

CALGARY

- ... is in the Canadian province of Alberta.
- ... is on the flat prairies but near the Rockies.
- ... was a few houses when the railway arrived in 1883.
- ... became rich after oil was found in Alberta.
- ... goes cowboy- and cowgirl-crazy every summer.
- ... often has snow that you need to clear in the cold winters.

Internet tasks

How many people live there? What happens every July? How far is it to the Rockies?

C

A

B

F

D

E

1 26 **Listen to Adam and his sister Trish at home in Calgary. Why are they fed up today?**

1 27

Find the best title for what Adam is saying:

Winter sports | Adam hates snow | Winter and summer | Adams's opinion about winter

“When we get a very big dump of snow in Calgary I can't drive my car. I only just got my P (probationary driver's license) after my sixteenth birthday. My parents think it's too dangerous for me after bad snow. But usually roads are cleared quickly. We expect snow in Canada!

But winter is fun because there are so many good things to do. I go snowshoeing, and I learned skating almost before walking!

If there's snow, I get my favourite chore, of course – clearing the sidewalk in front of the house. Yuk! But you can't have snow out front – that's the law. And in our family it's my job. I sometimes hope for a nice warm Chinook ...

And if there's no snow in Calgary, we go to the Rockies. Mom and dad ski, but Trish and I like snowboarding. We often go to Whistler and we stay at the cottage on weekends. That's great! It belongs to my grandparents, but they fly to resorts in Florida or Mexico for a few months every winter.”

► W 1

TASK

Make notes about winter where you live. Then talk to the class.

Some ideas:
- **weather:** What are winters usually like? How often does it snow? Is snow a problem?
- **activities:** What activities are popular? What do you do? What equipment do you have?
- **holidays:** Are there resorts near where you live? Do you sometimes go to a resort?
- **opinions:** What do you like/dislike about winter?

A–B
1 28, 29

A Gemma and her sister Kate were born in England, but their family moved to Calgary last year. Gemma is writing an email to her friend in England.

Hi Megan,

How is Bedford? Wet as always? Living in Calgary is so different. Winter is really cold here, and there's lots of snow.

I must tell you about something that happened a few days ago. I can't skate, but other kids at high school skate really well. If you live in Canada, you skate. So last week Kate and I bought some skates – a very good brand – and went to a park.

We went onto the ice very carefully. Kate is a good skateboarder, so she learned easily. She soon skated quite well. But I found it much more difficult. At first Kate held me and it was OK. I walked very slowly. Then I tried alone and I fell over very quickly. It happened over and over again! I was so fed up.

Then suddenly somebody held out a hand to me. It was a Canadian boy. (And very fit – "cute" they say here.) He skated fantastically, of course. But he didn't laugh at me. He just helped me. I wanted to get off the ice quickly, so he picked me up and carried me! I laughed so loudly. (Kate took these photos.)

CHECKPOINT

Adverbien der Art und Weise sagen, wie etwas getan wird. Meist enden sie auf *-ly*.
Gemma skated **badly**. She laughed **loudly**.

Beachte: Adam is a good skater. He skates **well**.

► Summary, p. 48

Exercise 1: Kate is telling a friend about the day in the park.

→ badly • easily • quickly • slowly • well

1 Gemma was a bad skater. She skated ...
2 She tried to be quick. She walked too ... and she fell.
3 A Canadian boy helped her. He was a good skater. He skated really ...
4 At first I was careful. I moved very ...
5 Skating was easy for me. I learned ...

Exercise 2: How good are you at these activities?

→ well • badly • quite well

1 I sing ...
2 I cook ...
3 I paint ...
4 I play video games ...
5 I skate ...
6 I ...

► W 2, 3

carefully, well

B From Gemma's diary:

Jan	8th	I met a boy called Adam today. I gave him my phone number. – If he calls, it'll be great.
	10th	Adam and I will have our first date tomorrow. (Dinner and a movie.)
Feb	8th	It's our first month anniversary at the weekend. – If it's a cold day, Adam and I will go ice skating again. – If it's warmer, we'll hire inline skates in the park.
April	14th	Everybody is planning grad (graduation) in two months. It's a really big day and Adam wants to go with me! Lots of girls already have special dresses for the dinner dance. I can't find a good one. But mum has had an idea. – If we go to Edmonton, we can try the shops in the big mall.
May	20th	It's Pyjama day at school on Monday. Adam says it's great. – I'll only wear pyjamas if he does too! And on Friday it's Parents at school day. – If your parents come, they sit in your lessons. No way!
June	19th	It's grad tomorrow! First it's the dinner dance with parents. Then it's after grad, a party without parents. – If you go to after grad, you stay up till breakfast. – Then you all eat pancakes together, if you're still awake!

My valentine's card (Adam's joke)

I think this is a cool dress!

Exercise 3: Adverts for graduation in the high school magazine: Can you finish them?

1

If you're looking for grad clothes, …

2 If you choose *Quality* photos, …

3

If you need cool transport, …

4

If you want to look terrific at grad, …

5 If you want a great "after grad" party, …

6 *If you're still awake in the morning, …*

→ you'll always remember graduation. come to the *Rocky Hotel*. have breakfast at *Sunny's*. you must try *Cool Clothes*. call *Flash Cars*. your day should start at *Stars* beauticians.

▸W 4, 5

If it's a cold day, we'll go ice skating.

LISTENING – Asking for help

1 30–32

1 **Look at the photos. What are all the people doing?**

A

B

C

D

2 **There are only three dialogues. Listen to them and find the three photos.**
Dialogue 1 – Photo ...

3 **Listen to dialogue 1. Who says this?**

Carl • Mrs Hale

1 I have a problem.
2 Can you drive over?
3 I can't come now.
4 You can walk home.

4 **Listen to dialogue 2. True or false?**
1 Lucy is selling software.
2 Bob is using online banking.
3 Bob can't start the computer.
4 Bob can't print something.

5 **Listen to dialogue 3. Finish the sentences.**
1 Molly is calling ... **a)** her boy friend. **b)** her uncle. **c)** her father.
2 Molly has bought ... **a)** a *Dash* T-shirt. **b)** a *Dash* sweatshirt. **c)** a book called *Dash*.
3 Her father would like a science fiction ... **a)** game. **b)** book. **c)** poster.

▶ W 6–8

READING – Opinions for and against

1 **Read the article on page 43. Answer these questions about it. Give short answers.**
1 Where does Naomi Klein come from?
2 Has Naomi Klein always been against logos?
3 Where do the big companies make their goods?

2 **Find the sentence in the article that tells you this.**
1 *No logo* became a popular book.
2 As a teenager Naomi had a job.
3 Naomi doesn't like big companies.
4 Corporations don't pay well.

3 **Look at the readers' opinions. Are they for or against?**
1 Gemma – *for* 2 Kelly – 3 Carl 4 Steve 5 Annie 6 Marie

4 **Dictionary work: What are the words in blue in German?**
1 What's the latest console?
2 They make millions of dollars.
3 In the end we think we need their goods.
4 We have less choice.

▶ W 9

COOL CANADA *For and against* – Our page of opinions

We love goods with brand names on them. Logos are all around us. And teenagers are no different to other people.

No logo?

What brand of jeans do you wear?
What sports shoes are *in* at the moment?
What's hot and what's not?
What brand of MP3 player is coolest?
What's the latest *must-have* games console?

Naomi Klein was born in 1970 in Montreal, Quebec.
www.naomiklein.org

A good idea?

Not everyone thinks logos and big brands are a good idea. Canadian journalist Naomi Klein doesn't. In 2000 she wrote a bestseller about them. Its name? *No logo.*

Mall rat

But she didn't always think that way. As a child and teenager Klein loved branded toys and clothes with logos. Her Saturday job was at the clothes store with the best logo. She shopped for brands at the mall like everybody else. She says she was a real mall rat.

Opinions

Now Klein is critical of the big multinational corporations – the companies that sell the same things all over the world. They make millions of dollars, but they often pay people in developing countries badly. A company paid one big basketball star more than all the thousands of people who made the shoes with his name on them.

In her opinion the big companies want to take over the world: They want to sell us a way of life. In the end we think we need their goods to be happy.

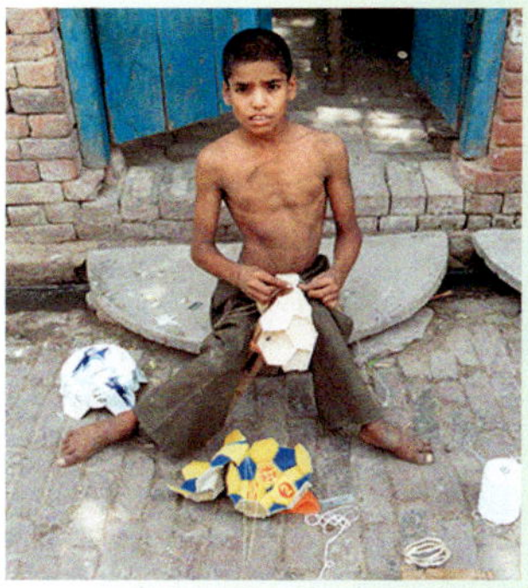

A small boy in India who is making footballs

Rich and poor

Poor countries become dependent on corporations because poor people need the work. The people there often have terrible working conditions – even children. In rich countries the small shops and firms close. In the end we have less choice. Towns all have the same shops. Countries have the same brands. The corporations have too much power.

Those are Naomi Klein's opinions. We asked some of our readers. ✔ for or ✘ against?

Gemma (Calgary): *I like brands. A brand means good quality.*
Kelly (Saskatoon): *Every town has the same shops. It's boring.*
Carl (Toronto): *I like my own style, not what companies say.*
Steve (Vancouver): *Logos are just fun. I like the latest fashions.*
Annie (Ottawa): *Big corporations give work to poor countries. In poor countries, children usually work. Their families need the money.*
Marie (Quebec City): *I prefer local shops and cafés. Our local cafés have gone. There's just one big chain.*

COOL CANADA magazine

SPEAKING – Talking about your interests

What's your favourite activity?
My favourite activity is ...
... playing video games.
... swimming.
... chatting on the Internet.
...

When/Where do you do it?

I	play video games	every evening.
	swim	at a club.
	chat	...
	...	

What things do you do?
I play with friends.
I practise a lot and go to competitions.
I download music and watch video clips.
I sometimes ...

How long have you had this interest?
I've had this interest for six months / ...

Why do you like doing it?
I think it's exciting/fun/healthy/...

I love	finding out about new bands.
	being active.
	being outdoors.
	chilling out.
	...

SITUATIONS

1 Wie sagst du das auf Englisch?

1 Schwimmen ist meine Lieblingsbeschäftigung.
2 Ich chatte jeden Abend im Internet.
3 Ich schaue mir lustige Videoclips an.
4 Ich interessiere mich seit einem Jahr dafür.
5 Ich bin gern draußen.

2 Wie würdest du jemanden fragen ...

1 ... was ihre/seine Lieblingsbeschäftigung ist?
2 ... wann sie/er Tennis spielt?
3 ... wie lange sie/er sich dafür interessiert?
4 ... warum sie/er es gern tut?

SCENE

1 33

Gary is telling his class about his favourite activity.

1 Why does Gary like it? (Find three reasons.)

My favorite activity is dirt biking. On weekends the guys and I put our dirt bikes on a truck. We take Highway 99 to Squamish Adventure Centre. It's an hour away from Vancouver. You can get there easily. We ride on dirt tracks. We camp and fish there too. We've visited Squamish for three months now. There are lots of other outdoor activities at Squamish too. But riding the bikes is exciting. Dirt biking is fun, and best of all, I like being outdoors.

2 The students interviewed Gary. Read his answers. What were their questions?

STUDENTS

Do only boys do the activity?
Can you ride in winter?
How long have you had that bike?
How often do you go?
What other activities do you do there?
Is riding a dirt bike very hard?

GARY

– Canoeing, climbing, hiking.
– Learning only takes a few minutes.
– No. Girls sometimes come.
– Since last fall.
– About twice a month.
– Yes, here's a photo from last November.

3 Make four more questions for Gary.

Do	the park	stay open in winter?
Does	you	think it's dangerous?
	a bike	get a lot of visitors?
	people	cost a lot?

● 4 Can you think of more questions?

1 Can you ...?
2 How long ...?
3 How far ...?
4 Why ...?

▸ W 10

PARTNER WORK

Role-play: Interview a partner about a free time activity.
Partner A: Look at page 84. **Partner B: Look at this page.**

Dialogue 1

- Ask about your partner's activity.
- Make notes about the activity.
- Then check your notes together.

→ Useful questions
- What's your ...?
- When/Where ...?
- What things do you like/play/...
- How long ...?
- Why do you ...?

Dialogue 2

Answer questions about your activity.

- playing video games
- every evening / at home
- car races / sports
- for two years
- fun, interesting

▸ W 11

CLASS REPORT

Give a talk about a favourite activity. Then answer questions about it.

Step 1	Step 2	Step 3	Step 4
Make notes. • What? • When/Where ...?	**Practise your talk.**	**Give a talk to the class.**	**Answer students' questions.**

→ collecting posters/... • dancing • doing a sport • jogging
looking after animals • meeting friends • reading • riding a bike
shopping • skating • taking photos • watching TV/football • ...

LANGUAGE

1 Gemma's friend, Megan, hopes to visit Canada. What can Gemma tell her?

a) Do you have six ideas for her?

If you visit Canada,	you can ...
If you come in the winter,	you'll ...
If you come in the summer,	you must ...
	you should ...
	you won't ...

... meet Adam.

... go snowboarding in the Rockies.

... go skating.

... watch a hockey game.

... visit my high school.

... eat Canadian pancakes.

... stay at our house.

... bring your camera.

... hike in the Rockies.

b) What would you like to tell an English visitor?

If you come to Bavaria ...

1 ... you can ...	**3** ... you must ...	**5** ... don't ...
2 ... you'll like ...	**4** ... you should ...	**6** ... you won't ...

2 Gemma is calling a friend about grad next week. What will/won't happen?

9 a.m. beautician
11 a.m. hairdresser's
3 p.m. Adam

It (not be) a quiet day! First I (go) to the beautician.
Then I (be) at the hairdresser's.
At 3 p.m. Adam (arrive). He (bring) a flower for my dress. I hope he (not forget) it.
At 5 p.m. the car (arrive). The dinner dance (begin) at 6 o'clock. It (finish) about 10 p.m.
The after grad party (be) at the *Maple Leaf Hotel*. It (begin) ... about 11 p.m.
It (not finish) until the next morning.

● 3 Gemma's parents are talking about her driving test. Put in the adverbs.

She passed! Was the test easy? – Yes, she passed ...
Was she nervous? – Only at first. She drove ... at first.
Some young drivers are dangerous. – But Gemma won't drive ...
I hope she'll be a careful driver. – Yes, I'm sure she'll drive ...
Will she be a good driver? – Yes, I think she'll drive very ...

4 People or things? Words with the ending *-er*. Make two lists.

a) people
customer
...

→ customer • dancer • drummer • firefighter • flower
letter • lover • miner • owner • river • shoplifter
skyscraper • soccer • teenager • vacuum cleaner

b) things
flower
...

► W 12–14

WRITING

- Kurze Sätze kannst du oft miteinander verbinden.
- Dazu verwendest du Konjunktionen wie *and, but, because, …*

1 Write about the picture. Use a word and join two sentences to make one.

→ but • because • so • when

Jake likes listening to rap. He's in his room.
He often listens to rap. It's his favourite music.
Last week he had a great new album. He played it loudly.
He listened to the music. He didn't listen for very long.

2 Finish the sentences to tell the story.

Jake's mother was …
She had a magazine and …
But she couldn't read because …

Jake played his music …
His mother was angry so …
His mother shouted because …

→ … she was so angry. • … she wanted to read. • … really loudly.
… in the living room. • … she went to his room. • … the music was so loud.

3 Make the sentences.

- Jake's / and / A week later / 16th / presents / some / was / birthday / it / got / he
- an MP3 player / very / because / He / was / surprised / gave / mother / his / him
- happy / when/ was / Jake / with / very / present / he / his / it / saw

● **4 Finish the story.**

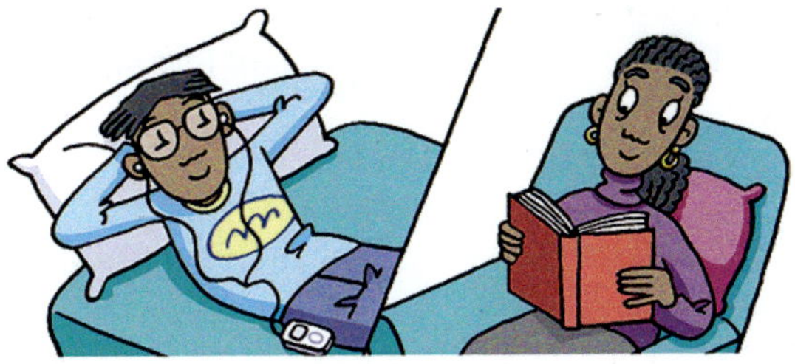

- später – Lieblingslieder – MP3-Player – neue Lieder herunterladen
- liegen – neue Raps und Lieblingsmusik zuhören
- Wohnzimmer – Buch lesen – beide glücklich

► W 15

Adverbien *(adverbs)*

Adverbien der Art und Weise *(adverbs)* sagen, wie etwas geschieht oder getan wird. Oft enden sie auf *-ly*.

John is a bad skater. He skates **badly**.

Now move **slowly** towards me.

Please speak slowly. Bitte sprechen Sie langsam.
Please don't play the music so loudly. Bitte spielen Sie die Musik nicht so laut.

! Beachte die Schreibweise:
angry – angr**ily**, beautiful – beautifu**lly**, careful – carefu**lly**

! Beachte die Sonderformen:
Is she a good singer? Does she sing **well**? Ist sie eine gute Sängerin? Singt sie gut?
Does Tom swim **fast**? Schwimmt Tom schnell?
She works **hard** for her money. Sie arbeitet hart für ihr Geld.

if-Sätze

Ein *if*-Satz drückt eine Bedingung aus.

If it rains, we'll get very wet.

If I still feel ill tomorrow, I'll stay at home.

Im *if*-Teil des Satzes steht die Bedingung. Der andere Satzteil nennt die Folge (was passieren wird).

Der *if*-Teil kann am Anfang oder am Ende des Satzes stehen.

If it's fine, we'll play tennis tomorrow.
– Yes. We'll play tennis tomorrow if it's fine.

! Beachte: Kein *will/won't* im *if*-Teil des Satzes!

Sätze mit *if* sagen beispielsweise aus, unter welchen Bedingungen etwas ...

- ... geschehen wird: **will/won't**
  If my train is late, **I'll phone you.**
  Wenn mein Zug Verspätung hat, rufe ich dich an.
  If the tickets arrive next week, **it won't be a problem.**
  Wenn die Karten nächste Woche ankommen, wird es kein Problem sein.
- ... geschehen kann: **can/can't**
  We can meet later if you have time.
  Wir können uns später treffen, wenn du Zeit hast.
- ... geschehen soll: **should/shouldn't**
  If you like action films, **you should see *"Fire"*.**
  Wenn du Actionfilme magst, solltest du dir „Fire" anschauen.
- ... (immer) geschieht: If the Chinook comes, **we get warm weather.**
  Wenn der Chinook kommt, bekommen wir warmes Wetter.

Mit einem *if*-Satz kannst du auch einen Vorschlag machen:

If you're hungry, make a snack.

IN DIESER UNIT HAST DU WIEDERHOLT, WIE GESAGT WIRD, ...

... was in der Zukunft (nicht) passiert. ▸ Adam will arrive soon. He won't be late.

DU HAST GELERNT, WIE DU SAGST ...

... wie etwas getan wird.	▸ Sue drives carefully. She drives very well.
... was unter bestimmten Bedingungen geschehen wird.	▸ If it rains, we'll stay at home.
... was unter besimmten Bedingungen normalerweise geschieht.	▸ If there's no snow in Calgary, we go to the Rockies.
... was unter bestimmten Bedingungen geschehen kann.	▸ You can come for a meal at the weekend if you have time.
... was jemand unter bestimmten Bedingungen tun soll.	▸ If you're cold, put on a jumper. If you like the shoes, buy them!

DU KANNST AUCH VERSTEHEN, ...

... wie gesagt wird, dass etwas getan wurde. ▸ Oil was found in Alberta.

▸ EXAM PRACTICE p. 91

▸ W Test yourself 1–3

STORY 3

What sport does Mallory do?

Edmonton Teen Times, March 2008, p. 7

1 34

Mallory gets the gold!

Yesterday we reported on the *Alberta Tae Kwon Do Championship* in Calgary. Today we report from the last *Teen Competition*, where Mallory Johnston just won the gold. We talked to her after the competition.

Hi Mallory, congratulations on winning! How do you feel?

I'm really happy that I won. And I'm surprised too because there were so many other good people.

How long have you been learning tae kwon do?

I've been doing tae kwon do since I was ten. So I've been doing it for five years now.

Why did you start taking tae kwon do classes?

My mom thought I should do a sport and there was this tae kwon do school near our house. Through the window I saw some kids do tae kwon do and it looked like fun. At first I was scared, because it also looked hard. But one day I tried it – and I loved it!

What's tae kwon do and what do you like about it?

Tae kwon do is a sport from Korea. For me, it's about being strong as a girl and about protecting myself.

How often do you practise?

I go to classes two times a week and I also help out with classes for the younger kids.

Tell us a bit more about yourself.

I'm fifteen and I live in Calgary with my mom Laurie and my dog Ben. I was born in Calgary, so I've lived here all my life.

Do you speak English or French as a first language?

English is my first language. But my parents want me to learn French well because I can get a good job if I know both languages.

What school do you go to?

I go to *Western Canada High School*, I'm in grade 10. Our teachers speak French in most lessons, except for English.

What other places in Canada have you seen?

A place I love is Newfoundland in Eastern Canada. I've been there a couple of times. It has a really fantastic countryside, and we were right by the sea – something we don't have in Alberta of course. There are lots of forests and rocks and cliffs and interesting old towns in Newfoundland. I think it's just beautiful there. Another place I've been to is Quebec City. It was great because I could try my French in real life! It's an interesting old city with a big castle.

What do you like best about Calgary?

I really like that Calgary is a busy city, and that's also close to the Rocky Mountains. It takes about two hours by car. When I'm with my dad we sometimes drive there for a day to go hiking. My favourite area in Calgary is 17th Avenue, a neighbourhood with a lot of cool stores. I like to buy things that nobody else has.

What do you like better, summer or winter? Why?

I like both! In the summer you can go to the cottage and swim – and there's no school. And of course there's the *Calgary Stampede*, our huge cowboy and horse show. My mom likes the rodeo, but I often go to listen to the bands. The winter is fun too because you can skate outside with friends and play around in the snow.

What else do you do in your free time?

My other hobby is listening to pop songs. I love Nelly Furtado! Music is what I like best next to sports. In my free time I also talk to my friends on the phone or email them.

What do you do when you get together with your friends?

We go out for ice cream or hamburgers, or we go to the movies, or we walk around town, or we just go to each other's houses. On the weekends, we often go shopping. We mostly go to the smaller stores in the city. But sometimes we drive to the big malls because there are a lot of different stores, so there are a lot of different things to see and buy. And it's cheaper.

Thanks a lot, Mallory, and congratulations again!

Interview: Jutta Brendemühl

► W 16–18

Unit 4

Down under

Australia is often called "the land down under" ...

What things do people think of when they hear the word "Australia"?

People think of ...

- animals like kangaroos, ...
- famous places in Sydney like ...
- Aboriginal people, ...
- sports like ...
- Christmas ...

AND YOU?

What do you think of?

▸W 1

2 1 **Listen to the Australian radio programme about "the land down under". Does Simon like the map?**

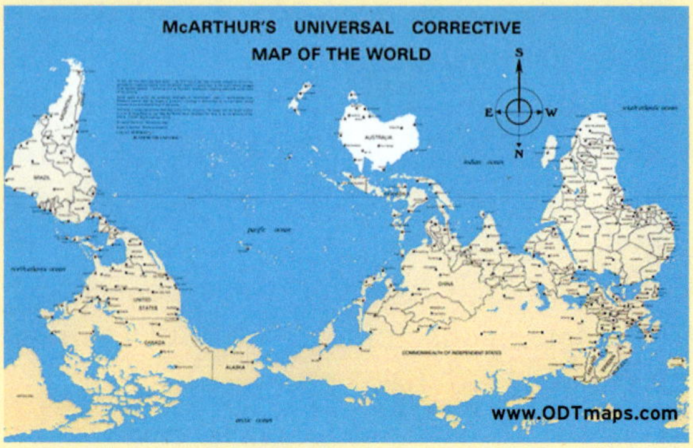

Look at the maps and pictures about Australia. Which information is correct?

Where are the cities?

a) Most big cities are in the north.
b) Most big cities are on the coast.

How far away?

a) Berlin is nearer than Los Angeles.
b) Los Angeles is nearer than Berlin.

How big is Australia?

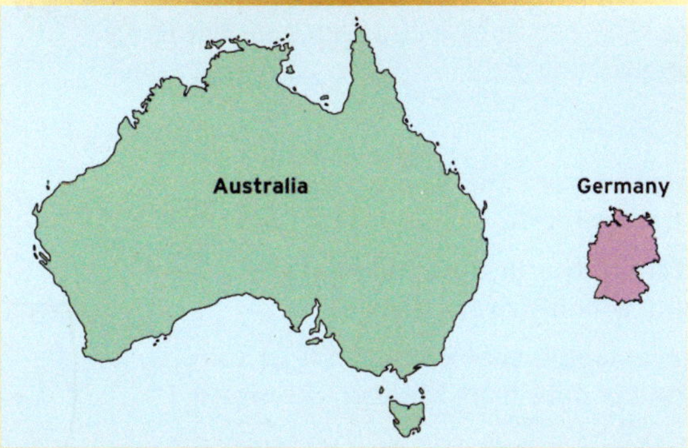

a) Australia is much bigger than Germany.
b) Germany is as big as Australia.

What's its capital?

a) The capital is Canberra with the parliament.
b) The capital is Sydney, the biggest city.

How many states?

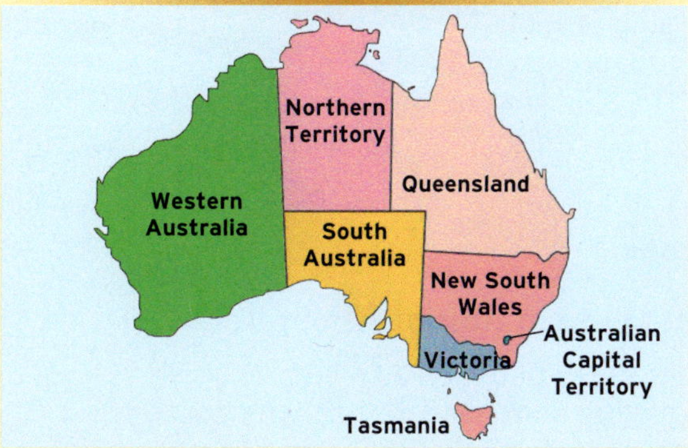

a) Australia has eight states and territories.
b) Australia has ten states and territories.

How many people per square kilometre?

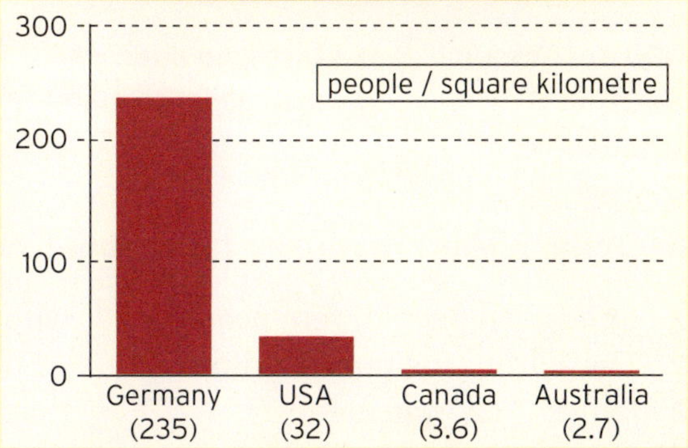

a) Australia has a lot of people for its size.
b) Australia has very few people for its size.

► W 2

A–B
2 2, 3

A

Who are the Australians?

The first Australians

Aboriginal people have been living in Australia for about 50,000 years. About one to three million Aboriginal people lived in Australia before the Europeans arrived. They were one of the world's oldest cultures. The Aboriginal people had no farms and they lived without harming the environment.

First immigrants

Ships from Europe sailed to Australia in the 16th and 17th centuries. In 1770 James Cook and 94 men arrived and made maps of parts of the coast. In 1788 Britain started settlements. For about 70 years it sent criminals to Australia as a punishment. When gold was found, other people went too. Europeans took land from the Aboriginal people and brought new illnesses to the continent. In 1900 there were only 50,000 Aboriginal people.

20th and 21st centuries

In the 20th century most immigrants came from Britain and Ireland. British people ("poms") paid £10 for the long sea journey. Australia needed more people for its farms and factories, so after 1945 people came from other parts of Europe too. Since the 1970s people have also been coming from Asia. Modern Australia has become a wealthy and successful country with people from all over the world.

Key facts

- **The first people who lived in Australia were the Aboriginal people. They were people who lived in a hard climate.**
- **Britain was the country which started the first settlements. Life in Australia was a punishment which Britain used.**
- **At first most new Australians were people that came from Britain. Australia is now a country that has people from all over the world.**

CHECKPOINT

Mit *who* ... kannst du mehr Informationen über Personen geben.
Aboriginal people were people **who** had no farms.

Mit *which* ... kannst du mehr Informationen über eine Sache geben.
The ship **which** arrived in 1770 was English.

Du kannst auch *that* statt *who* oder *which* verwenden.
Aboriginal people were people **that** had no farms. The ship **that** arrived was English.

▸Summary, p. 62

Exercise 1: Make more key facts about Australia.

1 Aboriginal people were people	who went to live in Australia from Britain.
2 The Europeans brought illnesses	who sailed to Australia in 1770.
3 James Cook was the man	that Europeans started were near the coast.
4 Australia is a country	that killed many Aboriginal people.
5 "Ten pound poms" were people	which is often hot and dry.
6 The first settlements	who lived closely with animals and plants.

▸W 3, 4

B

G'day.
Welcome to Oz and this brochure about our biggest city. I'll introduce myself: I'm Brucie. I have some tips for you while you are in Sydney. Visitors always enjoy themselves here. And here's my latest top tip for visitors ...

Spoil yourself in Sydney – climb the harbour bridge!

- The bridge was built in 1932.
- The bridge is 134 metres high.
- You can also climb at night.
- Two million people have climbed it since 1998.
- On the climb there are 1439 stairs.
- You can buy a special certificate or T-shirt.
- The oldest climber was Mrs Chris Müller, 100 years old.
- Climbers wear special grey clothes.

What some visitors have mentioned ...

"We really enjoyed ourselves on the bridge. We'll always remember it."
"Though Dad was frightened at first, he really enjoyed himself."
"You can't hurt yourself. You attach yourself to a line on the bridge."
"You can't take photos of yourself. That's a pity. But there's a camera at the top. Mum likes the photo of herself."

BRIDGECLIMB SYDNEY®
FOR THE CLIMB OF YOUR LIFE!™

Details and FAQ:
http://www.bridgeclimb.com

CHECKPOINT

Reflexivpronomen

Singular mit *-self*:	I – **myself**	you – **yourself**	he – **himself**	she – **herself**
Plural mit *-selves*:	we – **ourselves**	you – **yourselves**	they – **themselves**	

▸ Summary, p. 63

Exercise 2: Some FAQ on the bridge website. Put in the right form of *-self/-selves*.

FAQ 1 Will we enjoy ...? – All our visitors enjoy ...
FAQ 2 Will I hurt ... ? – No, you won't hurt ...
FAQ 3 Can we take photos of ...? – No. You can't take photos of ...
FAQ 4 Do older visitors enjoy ...? – Yes! Older visitors enjoy ... too.
FAQ 5 How do I attach ... to the bridge? – You attach ... with a line.

▸ W 5

myself, yourself, ourselves, yourselves

LISTENING – *G'day Oz* podcast

2 ◉ 4

1 Look at the photos. Is the podcast about Aboriginal or immigrant music?

drum

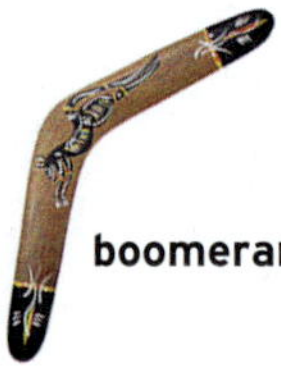
boomerang

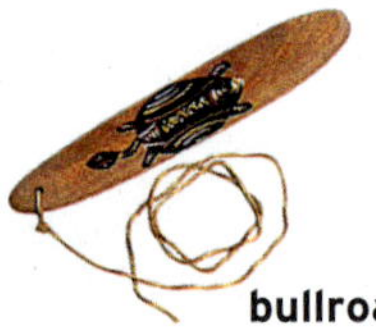
bullroarer

didgeridoo

2 Listen to the podcast. Which of the things don't they mention?

3 What are the right answers to the questions about the podcast?

1 Who's the *G'day Oz* podcast for?
  a) Music fans. **b)** New immigrants. **c)** Aboriginal people.
2 Where does Sheila work? **a)** In Alice Springs. **b)** In a music shop. **c)** In a museum.
3 What's important in Aboriginal culture?
  a) Writing and reading. **b)** Singing and dancing. **c)** Eating and drinking.
4 Who plays the music at ceremonies? **a)** Men. **b)** Women. **c)** Men and women.

4 Answer the questions about the podcast.

1 Is the man who plays the instruments an Aboriginal man?
2 Do all didgeridoos sound the same?
3 Are most didgeridoos longer or shorter than a metre?
4 Is playing the didgeridoo easy?

▸W 6–8

READING – Travel report

1 Read the text on page 57. Then answer the questions.

1 What is Uluru made of?
2 Why did Uluru have no tourists 150 years ago?
3 What were Liam's two activities?
4 What was the first thing that happened on the first day?

2 True, false or not in the text?

1 There's a river under Uluru.
2 Tourists do some things that Aboriginal people don't like.
3 Aboriginal people have made pictures about their legends.

3 Find the right ending.

1 Making Uluru … **a)** happened 500 million years ago. **b)** took 500 million years.
2 Almost half a million people visit Uluru … **a)** in a year. **b)** in some years.
3 Over the land, before time began … **a)** there was no sun. **b)** there was only the sun.

4 Dictionary work: Find a word in the text that means:

1 Entfernung
2 Erlebnis
3 heilig
4 Gemälde
5 Schlange
6 Angriff

▸W 9

Uluru

What makes it so special?

TINA GROVE (geologist)
Uluru (Ayers Rock) is in the outback in Australia. It's a sandstone mass that is 348 metres high. The distance round it is over 9 kilometres. It was formed over a period of 500 million years. Water made the marks on it.

LIAM STRONG (tourist)
No European saw the rock until 1872. Now almost half a million tourists come every year. I've been taking some great photos today. The colours change over the day: grey – orange – red. Most people climb the rock. It's a great experience. I've been enjoying myself here.

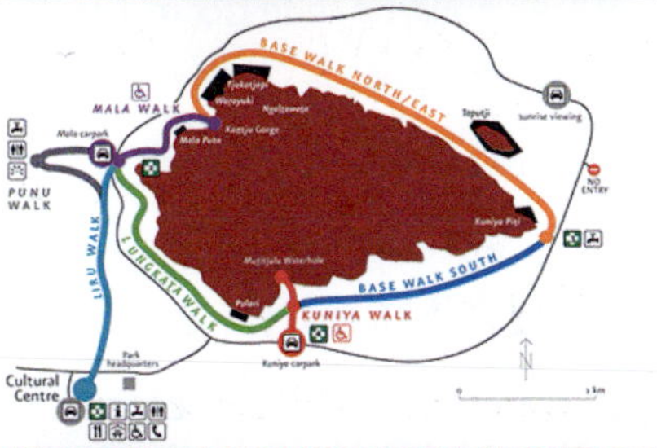

And Aboriginal people?
They say you shouldn't climb Uluru – it's a sacred place. They believe it was made before time began. The first spirits came as animals. There are many legends and they have songs and paintings about them.
Tourists sometimes take stones away. But Aboriginal people say that they'll be sorry later because the stones will bring them bad luck.

How Uluru was made – an Aboriginal legend

In the beginning the land was empty. There was no sun in the sky.
The sun, the stars and the spirits slept below the land. On the first day, the sun went up into the sky. The land became warm. Life began, with spirits, animals and plants.

Some quiet, friendly snake spirits lived near a watering hole in the outback. One day there was an attack by some other, dangerous snake spirits. There were big battles with lots of red blood. That place became Uluru. You can still see the red rocks, strange marks where these things happened.

SPEAKING – Talking about people

General information
Where does ... live? – He/She lives in ...
What nationality is he/she? – He's/She's Australian/...
Where does his/her family come from?
– They come from ...
Does he/she have brothers or sisters?

Dear Datefinder.com,
I live in Alice Springs. I'm good-looking. I'd like to meet a woman who likes a quiet life and hates the big city...

Describing people
What does he/she look like?
– He's/She's tall/short/good-looking/...
– He has short/long/fair/dark/black/brown hair / glasses.
What's he/she like?
– He's/She's friendly/clever/lazy/cool/serious/laid-back/quiet/noisy/...
What does he/she often wear? – He/She often wears ...
What's he/she wearing? – At the moment he's/she's wearing ...

People's activities
What's his/her job? – He's/She's a ...
What does he/she do in his/her free time? – He/She plays/reads/listens to ...
Does he/she play/like/...?
Is he/she the one who ...?

SITUATIONS

1 Wie würdest du dich nach einem Mädchen erkundigen, ...

1 ... ob sie Geschwister hat?
2 ... wie sie aussieht?
3 ... wie sie ist?
4 ... was sie gerade trägt?

2 Wie beantwortest du diese Fragen über dich?

1 What do you look like?
2 What kind of a person are you?
3 What do you often wear?
4 Are you a person who plays sport?
5 Are you a person who likes music?

► W 10

GAME – Who's the student?

- Make two teams.
- A team gets a card with the name of a student in class.
- They make notes and then say four things about him/her.
- The other team has to guess the student's name.
  They can ask four questions. (A guess counts as a question.)
- If they guess the right name, they win the card.
- The team with the most cards wins.

SCENE

1 Describe the teenagers in the photo at a summer camp in Australia.

→
- One boy/girl is wearing ...
- He's/She's standing next to / between ...

2 5 **2 A friend took a photo with Jack's mobile. Jack has just sent the photo to his parents. Who's his best friend?**

MUM I like the photo. You have some nice friends there.
JACK Yes, they're good mates. I get on well with them. Specially Sam.
MUM Which boy is he? Is he the boy who is wearing the green top?
JACK Yes. I'm standing next to him in the photo. He lives in Sydney too.
MUM What's he like?
JACK He's fun. He has a really good sense of humour. And he's very good at sports.
MUM Does he surf?
JACK Yes. We'll meet up when we're back home. The other guy is Lachlan. He's cool too, but he lives in Brisbane. The girl on the left is his sister, Jessica.
MUM And the other girl?
JACK That's Holly. She's OK, but she's a bit quiet and serious.

3 What are the names of the teenagers in the photo, from left to right?

► W 11, 12

PARTNER WORK

Interpreting practice: Work with two other partners. Then change your roles.

Partner A: You don't speak English. Look at page 85.
Partner B: You must help A and C. Look at this page.
Partner C: You don't speak German. Look at page 88.

Dialogue 1: At an information desk in a shopping mall

PARTNER A ⇨ YOU

PARTNER C ⇨ YOU

...

● Dialogue 2: At a police station

PARTNER A ⇨ YOU

PARTNER C ⇨ YOU

...

LANGUAGE

1 Describe some Australian animals.

A kangaroo is A crocodile is A koala is A kookaburra is An emu is	an animal a bird	that	lives in trees and eats leaves. can jump a long way. lives in rivers. can't fly like other birds. makes a sound like laughing.

2 Explain some things in Germany for a visitor from another country.

1 The Oktoberfest is a festival that ...
2 Munich is the city that ...
3 Nikolaus is a man who ...
4 Lebkuchen is cake that ...

5 Dirk Novitzki is a man who ...
6 Nena is a woman who ...
7 Sandmännchen is a man who ...
8 The Zugspitze is a mountain that ...

3 Some facts about Australia

a) Make some comparisons.

1 Summer in Alice Springs – summer in Tasmania (hot)
Summer in Alice Springs is hotter than summer in Tasmania.
2 Germany – Australia (small) *Germany is ...*
3 Sydney – Canberra (big)
4 Christmas in Germany – Christmas in Australia (cold)

b) Finish the information.

1 Australia is the (big) island in the world. *Australia is the biggest island in the world.*
2 Australia is the (small) continent in the world.
3 (Many) people in Australia live in ten cities.
4 Asia is Australia's (near) neighbour.

▸ W 13–15

CHECKPOINT

Vergleiche
Austria is **smaller** than Germany. Switzerland is the **smallest** of the three countries.

Beachte dabei die Schreibweisen:
big – bi**gg**er – bi**gg**est hot – ho**tt**er – ho**tt**est late – later – latest

Sonderformen: good – **better** – **best** bad – **worse** – **worst** many – **more** – **most**

4 What are these things?

Tip: The first letters of the ten words make something that will help you with your English.

1 Money that you use in Australia. *dollar*
2 A country that has the sea round it.
3 A person who buys things in a shop.
4 The day that comes after Wednesday.
5 A person who lives in a new country.
6 A word that is the opposite of indoors.
7 Somebody who lives near you.
8 The first people who lived in Australia.
9 A place that sells meals and drinks.
10 The day that came before today.

WRITING

1 Sarah's visit to Australia: Find the right English sentences and tell the story.

Sarah is from England. Last year she visited her cousin Darren in Australia. It was …

1. Weihnachten
2. Wetter
3. Aktivitäten
4. Stimmung
5. Gründe
6. Idee
7. Telefon
8. Beantwortung des Telefons
9. Grüße
10. Uhrzeit

- Sarah and some friends sat on the beach, played games and swam.
- She took out her mobile and rang home.
- At first nobody answered but then she heard her mother.
- Sarah said, "Happy Christmas, mum! What's the weather like at home?"
- Then Sarah had a good idea.
- Sarah missed her family at home with their special meal and the presents.
- Her mother was surprised because it was only 4 a.m. in England!
- The Australians enjoyed themselves, but Sarah was sad.
- The weather was sunny and hot.
- It was Christmas Day.

2 Begin a story about Alex in Sydney.

Beteiligte Person
Alex comes from Germany and last month …

Besuchsziel
He wanted to visit the Australian Museum because …

Reiseart
He travelled by underground because …

Ankunft
He arrived at Museum station and …

● 3 Finish the story about Alex in Sydney.

Problem **Gefühle** **Gründe**

▸ W 16

Relativsätze mit *who, which, that*

Gareth was the singer **who** won the competition.

Here's the sweatshirt **which** I got last week.

I like the great poster **that** you painted.

Solche Sätze mit *who/which/that* werden Relativsätze *(relative clauses)* genannt. Der Satzteil mit *who/which/that* gibt zusätzliche Informationen über eine bereits genannte Person oder Sache.

- **who** wird nach Personen benutzt:

This is the boy **who** I met on holiday.

Is Lachlan the boy who lives in Brisbane?
Ist Lachlan der Junge, der in Brisbane lebt?
I have a friend who works in Canada.
Ich habe einen Freund, der in Kanada arbeitet.

- **which** wird nach Dingen benutzt:

I like the jeans **which** are in the window.

Is Alice Springs the town which is nearest to Uluru? Ist Alice Springs die Stadt, die Uluru am nächsten liegt?
The didgeridoo is an instrument which comes from Australia. Das Didgeridoo ist ein Instrument, das aus Australien kommt.

- **that** kannst du – nach Personen und auch Dingen – statt *who/which* verwenden.

Tina is the woman that found the money. Tina ist die Frau, die das Geld gefunden hat.
I like the cinema that is in the mall. Ich mag das Kino, das im Einkaufszentrum ist.

myself, yourself, ...

Diese Wörter heißen Reflexivpronomen *(reflexive pronouns)* oder rückbezügliche Fürwörter. Du verwendest sie nach einem Verb, wenn z. B. die Handlung dich selbst betrifft.

Anna is washing **herself**.

The Wilsons enjoyed **themselves** on holiday.

Im Singular enden die Pronomen auf *-self*. Im Plural enden sie auf *-selves*.

I – **my**self	we – **our**selves
you – **your**self	your – **your**selves
he – **him**self	they – **them**selves
she – **her**self	
it – **it**self	

! Häufige Verben mit *-self/-selves*: **hurt • enjoy • help • look at**

Beachte auch: Help yourselves! Nehmt euch!
Enjoy yourself! Amüsier dich gut! / Viel Spaß!

IN DIESER UNIT HAST DU WIEDERHOLT, WIE ...

... Dinge miteinander verglichen werden. ▸ *Sydney is larger than Canberra. It's the largest city in Australia.*

DU HAST GELERNT, WIE ...

... du weitere Informationen über eine Sache gibst. ▸ *This is the film which won an Oscar. This is the film that won an Oscar.*

... du weitere Informationen über eine Person gibst. ▸ *Fuang is the boy who comes from China. They're the girls who make a podcast.*

... du sagst, dass eine Handlung dich (selbst) betrifft. ▸ *I hurt myself yesterday. I bought a camera for myself.*

DU KANNST AUCH VERSTEHEN, WIE GESAGT WIRD, ...

... dass eine Handlung seit einiger Zeit im Gange ist. ▸ *Aboriginal people have been living in Australia for at least 50,000 years.*

▸ EXAM PRACTICE p. 92

▸ W Test yourself 1–4

What happened on the trip to the Australian bush?

Don't feed the dingoes!

2 ◎ 6, 7

"Ten days in the bush sounds like a great holiday!" Steve thought. Mike, Steve's friend, had the idea and he asked his dad to go camping with them. They started from their hometown Brisbane and after crossing by ferry from the mainland, they arrived late in the evening at a bush camp on Fraser Island. First they put up their tent. Then they had a barbecue. It was late at night and while they were eating Steve heard strange sounds in the bush. They sat by the fire and chatted for a long time about their holiday plans.

Steve wanted to throw the barbecue scraps into the bush. But Mike's father stopped him, "Don't throw food into the bush. There are lots of dingoes around here. If they find the food, then they'll know we're here." Steve laughed. He couldn't believe that dingoes were dangerous.

But Mike's dad was very serious. "Dingoes can be dangerous. Some years ago they killed a baby at a campsite in Uluru. They also killed a young boy here on the other side of Fraser Island."

"Wow!" Steve said, "That's not far from here ..."

They went into the tent but Steve couldn't sleep. He thought about the dingoes and listened to the sounds outside the tent. But a few minutes later he fell asleep.

The sound of kookaburras woke Steve up. He looked at Mike, who was still asleep. But Steve couldn't sleep because it was so hot in the tent. So he put on his shorts and went outside. It was still very early. He decided to go for a walk along the beach in the morning sun. He looked around. There were only the two tents and the Land Rover behind him.

Nobody was on the beach. Steve sat down on the sand and looked over towards the sea. Suddenly he saw some dark shadows in the distance. He didn't know what they were, but they were getting closer and closer to him. He stood up. They were dingoes, four dingoes! Steve tried not to panic. The dingoes were coming towards him. He went slowly backwards. Then he turned and started to run. But the dingoes followed him quickly and soon there were only a few metres between him and the dingoes. He began to scream as loudly as he could and hoped that somebody would hear him.

Suddenly the dingoes were all around him. Steve stopped. They looked dangerous. There was no way out. He thought about the baby at Uluru and the young boy that the dingoes had killed here on the island. He didn't want to die. He screamed again: "Mike! Help!"

Then he saw Mike and his father. They ran towards him with sticks in their hands. Mike's dad shouted and threw his stick at one of the dingoes. It ran away, but the other dingoes didn't move. When Mike came nearer they followed the other dingo. Mike's dad came and put his hand on Steve's shoulder. "It's OK, mate, we're here now." Steve tried to smile, "Yeah! I didn't want to feed the dingoes!"

Written by Peter Bulkeley

► W 17–19

2 ◎ 8–12

OZ! AUSTRALIA MAGAZINE

Two Australian ideas

A school of the air …

Young children who live in the outback have no school. But since 1951 Australia has had the special *School of the Air*. At first they had live radio classes of 20–30 pupils. Now lessons use satellite technology and computers. This means that the pupils can speak to, hear and see their teacher. But so far, the teacher can't see the pupils …

And a flying doctor …

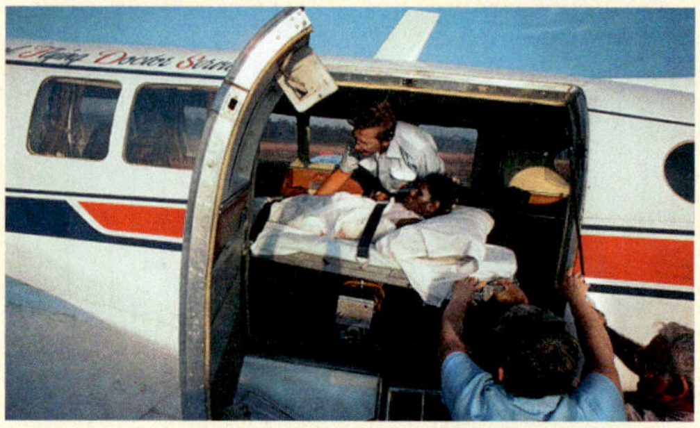

People in the outback live hundreds of miles from a hospital. If they are very ill, their life is in danger. They're a long way from a doctor. So in 1928 the first *Flying Doctor Service* began. A plane with a doctor is called by radio and the patient is taken to hospital in a city.

Two Australian railways

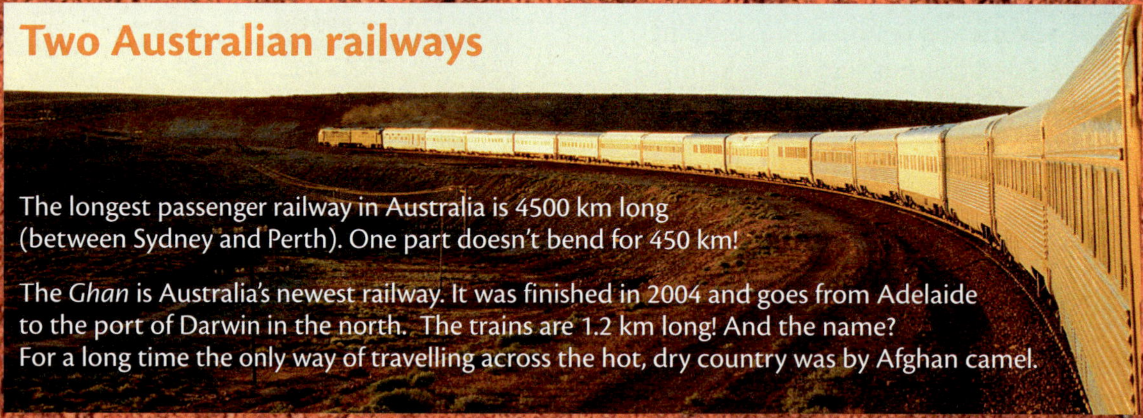

The longest passenger railway in Australia is 4500 km long (between Sydney and Perth). One part doesn't bend for 450 km!

The *Ghan* is Australia's newest railway. It was finished in 2004 and goes from Adelaide to the port of Darwin in the north. The trains are 1.2 km long! And the name? For a long time the only way of travelling across the hot, dry country was by Afghan camel.

*QUIZ – Don't you understand Strine?

Australians have their own kind of English with their own slang words. Just for fun: Can you guess what these words and phrases mean?

1 a sheila
2 a tinny
3 No worries!
4 a barbie
5 this arvo
6 G'day!
7 a scratchie
8 sunnies
9 mate

An Australian band

YOTHU YINDI

What does it mean? – It's from an Aboriginal language and means "mother and child".

What is it? – An Australian rock band.

What kind of music? – It's a mix of western rock and Aboriginal music.

The band is Aboriginal? – Yes, most singers and musicians are Aboriginal.

What instruments? – They play western and Aboriginal instruments.

Have they made albums? – Yes. They've made over ten very successful albums.

Do they play abroad? – They've had tours in Europe, Asia, North America and South Africa.

And Germany? – Of course, several times. They've toured with Peter Maffay.

Their biggest hit? – "Treaty".

What's it about? – A land treaty with the Aboriginal people. A promise on Australia's 200th birthday, in 1988 …

http://www.yothuyindi.com/

*SONG – Treaty

Well I heard it on the radio,
And I saw it on the television.
Back in 1988, all those talking politicians.
Words are easy, words are cheap,
Much cheaper than our priceless land.
But promises can disappear,
Just like writing in the sand.

Treaty yeah, treaty now …
Nhima djat'... gutjuk.

This land was never given up.
This land was never bought and sold.
The planting of the Union Jack,
Never changed our law at all.
Now two rivers run their course
Separated for so long
I'm dreaming of a brighter day,
When the waters will be one.

Treaty yeah, treaty now …
Nhema … gumurrtjarrk nhe ya

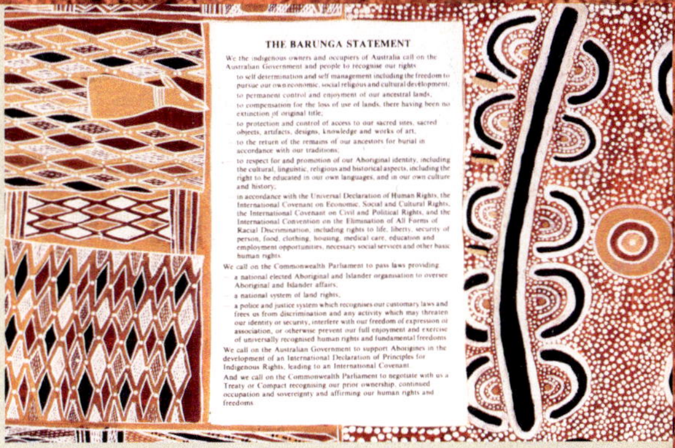

THE BARUNGA STATEMENT

We the indigenous owners and occupiers of Australia call on the Australian Government and people to recognise our rights

- to self determination and self management including the freedom to pursue our own economic, social religous and cultural development;
- to permanent control and enjoyment of our ancestral lands;
- to compensation for the loss of use of lands, there having been no extinction of original title;
- to protection and control of access to our sacred sites, sacred objects, artifacts, designs, knowledge and works of art;
- to the return of the remains of our ancestors for burial in accordance with our traditions;
- to respect for and promotion of our Aboriginal identity, including the cultural, linguistic, religious and historical aspects, including the right to be educated in our own languages, and in our own culture and history;
- in accordance with the Universal Declaration of Human Rights, the International Covenant on Economic, Social and Cultural Rights, the International Covenant on Civil and Political Rights, and the International Convention on the Elimination of All Forms of Racial Discrimination, including rights to life, liberty, security of person, food, clothing, housing, medical care, education and employment opportunities, necessary social services and other basic human rights.

We call on the Commonwealth Parliament to pass laws providing

- a national elected Aboriginal and Islander organisation to oversee Aboriginal and Islander affairs;
- a national system of land rights;
- a police and justice system which recognises our customary laws and frees us from discrimination and any activity which may threaten our identity or security, interfere with our freedom of expression or association, or otherwise prevent our full enjoyment and exercise of universally recognised human rights and fundamental freedoms.

We call on the Australian Government to support Aborigines in the development of an International Declaration of Principles for Indigenous Rights, leading to an International Covenant.

And we call on the Commonwealth Parliament to negotiate with us a Treaty or Compact recognising our prior ownership, continued occupation and sovereignty and affirming our human rights and freedoms.

Promises – disappear – priceless land – destiny

Treaty yeah, treaty now …

Well I heard it on the radio,
And I saw it on the television.
But promises can be disappear
Just like writing in the sand

Treaty yeah, treaty now …

Unit 5

A better life

Why do people emigrate to Australia?

2 13

One in four Australians was born in another country

DILIP
I came because of the good jobs here.

SARAH
We just love the climate. Back in Scotland it was often rainy and cold.

HELMUT
The lifestyle here is fantastic – we work hard and we play hard. We're near a beach too.

LOI
We have a nice house in a city with clean air, much better than our small flat in China.

JIM
I came because my son lived here already.

CARLA
We came to give our children a good start in life.

▸W 1

What was the most important reason for each of those new Australians?

- Better weather
- A better future for children
- Better houses, clean cities
- More jobs and opportunities
- Other family members
- A life with sport and outdoor activities

2 14

Listen to the interview with Sunaina for her school newspaper.
How old was she when she came to Australia?

People emigrate for different reasons.

Silke
- Germany
- Canada
- liked the lifestyle

Silke was born in Germany.
She emigrated to Canada.
She emigrated because she liked the Canadian lifestyle.

Raoul
- Mexico
- the USA
- needed work

Raoul was born in ...
He emigrated to ...
He emigrated because ...

AND YOU?

I wouldn't like to emigrate. / I'd like to emigrate to ... because ...

▸W 2

TALK – Somebody who emigrated to another country

First make notes. Then talk to the class.

→ a friend • a neighbour • your family • somebody famous

Who?	I'll talk about somebody who	came to Germany. left Germany.
	My talk is about ...	
Where?	... emigrated from ... to ...	
When?	He/She/They/We emigrated in (about) ...	
Why?	He/She/They/We wanted	a different lifestyle. a better climate. work. a life without war. a better job. a better life. a safer life. to be with a family.
How?	I think life in the new country was hard/easy.	
	He/She/They/We	had (didn't have) family/friends there. spoke (didn't speak) the language. had to (didn't have to) understand a different lifestyle. found (didn't find) the people friendly.

A–B
2 15, 16

A Every year about 50,000 British people emigrate to Australia.

Emigrating to Australia

PLAN
- get information
- surf the Internet

APPLY
- check your points
- fill in forms
- have medicals
- get a visa

MOVE
- sell house & pack
- fly to Australia

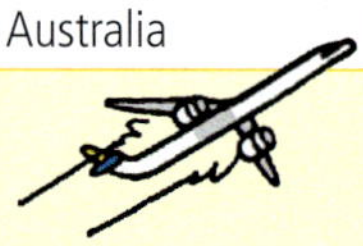

SETTLE IN
- find a home
- find jobs and school
- find a house

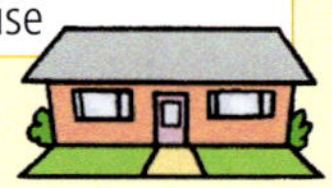

Planning

ALAN Living in Australia was always our dream. Pat and I often talked about a new life in the sun in a young country.
PAT On January 1st – a new year – we made our big decision. We got information, surfed the Internet and visited a special exhibition in Glasgow.

Applying

ALAN You need a number of points for an immigration visa. We were young; we had jobs that Australia needed (I'm a plumber. Pat is a police officer.). We had some savings. So we had enough visa points.
PAT We sent off a lot of forms. Then we told our parents. They were very surprised and sad. Then we had our medicals and waited a long time. We read a lot and chose Perth for our new home. After six months our visas came.

Moving

PAT In December things happened quickly. We sold our house and most of our furniture. But when we packed our things we still needed 80 boxes!
ALAN Over Christmas we stayed with my parents and then in January we booked seats on a plane – one way! At the airport in February we all cried and felt very sad when we said goodbye.

Settling in

PAT At first things were very difficult. We needed a home, jobs, a school and lots of papers. We didn't have our boxes. They were still on a ship somewhere.
ALAN In March we rented a house. I found a job and in May Pat got one too. In August we found our home and moved. Four bedrooms, a swimming pool. Emigrating wasn't easy. We've been here for three years now.

CHECKPOINT

Mit *simple past*-Form erzählst du, was in der Vergangenheit geschah.
Regelmäßige Verben: The Dunbars **emigrated** three years ago. They **moved** to Australia.
Unregelmäßige Verben: They **flew** to Australia. They **found** a good house.

▸Summary, p.78

Exercise 1: Planning and applying: What happened?
In January they got information and they surfed the Internet.
In February they went to ... and they ...
In March ...

- **January** *information – Internet*
- **February** *Glasgow – exhibition*
- **March** *visa forms – parents*
- **April–September** *medicals – books*
- **November** *visas – Perth*

Exercise 2: Moving and settling in: What happened from December to August?
In December they sold their house and they ...

▸W 3

simple past (Wdh.)

B Amber (16) and Ryan (13) moved to Perth with their parents three years ago.

Living in Australia

AMBER At first it was exciting here. Australian cities are so clean and modern. And it was warm and sunny every day. But then we missed our friends, grandparents, cousins, and even our favourite TV programmes and food.
Our school is better here, but settling in was more difficult than I expected. I talked to girls at school about it but Australians don't really understand. They say poms always complain all the time.

Slip, Slop, Slap!
Slip on a shirt,
slop on sunscreen
and slap on a hat,
Slip, Slop, Slap!
You can stop skin cancer
– say: "Slip, Slop, Slap!"

RYAN You can do more things outdoors here. Barbecues are more successful here than in the Scottish rain! But the sun is hotter and more dangerous here because of skin cancer. You need a hat and sunscreen all the time. You have to be more careful than in Scotland.
The animals here were more unpleasant than I expected. I'm talking about lizards, enormous spiders and flies. (The flies are the most annoying – they sometimes follow you everywhere. Worse than midges in Scotland!)

AMBER The lifestyle is more relaxed here than in Britain. We go to the beach every weekend, hang out with our friends and skate, surf or swim. It's easier to make new friends here. I think people are friendlier. In Australia everybody wants to be your mate.

RYAN People at home think that Australia is just the outback. But most Australians live in cities on the coast, in houses like ours. The cities have big suburbs. Our bus journey from Mullaloo to the centre of Perth takes 40 minutes.

AMBER In Scotland we usually went on holiday to Spain, and we sometimes took a cheap flight to another country for a weekend.
You can't do that in Perth! Perth is so far from everywhere else. But I love living here now.

CHECKPOINT

Vergleiche mit Steigerungsformen

- **-er/-est:** warm – warm**er** – warm**est** late – lat**er** – lat**est**
- **more/most:** difficult – **more** difficult – **most** difficult

▸ Summary, p. 79

Exercise 3: Australia and Scotland. What do Ryan and Amber think about Australia?

1 ... are cleaner. *The cities are cleaner.*
2 ... is warmer.
3 ... is better.
4 ... are more successful.
5 ... is more dangerous.
6 ... are more annoying.
7 ... is more relaxed.
8 ... are friendlier.

▸ W 4, 5

LISTENING – Three scenes on a plane journey

2 17–19

1 Scene 1: Amy and Jack are waiting for their plane.

a) Listen and make notes.

Where are they going? What are their seat numbers?

b) Listen to Scene 1 again. Finish the sentences about the scene.

1 The plane is very ... **a)** small. **b)** empty. **c)** big.
2 The seat numbers are on ... **a)** the boarding cards. **b)** a board. **c)** the passports.
3 Amy and Jack must now ... **a)** wait. **b)** get on the plane. **c)** get new boarding cards.

2 Scene 2: On the plane. True (T) or false (F)?

1 The plane has landed.
2 The time is now 7.30 p.m.
3 They've found some passports.
4 The plane has arrived late.
5 The flight came from Singapore.

3 Scene 3: At Kingsford Smith airport. Who said it: Amy or Jack?

1 Two days there without my suitcase was no joke.
2 We're visiting my friends here first.
3 I've been before. I worked here for a year.

► W 6–8

READING – A real-life story

1 Read the story on page 73. Here are some titles for the parts of the story. Put them in the right order (1–6).

(A) Finding the accident (B) Two radio calls (C) Flying to Perth (D) A dangerous landing (E) Planning the day (F) Arriving at the accident

1 *(E)* 2 ... 3 4 5 6

2 Answer the questions. You can write short answers.

1 Why did the plane land on the road?
2 What were the two problems about landing on the road?
3 How far was the flight to the hospital?

3 Which expression in the story tells you ...

1 ... that somebody phoned the pilot?
2 ... that it wasn't a small accident?
3 ... how they told people at the accident what they had to do?
4 ... that Lee's landing went well?

4 Dictionary work: Find words in the text that mean:

1 gewöhnlich
2 Flugplatz
3 Richtung
4 Kettensäge
5 Äste
6 erleichtert

► W 9

A true-life Royal Flying Doctor story

Only one place to land

It was early one day in September. At Kalgoorlie Flying Doctor base, Western Australia, Captain Lee, the pilot, checked his jobs for the day. He and a nurse had to take some people to hospital in Perth at 8.45 a.m. Just another ordinary job for the Flying Doctor Service.
Then there came a call for the Captain.

The call was about a road accident about 800 km away, between Laverton and Warburton. It wasn't clear how bad the accident was. Then ten minutes later there was another call. The accident was very serious, and the people needed help. Suddenly Captain Lee's day changed.

There were problems. There was no airfield near the accident, with only one place to land the plane – on the road! And it was a narrow road with trees along the sides. The road was narrower than the landing strip the plane needed.
Even worse, there was a strong wind in the outback too. How fast and dangerous for a landing was it? What direction did it come from?
A pilot needed that information. Before taking off Lee spoke to the chief pilot and asked him for his opinion. They talked about the problems, then sent a radio message with a two-part plan.

With a nurse and doctor on board, the plane took off and flew in the direction of Laverton. Then Captain Lee followed the road through the outback until he reached the accident. Lee flew very low over the accident so that he could see the road well. Below him he noticed a man with a chain saw who waved at the plane. Along the road, trees were already cut down. Good. That was the first part of the plan. But the second part of the plan?

Yes, there it was – a fire! A big, smoky fire that was made with the leafy branches from the trees. In the wind, the smoke didn't rise straight up. From the smoke Captain Lee could guess how strong the wind was. It wasn't accurate – but the plane had to land. It was the only way. He turned the plane and came down. Captain Lee held his breath …
It was one of Lee's best landings! The two passengers applauded. Captain Lee was relieved.

When the patient was on board, the plane turned and moved slowly back along the road. Lee noticed a small bend in the road. Then the plane turned and took off. Although the road had a bend, the plane rose into the air – on its way to the hospital in Perth almost 1,500 kilometres away.

SPEAKING – Talking about places

Describing a place
... is a town/village/place in ... It's near ...
It has a few / a lot of factories/houses/roads/mountains ...
It's a quiet/lively/busy/beautiful/old/modern/... place.

The place where you live
I live in ... I've always lived there. / I've lived there for ...
I live in a modern/big/old/small flat/house there.
Tourists often/sometimes/never visit it.

It's a lively place ...

A place that you have visited
I went there ... ago with ...
We saw/visited/enjoyed/looked ... We skied/skated/swam/hiked/...
It's popular for holidays/shopping/camping/winter sports/short visits/...

Your opinions about a place
I think ... is a very interesting/boring/exciting/lively/... place.
I enjoy (don't enjoy) living there. / I enjoyed (didn't enjoy) visiting it.

SITUATIONS

1 Wie sagst du, ...

1 ... wo du wohnst?
2 ... dass du schon immer in Bayern lebst?
3 ... dass Schönau ein beliebtes Ferienziel ist?
4 ... dass du die Stadt gern besucht hast?

2 The place where you live: Are these things true or false?

1 I live in a village.
2 I'd like to live in a village.
3 I live in Munich.
4 I've visited Munich.
5 Our cinema is very good.
6 Tourists don't come here.

TALK

2 20

Which of these things does Dan mention in his talk about Alice Springs?

→ the journey • animals • weather • a river • his opinion of it

I'll tell you about a visit to Alice Springs. It's a town in the outback. I visited it a year ago. Some mates and I drove from Adelaide. The journey took two days. It was our first time in the outback and we went in August. Though it was winter, it was so hot. We went to the famous dry boat races. We had a boat too, and we earned a lot of money for charity. The next day we walked round Alice and then drove to Uluru. I think it's an interesting place. We enjoyed visiting it.

INTERVIEW

2 21

Why doesn't Emma like living in Alice Springs? Find four things.

TOM So you live in Alice. How long have you lived here?
EMMA For two years. Sydney was more exciting. Alice is too small.
TOM What's it like here?
EMMA Tourists come in winter but it's quieter in summer. From October to May it's often over 40 degrees. And we're so far from the rest of the world.

TOM But the *Ghan* train comes twice a week?
EMMA It's expensive – and mainly for tourists. The journey takes days.
TOM Is Alice a friendly place?
EMMA People are friendly, but it's very boring here for teenagers. The town and some Aboriginal people have bad alcohol problems too.
TOM So life in Alice isn't always easy?
EMMA No, it isn't. There are dangerous snakes too! Last week our cat brought a Western Brown into our kitchen! I don't really like living in Alice.

► W 10

PARTNER WORK

Interpreting practice: Work with two other partners. Then change your roles.

Partner A: You don't speak English. Look at page 86.
Partner B: You must help A and C. Look at this page.
Partner C: You don't speak German. Look at page 89.

Dialogue 1: At a backpacker hostel in Sydney

PARTNER A ⇨ YOU

PARTNER C ⇨ YOU

…

● **Dialogue 2: At the Alice Springs tourist office**

PARTNER A ⇨ YOU

PARTNER C ⇨ YOU

…

► W 11

LANGUAGE

1 A story: How the kangaroo got its name. Put in the right *simple past* forms.

asked • came • got • knew • meant • said • saw • was • were

1 Two hundred years ago Europeans ... to Australia.
2 They ... a very strange animal.
3 It ... different from other animals that they ...
4 The Europeans ... very surprised and they ... the Aboriginal people for its name.
5 They ... "kangaroo", which ... "I don't understand" in their language.
6 So that's how the animal ... its English name.

2 A famous Australian: Put in the *simple past* forms.

Steve Irwin *(be)* born in Melbourne in 1962. His parents *(be)* animal experts and they *(have)* a zoo. Steve *(grow up)* with animals and *(love)* them. He *(know)* a lot about crocodiles. When a big crocodile *(be)* in a town, the people there *(call)* him. He *(catch)* the animal and *(put)* it in his park. Steve *(become)* famous when he *(make)* some TV shows. People *(call)* him *The Crocodile Hunter*. He also *(hold)* dangerous snakes.
In 2006 a dangerous fish *(kill)* him in the sea near Queensland. A few days later thousands of people *(come)* to Australia Zoo and *(remember)* him. 300 million people around the world *(watch)* on TV.

3 Choosing where you live
a) Living in a city or village. What do you think? Write six sentences.

A city A village	is	more interesting more boring more exciting nicer	more dangerous more expensive better safer	than	a village. a city.

**b) Which country? You've read about Canada and Australia.
What do you think about them and Germany? What are your ideas?**
I think that ... is more ... / ...er than ...

▸ W 12–14

4 Find the right endings and make the adjectives.

1 comfort...	4 rain...	7 health...	10 cloud...
2 luck...	5 help...	8 interest...	11 danger...
3 use...	6 care...	9 success...	12 snow...

\+ -able, -ous, -ful, -ing, -y =?

WRITING

1 Look at the job adverts and the two applications. Who wants which job?

Job A

ESPRESSO

Head barista/manager

For busy Sydney coffee shop.
Senior job with a good future.
You must have two years experience as a manager.
Phone for application form: Greg Mills, manager 6654493

Job B

Beans Coffee shop

Friendly barista needed

In Brisbane (Kedron area). Some experience would be useful. You must enjoy meeting young people. 30 hours a week. Backpackers welcome.
Send résumé by email to beans@sox.com

Re: Job advertisement

Dear Sir or Madam,

I saw your job advert for a barista in *Metro Newspaper*. I come from England and I am spending a year in Australia. I have been here for four months now. I have been working in Sydney. I have worked part-time in a café for a month and I have been a barista in a *Brownlove* coffee shop for three months. I would like to live in Brisbane for about two months.

I am sending my résumé as an attachment.

I hope I can meet you next week.

Cathy Steel

Job	*barista/manager*
Personal details	
First name	*Gavin*
Family name	*Peters*
Age	*23*
Gender: Male	*X*
Female	
Address	
Street	*77 Beach Road*
Suburb/Town	*Manly, Sydney*
State	*NSW*
Post code	*2096*
Phone number	*02 9967 4664*
Experience	
Present job	*barista*
Company	*John Sears Coffee*
Time at present job	*3 years*

2 Write an email for a job as a shop assistant.

Tip: You'll find useful phrases in Cathy's email.

1. Du hast eine Anzeige im *Perth Express* gesehen.
2. Du kommst aus Deutschland und bist seit drei Monaten in Australien.
3. Du hast in Deutschland Teilzeit in einem Sportgeschäft gearbeitet.
4. Du willst gern in Perth arbeiten.
5. Du sendest auch deinen Lebenslauf.

● 3 You're interested in a job as a babysitter. Write a letter.

Schreibe: ... wo du die Anzeige gesehen hast.
... wie lange du Englisch lernst.
... dass du Englisch besser sprichst als schreibst.
... dass du kleine Geschwister hast.
... dass du in der Nähe wohnst.
... dass du die Familie nächste Woche besuchen kannst.

Babysitter needed by English-speaking family. Weekends and Friday evenings about four times a month. House in Würzburger Straße. Please write to Sarah Sampson, Lokalkurier Box 6787

Dear Ms Sampson,

...

▸ W 15

SUMMARY

simple past (Wiederholung)

Mit der einfachen Vergangenheitsform *simple past* sagst du, was zu einem bestimmten Zeitpunkt in der Vergangenheit geschah, z. B. in Berichten oder Erzählungen.

We **arrived** ten minutes early.
Our plane **landed** at 2.30.

I **had** an accident yesterday.
I **fell** and **broke** my finger.

Aussagen

Regelmäßige Verben enden auf *-ed*:

Tom walk**ed** to school yesterday.
It rain**ed** every day last week.

Unregelmäßige Verben haben eigene Formen (vgl. S. 164/165):

Jo Hill **won** a swimming race in Sydney.
We **flew** to Munich and **drove** to Austria.

Verneinungen

didn't + infinitive

We **didn't go** to the cinema.
We went to the shops.

I didn't buy the DVD.
Ich habe die DVD nicht gekauft

Fragen

Did + infinitive

Did you **get** my letter?
– Yes, I got it yesterday.

Did you read about Tom?
Hast du über Tom gelesen?

! Die *simple past*-Form wird dort verwendet, wo im Deutschen oft das Perfekt steht.

Typische Zeitausdrücke der Vergangenheit im *simple past*:

yesterday • last year • ... ago • last March • in 2007

SALLY
I went to the cinema with Dean yesterday. After the film we ate at an Indian restaurant. The film was very good but we didn't really enjoy the food. Ich bin gestern mit Dean ins Kino gegangen. Nach dem Film sind wir indisch essen gewesen. Der Film hat uns gut gefallen, aber das Essen hat uns eigentlich nicht so recht geschmeckt.

comparison (Wiederholung)

Manchmal willst du Personen oder Sachen miteinander vergleichen.

Dave is **younger** than his brother Brad.

I like the *Wheel* **better**.
It's **more exciting** than *Fun Cars*.

- Bei einsilbigen sowie zweisilbigen Adjektiven mit der Endung *-y* werden Steigerungsformen mit *-er/-est* benutzt:

Planes are faster than cars.
Is Melbourne bigger than Canberra?

Which is the funniest story?
Liv is the friendliest girl.

! Besondere Formen:

good – better – best
bad – worse – worst

Who's the best football player on the team?
What's the worst thing that has happened to you?

- Bei mehrsilbigen Adjektiven werden Steigerungsformen mit *more ..., most ...* benutzt:

Rock is more popular than jazz.

This is one of the most dangerous snakes in the world

! Folgende Adjektive, die mit *more..., most ...* gesteigert werden, kennst du schon:

boring • difficult • expensive • famous • frightened • interesting • modern • popular

IN DIESER UNIT HAST DU WIEDERHOLT, WIE ...

... über Vergangenes gesprochen wird.	► *We lived in Scotland but we emigrated.* *We came to Perth three years ago.* *We didn't miss the Scottish weather.*
... Dinge miteinander verglichen werden.	► *The sun is more dangerous here than in Scotland.* *You should be more careful in the sun.* *It's most dangerous season too.*

► EXAM PRACTICE p. 92/93

► W Test yourself 1–3

What about the day when you wake up in the morning and everything is different?

Tomorrow, when the war began

2 22–27

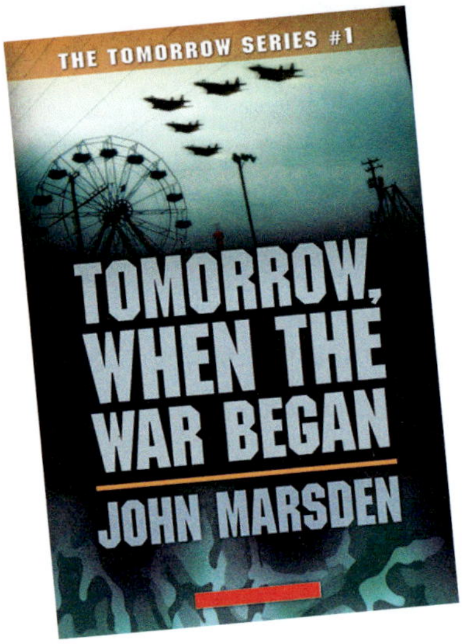

The Australian youth bestseller "Tomorrow, when the war began" is about a group of Australian teenagers and their fight to survive[1]. One of the seven characters[2] in the story is Ellie. She's telling the story. All the teenagers are country kids who can drive a car, use guns, work with animals and know a lot about the bush. In their Christmas holidays Ellie and Corrie decide to go camping in the bush with their friends Homer, Lee, Kevin, Robyn and Fiona.

[1] survive [sə'vaɪv] *überleben* [2] character ['kærəktə] *Person (in einem Buch/Film)*

"So: it all began when Corrie and I said we wanted to go bush, go feral[1] for a few days over the Christmas holidays. It was just one of those stupid things: 'Oh wouldn't it be great if ...' We'd camped out quite often, been doing it since we were kids, taking the motorbikes[2] all loaded with gear[3] and going down to the river, sleeping under the stars, or slinging[4] a bit of canvas[5] between two trees on cold nights. So we were used to[6] that. Sometimes another friend would come along, Robyn or Fi usually. Never boys. At that age you think boys have as much personality[7] as coat hangers[8], and you don't notice their looks[9]. Then you grow up.

Well there we were, only weeks ago, though I can hardly[10] believe it, lying in front of the television[11] watching some junk and talking about the holidays. Corrie said, 'We haven't been down to the river for ages. Let's do that.'

'OK. Hey, let's ask Dad if we can have the Land Rover.'

'OK. Hey, let's see if Kevin and Homer want to come.'

'God[12] yeah, boys! But we'd never be allowed.'

'I reckon[13] we might[14]. It's worth a try[15].'

'OK. Hey, if we get the Land Rover, let's go farther[16]. Wouldn't it be great if we could go right up to Tailor's and into Hell.'

'Yeah OK, let's ask.'"

(taken from "Tomorrow, When the War Began", p.3)

The teenagers enjoy life in the bush. They spend their first night sitting around the fire and talking. They're excited to be at that strange place in the bush called "Hell". The next morning they sleep in and don't do a lot. The most exciting experience is a snake in Homer's sleeping bag. On their second night in the bush something strange happens.

---

[1] go bush, go feral ['ferəl] *in den Busch rausfahren und in der Wildnis leben* [2] motorbike ['məʊtəbaɪk] *Motorrad* [3] loaded with gear [ləʊdɪd wɪθ 'gɪə] *mit Ausrüstung beladen* [4] sling (informal) [slɪŋ] *aufhängen* [5] canvas ['kænvəs] *Segeltuch* [6] used to that ['juːst tu] *daran gewöhnt* [7] personality [pɜːsə'næləti] *Persönlichkeit* [8] coat hanger ['kəʊt hæŋə] *Kleiderbügel* [9] their looks [lʊks] *ihr Aussehen* [10] hardly ['hɑːdli] *kaum* [11] television ['telɪvɪʒn] *Fernsehen* [12] God! [gɒd] *Mein Gott!* [13] reckon ['rekən] *glauben* [14] might [maɪt] *könnte/n (vielleicht)* [15] it's worth a try ['wɜːθ ə 'trai] *man kann's ja mal versuchen* [16] farther ['fɑːðə] *weiter weg*

"I got back to the sleeping bag and Fi said sleepily[1]: 'What was that noise?' It seemed that she was the only one awake, though I could hardly believe it.
'Planes,' I said.
'Mmmm, I thought so,' she said. 'Coming back from Commem Day[2], I suppose[3].'
Of course, I thought. That's what it'll be.
I started to drift[4] into a kind of sleep, restless[5] and full of wild dreams. It still hadn't occurred[6] to me that there was anything strange about dozens of aircraft[7] flying fast and low[8] at night without lights. It wasn't till much later that I even realised[9] they'd had no lights.
In the morning, at breakfast, Robyn said, 'Did anyone[10] else hear those planes last night?'
'Yes,' I said. 'I was up. I'd been to the toilet.'
'They just never stopped,' Robyn said. 'Must have been hundreds.'
'There were six lots[11],' I said. 'Close together and really low. But I thought you slept through it. Fi was the only one who said anything.'
Robyn stared[12] at me. 'Six lots! There were dozens and dozens, all night long. And Fi was asleep. I thought you were too. Lee and I were counting them but everyone else snored away[13].'
'God,' I said, starting to realise, 'I must have heard a different lot to[14] you.'
'I didn't hear anything,' said Kevin (...).
'It's probably[15] the start of World War Three,' said Lee. 'We've probably been invaded[16] and don't even know.'
'Yes,' said Corrie from her sleeping bag. 'We're so cut off[17] here. Anything could happen in the outside world and we'd never hear about it.'"

(taken from "Tomorrow, When the War Began", p.38/39)

[1] sleepily ['sli:pɪli] *verschlafen* [2] Commem Day [kə'mem deɪ] *Gedenktag* [3] I suppose [sə'pəʊz] *ich glaube* [4] drift into sleep [drɪft] *langsam einschlafen* [5] restless ['restles] *unruhig* [6] it hadn't occurred to me [ə'kɜ:d] *es war mir nicht in den Sinn gekommen* [7] dozens of aircraft ['dʌznz əv 'eəkrɑft] *Dutzende Flugzeuge* [8] low [ləʊ] *niedrig* [9] I realised ['rɪəlaɪzd] *mir wurde klar* [10] anyone ['eniwʌn] *jemand* [11] six lots *sechs Gruppen* [12] stare at [steə] *anstarren* [13] snore away [snɔ:] *vor sich hin schnarchen* [14] a different lot to you *eine andere Gruppe als ihr* [15] probably ['prɒbəbli] *wahrscheinlich* [16] we've been invaded [ɪn'veɪdɪd] *unser Land wurde überfallen* [17] we're so cut off here *wir sind hier so von allem abgeschnitten*

The teenagers stay in the bush for a week. When they come back everything has changed in their hometown Wirrawee. Lots of people are missing, the farms are empty and their pets and animals are dead. There is no sign of a fight and the kids are on their own. The young people form three groups. They find out that their country has been invaded by a foreign power[1] and most people have been captured[2]. Ellie's group is discovered[3] by some foreign soldiers[4] but they escape. In the other group Lee has been shot[5] in the leg. They free Lee and go back to Hell. They reflect on[6] how they took so many things for granted[7] – safety[8], school, parents, normality[9]. Now they have to decide what they should do. How can they help their relatives and all the other people of Wirrawee? They are no superheroes[10], only teenagers. What can they do? Either[11] they come out and fight, risking[12] their own lives, or they hide[13] in the bush, wait for help and don't help their families. The teenagers decide to fight.

The first book of the "Tomorrow" series[14] "Tomorrow, when the war began" was successful and got some prizes. In the other six books the teenagers get more involved[15] in the war. The "Tomorrow" series shows the horror[16] of war and how, even if you survive until the end like Ellie, you are changed forever[17].

John Marsden was born in Victoria, Australia in 1950. He loved reading and writing from an early age. At the age of nine he decided he wanted to become an author[18]. After school he went to university to study law but left.
He tried different jobs for ten years to earn money.
At the age of 28 he began a teaching course[19] and became more interested in writing and teaching[20]. John Marsden has now sold more than 2.5 million books in Australia. You can visit his website at www.johnmarsden.com.

▸ W 16–18

---

[1] a foreign power [fɒrən 'paʊə] *eine fremde Macht* [2] they have been captured ['kæptʃəd] *sie wurden gefangen genommen*
[3] the group is discovered [dɪ'skʌvəd] *die Gruppe wird entdeckt* [4] soldier ['səʊldʒə] *Soldat/in*
[5] he has been shot in the leg *ihm wurde ins Bein geschossen* [6] reflect on [rɪ'flekt] *nachdenken über*
[7] take things for granted [fə 'grɑntɪd] *Dinge für selbstverständlich halten* [8] safety ['seɪfti] *Sicherheit*
[9] normality [nɔː'mæləti] *Normalität* [10] superhero, pl. superheroes ['suːpəhɪərəʊ] *Superheld/in*
[11] either ... or ['aɪðə] *entweder ... oder* [12] risk [rɪsk] *riskieren, aufs Spiel setzen* [13] hide [haɪd] *(sich) verstecken*
[14] series, pl. series ['sɪəriːz] *Serie* [15] get involved in [ɪn'vɒlvd] *verstrickt werden in* [16] horror ['hɒrə] *Schrecken*
[17] forever [fər'evə] *für immer, ewig* [18] author ['ɔːθə] *Autor/in, Schriftsteller/in*
[19] teaching course ['tiːtʃɪŋ kɔːs] *Ausbildung zum/zur Lehrer/in* [20] teach [tiːtʃ] *unterrichten*

PARTNER A PAGES

UNIT 1 (p. 15)

Interpreting practice: Work with two other partners. Then change your roles.
You're Partner A. You speak German in the dialogue. Partner B will speak English for you.

Dialogue 1: At a reception in a hostel

YOU Gibt es Internetanschluss hier?
PARTNER B ...
PARTNER C ...
PARTNER B ...
YOU Das ist schade. Gibt es in der Nähe ein Internet-Café?
PARTNER B ...
PARTNER C ...
PARTNER B ...
YOU Super, aber wo ist das nächste Internet-Café?
PARTNER B ...
PARTNER C ...
PARTNER B ...

● Dialogue 2: At a snack bar

YOU Haben die Hotdogs Schweinefleisch drin?
PARTNER B ...
PARTNER C ...
PARTNER B ...
YOU Dann möchte ich keinen Hotdog. Kauf für mich lieber einen Hamburger. Und ich hätte gern auch eine Dose *Fruity*.
PARTNER B ...
PARTNER C ...
PARTNER B ...
YOU Lieber Senf, aber nicht zuviel.
PARTNER B ...
PARTNER C ...
PARTNER B ...
YOU Was kostet das alles?
PARTNER B ...
PARTNER C ...
PARTNER B ...

UNIT 3 (p. 45)

Role-play: Interview a partner about a free time activity.
You're partner A.

Dialogue 1
Answer questions about your activity.

- winter sports
- every winter / Austria
- snowboarding/skiing
- for about five years
- exciting, healthy

Dialogue 2
- Ask about your partner's activity.
- Make notes about the activity.
- Then check your notes together.

→ Useful questions
- What's your ...?
- When/Where ...?
- What things do you like/play/...
- How long ...?
- Why do you ...?

UNIT 4 (p. 59)

Interpreting practice: Work with two other partners. Then change your roles.
You're Partner A. You'll speak German in the dialogue. Partner B will speak English for you.

Dialogue 1: At an information desk in a shopping mall

YOU Ich weiß nicht, wo mein kleiner Sohn ist. Wir waren vor dem Restaurant. Dann war er plötzlich weg.
PARTNER B ...
PARTNER C ...
PARTNER B ...
YOU Er ist sieben Jahre alt. Er hat kurze, dunkle Haare. Er trägt eine Brille.
PARTNER B ...
PARTNER C ...
PARTNER B ...
YOU Er trägt blaue Jeans und er hat ein rotes Oberteil an – ein Sweatshirt mit einem Flugzeug darauf.
PARTNER B ...
PARTNER C ...
PARTNER B ...
YOU Vielen Dank. Können Sie das jetzt tun?
PARTNER B ...

● Dialogue 2: At a police station

YOU Ein Mann hat meine Kamera gestohlen. Ich habe ihn gesehen.
PARTNER B ...
PARTNER C ...
PARTNER B ...
YOU Er war jung. Ungefähr 18 oder 20 Jahre alt.
PARTNER B ...
PARTNER C ...
PARTNER B ...
YOU Er hatte blaue Jeans an. Und er trug einen schwarz-roten Pullover.
PARTNER B ...
PARTNER C ...
PARTNER B ...
YOU Ich denke, er hatte helle Haare und trug auch eine Brille.
PARTNER B ...
PARTNER C ...
PARTNER B ...

UNIT 5 (p. 75)

Interpreting practice: Work with two other partners. Then change your roles.
You're Partner A. You speak German in the dialogue. Partner B will speak English for you.

Dialogue 1: At a backpacker hostel in Sydney

YOU Toll, dass die beiden schon das Outback besucht haben. Wann waren sie dort? Wie sind sie dorthin gefahren?
PARTNER B ...
PARTNER C ...
PARTNER B ...
YOU Was haben sie dort gemacht?
PARTNER B ...
PARTNER C ...
PARTNER B ...
YOU Wie war Alice Springs?
PARTNER B ...
PARTNER C ...
PARTNER B ...
YOU Ja, das klingt sehr interessant. Wir müssen wirklich dorthin fahren.
PARTNER B ...

● Dialogue 2: At the Alice Springs tourist office

YOU Wir interessieren uns für das Leben der Ureinwohner und wollen auch Bilder kaufen.
PARTNER B ...
PARTNER C ...
PARTNER B ...
YOU Wir möchten vielleicht auch ein Didgeridoo kaufen.
PARTNER B ...
PARTNER C ...
PARTNER B ...
YOU Das ist vielleicht ein Problem, denn wir wollen auch andere Orte in Australien besuchen.
PARTNER B ...
PARTNER C ...
PARTNER B ...
YOU Vielen Dank für den Tipp. Was können wir noch in Alice Springs tun?
PARTNER B ...
PARTNER C ...
PARTNER B ...

UNIT 1 (p. 15)

Interpreting practice: Work with two other partners. Then change your roles.
You're Partner C. You speak English in the dialogue. You don't speak German. Partner B will speak German for you.

Dialogue 1: At a reception in a hostel

PARTNER A ...
PARTNER B ...
YOU Sorry, not today. All our computers are down. There's a problem with our provider.
PARTNER B ...
PARTNER A ...
PARTNER B ...
YOU Sure. There are lots of places in town.
PARTNER B ...
PARTNER A ...
PARTNER B ...
YOU Go to the first crossroads, then take a left. There's one next to the big building with a bank in it.
PARTNER B ...

● **Dialogue 2: At a snack bar**

PARTNER A ...
PARTNER B ...
YOU Yes, all these sausages are made with it.
PARTNER B ...
PARTNER A ...
PARTNER B ...
YOU Mustard or ketchup on the hamburger?
PARTNER B ...
PARTNER A ...
PARTNER B ...
YOU OK. One hamburger and one can of *Fruity*, then. Here you are.
PARTNER B ...
PARTNER A ...
PARTNER B ...
YOU $2.95, please
PARTNER B ...

UNIT 4 (p. 59)

Interpreting practice: Work with two other partners. Then change your roles.
You're Partner C. You'll speak English in the dialogue. You don't speak German. Partner B will speak German for you.

Dialogue 1: At an information desk in a shopping mall

PARTNER A ...
PARTNER B ...
YOU Don't worry. We'll soon find him. What does he look like?
PARTNER B ...
PARTNER A ...
PARTNER B ...
YOU OK. What's he wearing?
PARTNER B ...
PARTNER A ...
PARTNER B ...
YOU OK. I've written that down. I'll tell our security people. They'll look for him.
PARTNER B ...
PARTNER A ...
PARTNER B ...

● Dialogue 2: At a police station

PARTNER A ...
PARTNER B ...
YOU A man took your camera? Can you describe him?
PARTNER B ...
PARTNER A ...
PARTNER B ...
YOU And his clothes? What did he wear?
PARTNER B ...
PARTNER A ...
PARTNER B ...
YOU I see. Was he fair or dark?
PARTNER B ...
PARTNER A ...
PARTNER B ...
YOU Well, now I'll need some more details about yourself, please.
PARTNER B ...

UNIT 5 (p. 75)

Interpreting practice: Work with two other partners. Then change your roles.
You're Partner C. You'll speak English in the dialogue. You don't speak German. Partner B will speak German for you.

Dialogue 1: At a backpacker hostel in Sydney

PARTNER A …
PARTNER B …
YOU We went there two weeks ago. We travelled in a small bus with a backpacker tour group.
PARTNER B …
PARTNER A …
PARTNER B …
YOU We hiked in the outback near Alice Springs. And we visited Uluru of course.
And we talked to some Aboriginal people.
PARTNER B …
PARTNER A …
PARTNER B …
YOU The town was OK, but a bit boring. But Uluru is a fantastic place. I really enjoyed visiting it. You must go there.
PARTNER B …
PARTNER A …
PARTNER B …

● Dialogue 2: At the Alice Springs tourist office

PARTNER A …
PARTNER B …
YOU Alice Springs has lots of shops with Aboriginal art and instruments. The Aboriginal Art and Culture Centre is very good. Tourists often visit it.
PARTNER B …
PARTNER A …
PARTNER B …
YOU The shop has lots of interesting things. They have didgeridoos too. But they're very big, you know.
PARTNER B …
PARTNER A …
PARTNER B …
YOU If you go to a good shop, that isn't a problem. They will send it to your home in Germany for you.
PARTNER B …
PARTNER A …
PARTNER B …
YOU There are lots of interesting activities. Thousands of tourists visit Alice Springs every winter. You can hike in the outback, you know.
PARTNER B …

UNIT 1

1 Put in the right form (*simple present* or *present progressive*).

This is David. He's a tour guide. He (come) from Johannesburg. He (show) tourists his city every day. He usually (take) groups of six people. He (drive) a bus. Today David (take) a group to Soweto. At the moment they (eat) an African meal.

2 Put in the right preposition to go with the verb.

1 Are you listening ... a good album?
2 I work as a babysitter. I look ... a small child.
3 Hello. Are you waiting ... me?
4 Can you ask ... two tickets in English?
5 What time to you get ... in the mornings?

3 Write the word that shouldn't be in the group.

1 German • French • Canada • English • Spanish
2 speak • shout • say • swim • answer • ask
3 visitor • tourist • backpacker • nurse • passenger
4 suitcase • bag • rucksack • tent • backpack
5 group • family • nation • ostrich • crowd
6 tree • house • hotel • tent • youth hostel

UNIT 2

1 Put in the right tense of the verb.

1 This is Ella. She ... (live) in Nunavut.
2 Her parents ... (have) their house in Iqaluit for three years.
3 A few weeks ago she ... (visit) her uncle with her family.
4 First they ... (travel) to Churchill and then they ... (fly) to Toronto.
5 When she was there Ella ... (spend) a lot of time at the shops, but she ... (not like) the traffic.
6 But today she's at home. She ... (be) back at school for a week.

2 Find two more examples for each group.

1 **clothes:** T-shirt, jeans, ...
2 **jobs:** doctor, mechanic, ...
3 **vegetables:** potato, bean, ...
4 **drinks:** lemonade, water, ...
5 **rooms:** bedroom, hall, ...
6 **seasons:** winter, summer, ...

3 Pat is waiting for a plane at Calgary airport. Write the phone dialogue with the missing words.

→ that's a pity • for • how long • can have
I'm waiting • don't leave • didn't leave • will arrive

PAT Hi, Dad. I'm still in Calgary. We're late. Our plane ... here on time.
DAD ...! Do you know when it ... here?
PAT In about three hours, I guess. So ... home.
DAD It's too late. ... at the airport.
PAT ... have you been there?
DAD I've been here ... an hour.
PAT Perhaps you ... lunch!

UNIT 3

1 Du hast ein sympathisches Paar aus Kanada kennen gelernt.

1 Frage sie, wie lange sie schon in Bayern sind.
2 Frage sie, ob sie Bayern mögen.
3 Frage sie, wie lange sie in Deutschland bleiben werden.
4 Sage, dass wenn sie Fußball mögen, sie morgen ein gutes Spiel sehen können.
5 Sage, du wirst dich mit ihnen um 14 Uhr treffen.
6 Sage, du hoffst, dass es nicht regnen wird.

2 Setze das passende Adverb ein.

1 It's a very slow train. It travels very *slowly*.
2 The accident was very quick. The accident happened very ...
4 Anna is a beautiful singer. She sings ...
5 Tom is good at cooking. He cooks very ...

3 What's the right word?

1 A tourist uses it to find the way. **a)** card **b)** ticket **c)** map
2 Where you carry things in your jeans. **a)** pocket **b)** bag **c)** cup
3 You need it to smell things. **a)** nurse **b)** noise **c)** nose
4 Girls and women wear it. **a)** dress **b)** diary **c)** doll
5 A place where things are made. **a)** fridge **b)** factory **c)** fence

UNIT 4

1 Finish the sentences with the right English words.

1 Lots of people fly on holiday because it has become much (billiger).
2 But a train is sometimes (am besten) when you go on holiday.
3 Planes aren't always quicker (als) trains.
4 Bus and train stations are usually (am nächsten) to the town centre.
5 In America (mehr) people travel by car than in other countries.

2 Fill in the right reflexive pronoun.

Example: Have a good time. I hope you enjoy *yourself*.

1 Sally saw ... on TV last week.
2 Can I introduce ...? My name is Bruce.
3 The man fell on the ice. He hurt ...
4 We loved our holiday. We really enjoyed ...

3 Join the sentences with the right word.

→ after • because • but • while

1 It took 24 hours ... Katrin arrived in Australia.
2 Katrin was tired ... the journey to Australia was so long.
3 She made new friends ... she was in Australia.
4 She visited many places ... she didn't visit Uluru.

UNIT 5

1 Put in the *simple past* form.

1 "Crocodile Dundee" ... (be) a very popular Australian film.
2 Paul Hogan ... (play) an Australian who ... (go) to New York.
3 He ... (come) from the outback in Australia.
4 In New York he ... (have) lots of adventures.
5 He ... (no understand) life in the big city.

2 Put in the right form.

Example: The blue bike is (nice) the red bike. *The blue bike is nicer than the red bike.*

1 Trains are (expensive) than buses.
2 Alice Springs is (hot) than London.
3 Your mobile is (good) than my mobile.
4 The train will be (late) than we expected.
5 In Australia the sun is (strong) and (dangerous) than in Ireland.

3 What's the right word?

1 The number after twelve. **a)** thirty **b)** thirsty **c)** thirteen
2 How you feel when you're nervous. **a)** angry **b)** frightened **c)** foggy
3 It has information about trains. **a)** timetable **b)** adult **c)** dictionary
4 They hang at the window. **a)** cushions **b)** curtains **c)** gardens
5 Can I ... a sausage, please? **a)** use **b)** have **c)** become

UNIT 2 (p. 23)

Answers

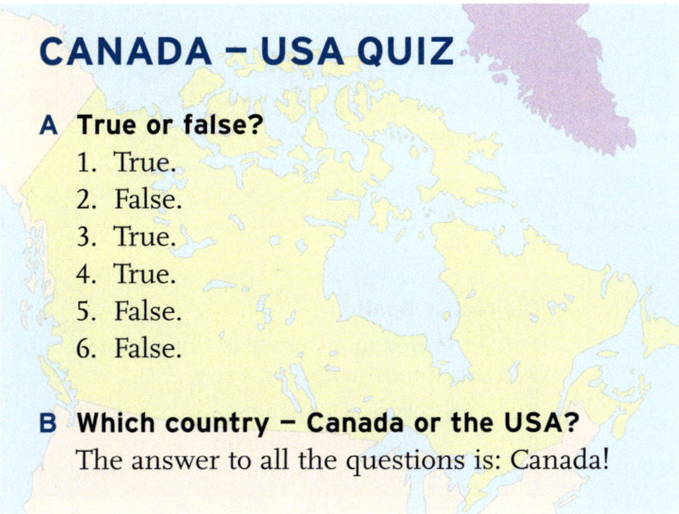

CANADA – USA QUIZ

A True or false?

1. True.
2. False.
3. True.
4. True.
5. False.
6. False.

B Which country – Canada or the USA?

The answer to all the questions is: Canada!

Schlüssel zu den Einträgen

Tipp
Jede Unit beginnt mit einem Lerntipp.

Wortschatz
Die **fett** gedruckten Wörter sollst du verstehen und benutzen können.

Seitenzahl
Das neue Wort kommt auf dieser Seite in der Unit vor.

Pfeile
verweisen auf die Kästen.

Wortschatz
Die normal gedruckten Wörter sollst du nur verstehen.

Die Lautschrift
zeigt dir die richtige Aussprache.

Unit 1

Unit 1

TIPP Wortgruppen

Du behältst Wörter besser, wenn du sie in Gruppen lernst. Du kannst die Gruppen auf unterschiedliche Weise zusammenstellen, je nachdem, wie es dir am meisten hilft. Hier sind einige Beispiele:

- **Gleicher Anfang:** *study – student – ...*
- **Gleiches Thema:** *traveller – passenger – backpacker – ...*
- **Einheiten:** *spring – summer – autumn – ...*
- **Ähnliches:** *lovely – beautiful – ...*
- **Gegensätze:** *true – false; war – ...*

Die blauen Kästen in diesem *Vocabulary* können dir Ideen geben.

Verkehrsmittel: *port → ship, boat; airport → plane; station → train*

Aufzählungen: ***once – twice** – three times – four times – five ... usw.*

peace – peaceful

English around the world

p. 8	**(video) podcast** ['pɒdkɑːst]	(Video-)Podcast *(Videodatei aus dem Internet)*	→ You can download this programme as a podcast.
	traveller ['trævələ]	Reisende/r	**Beachte die Schreibweise!** BE: *traveller*, AE: *traveler*
p. 9	**backpacker** ['bækpækə]	Rucksacktourist/in	
	work out [wɜːk 'aʊt]	herausbekommen	
	only ['əʊnli]	einzig, einzige(r/s)	→ You're my only real friend.
	sound [saʊnd]	klingen	→ Great idea! It sounds very interesting.
	nickname ['nɪkneɪm]	Spitzname	
	Strine *(informal)* [straɪn]	australisches Englisch	**Strine** In breitem australischen Dialekt wird "Australian" zu "Strine". Beispiele für AustE Wörter: *bickie = biscuit, dunny = toilet.*
	foreigner ['fɒrənə]	Ausländer/in	
	English **is spoken** [ɪz 'spəʊkən]	Englisch wird gesprochen	
	English **is understood** [ɪz ʌndə'stʊd]	Englisch wird verstanden	
	English **is needed** [ɪz 'niːdɪd]	Englisch wird gebraucht	
	you've **heard** – hear [hɜːd]	du hast gehört	

Presentation

p. 10	**township** ['taʊnʃɪp]	Township *(von Farbigen bewohnte Siedlung)*	***Townships*** entstanden während der Apartheid. Bekanntestes Beispiel ist Soweto in Johannesburg. Soweto steht für **So**uth **We**stern **To**wnships.
	it's called [kɔːld]	es wird genannt	
	the beat of the street [biːt əv ðə 'striːt]	der Rhythmus der Straße	
	concert ['kɒnsət]	Konzert	
	drugs [drʌgz]	Drogen; Medikamente	**Ein Wort, zwei Bedeutungen:** *dangerous drugs like heroin; special drugs for people with AIDS*
	violence ['vaɪələns]	Gewalt(tätigkeit)	
	AIDS [eɪdz]	Aids *(gefährliche Infektionskrankheit)*	
	suffer from ['sʌfə]	leiden an/unter	→ Many people in Africa suffer from malaria and AIDS.
	illness ['ɪlnəs]	Krankheit	
	fashion ['fæʃn]	Mode	→ the latest fashion
p. 11	**to**	(um) zu	**Achtung!** In dieser Bedeutung wird das Wort *to* immer mit dem Infinitiv gebraucht!
	view [vjuː]	ansehen, betrachten	
	lovely ['lʌvli]	wunderschön	
	braai [braɪ]	Grillfest *(südafrikanisch)*	aʊ h**ou**se, **ou**t ɜː w**o**rk, s**e**rve

Wortschatz
Außerdem gibt es noch *schräg* gedruckte Wörter. Sie kommen in Liedern, Reimen, Projekten usw. vor.

Die rechte Spalte
enthält Anwendungsbeispiele sowie Kästen mit weiterführenden Informationen.
Rot = Schwerpunkt: Grammatik
Blau = Schwerpunkt: Sprache
Gelb = Schwerpunkt: Kulturelle Besonderheiten

Unit 1

TIPP Wortgruppen

Du behältst Wörter besser, wenn du sie in Gruppen lernst. Du kannst die Gruppen auf unterschiedliche Weise zusammenstellen, je nachdem, wie es dir am meisten hilft. Hier sind einige Beispiele:

- **Gleicher Anfang:** *study – student – ...*
- **Gleiches Thema:** *traveller – passenger – backpacker – ...*
- **Einheiten:** *spring – summer – autumn – ...*
- **Ähnliches:** *lovely – beautiful – ...*
- **Gegensätze:** *true – false; war – ...*

Die blauen Kästen in diesem *Vocabulary* können dir Ideen geben.

→ **Verkehrsmittel:** *port → ship, boat; airport → plane; station → train*

→ **Aufzählungen:** ***once – twice*** *– three times – four times – five ... usw.*

→ *peace – peaceful*

English around the world

p. 8	**(video) podcast** ['pɒdkɑ:st]	(Video-)Podcast *(Videodatei aus dem Internet)*	→ You can download this programme as a podcast.
	traveller ['trævələ]	Reisende/r →	
p. 9	**backpacker** ['bækpækə]	Rucksacktourist/in	
	work out [wɜ:k 'aʊt]	herausbekommen	
	only ['əʊnli]	einzig, einzige(r/s)	→ You're my only real friend.
	sound [saʊnd]	klingen	→ Great idea! It sounds very interesting.
	nickname ['nɪkneɪm]	Spitzname	
	Strine *(informal)* [straɪn]	australisches Englisch →	
	foreigner ['fɒrənə]	Ausländer/in	
	English **is spoken** [ɪz 'spəʊkən]	Englisch wird gesprochen	
	English **is understood** [ɪz ʌndə'stʊd]	Englisch wird verstanden	
	English **is needed** [ɪz 'ni:dɪd]	Englisch wird gebraucht	
	you've **heard** → hear [hɜ:d]	du hast gehört	

→ **Beachte die Schreibweise!**
BE: *traveller*, AE: *traveler*

→ **Strine**
Im breiten australischen Dialekt wird „Australian" zu „Strine". Beispiele für AustE Wörter: *bickie = biscuit, dunny = toilet.*

Presentation

p. 10	**township** ['taʊnʃɪp]	Township *(von Farbigen bewohnte Siedlung)* →	
	it's called [kɔ:ld]	es wird genannt	
	the beat of the street [bi:t əv ðə 'stri:t]	der Rhythmus der Straße	
	concert ['kɒnsət]	Konzert	
	drugs [drʌgz]	Drogen; Medikamente →	
	violence ['vaɪələns]	Gewalt(tätigkeit)	
	AIDS [eɪdz]	Aids *(gefährliche Infektionskrankheit)*	
	suffer from ['sʌfə]	leiden an/unter	→ Many people in Africa suffer from malaria and AIDS.
	illness ['ɪlnəs]	Krankheit	
	fashion ['fæʃn]	Mode	→ the latest fashion
p. 11	**to**	(um) zu →	
	view [vju:]	ansehen, betrachten	
	lovely ['lʌvli]	wunderschön	
	braai [braɪ]	Grillfest *(südafrikanisch)*	

→ ***Townships*** entstanden während der Apartheid. Bekanntestes Beispiel ist Soweto in Johannesburg. Soweto steht für **So**uth **We**stern **To**wnships.

→ **Ein Wort, zwei Bedeutungen:**
dangerous drugs like heroin
special drugs for people with AIDS

→ **Achtung!**
In dieser Bedeutung wird das Wort *to* immer mit dem Infinitiv gebraucht!

aʊ **house, out** ɜ: w**or**k, s**er**ve

	Afrikaans [æfrɪ'kɑːns]	Afrikaans *(Sprache in Südafrika)* →	
	ostrich ['ɒstrɪtʃ]	Strauß *(Vogel)*	
	salad ['sæləd]	Salat *(Gericht)* →	
	cool off [kuːl 'ɒf]	(sich) abkühlen	
	by the way [baɪ ðə 'weɪ]	übrigens	→ Oh, by the way, have you finished your homework?
	fit [fɪt]	montieren	
	security [sɪ'kjʊərəti]	Sicherheit	
	keep [kiːp]	(be)halten	
	he kept → keep [kept]	er (be)hielt	
	keep him busy	ihn beschäftigen, ihm Arbeit machen	

→ **Afrikaans** entstand um 1770 aus dem Niederländischen, hat aber eine stark vereinfachte Grammatik.

→ **Vorsicht!**
Salad bezeichnet nur angemachten Salat, also ein Gericht, nicht Kopfsalat! Das wäre *lettuce*.

Skills

p. 12	**lion** ['laɪən]	Löwe	
	continent ['kɒntɪnənt]	Kontinent	
	false [fɔːls]	falsch	
p. 14	**onion** ['ʌnjən]	Zwiebel	
	mustard ['mʌstəd]	Senf	
p. 15	**reception** [rɪ'sepʃn]	Empfang *(Hotel, Jugendherberge etc.)*	
	couple ['kʌpl]	Paar	→ The couple are making plans for a holiday.
	hi there, **guys**! *(informal)* [gaɪz]	hallo Leute!	
	R8 = eight rand [rænd]	acht Rand *(südafrikanische Währung)* →	
	elephant ['elɪfənt]	Elefant	
	shark [ʃɑːk]	Hai	
	shark cage diving	Hai-Tauchen mit Käfigen	
	interpret [ɪn'tɜːprɪt]	übersetzen, dolmetschen	

→ **Rand (R)**
Ein Rand hat 100 Cent (c).
Ein Euro entspricht ca. 10 Rand.

Practice and Revision

p. 16	kaffir ['kæfə]	Kaffer *(abwertendes Wort für Farbige/n in Südafrika)*	⚠ Beleidigendes Wort
	South African [saʊθ 'æfrɪkən]	Südafrikaner/in; südafrikanisch	
p. 17	**passenger** ['pæsɪndʒə]	Passagier/in	

Summary

p. 19	**It's raining cats and dogs!**	Es gießt wie aus Kübeln!	

Story 1 – Who's your hero?

p. 20	**hero,** *(pl.)* **heroes** ['hɪərəʊ]	Held/in	
	decide [dɪ'saɪd]	(sich) entscheiden, beschließen	→ I can't decide what I want to eat. – Well, I've decided to try the lasagne.
	they weren't **allowed** to [ə'laʊd]	sie durften nicht	
	vote [vəʊt]	abstimmen, wählen *(bei einer politischen Wahl)* →	
	it **was called** [wəz 'kɔːld]	es wurde genannt	

→ *When you're 18, you're allowed to vote.*
Aber jdn. wählen = *vote for sb.*
Many South Africans voted for Nelson Mandela.

ɪ **e**scape, which ʃn constru**ction**

apartheid [ə'pɑːthaɪt]	Apartheid *(früheres System der Trennung zwischen Weißen und Farbigen in Südafrika)*	Das Wort **Apartheid** ist Afrikaans und kommt von *apart* = getrennt, einzeln, separat.

fight [faɪt]	kämpfen (gegen)	
they fought → **fight** [fɔːt]	sie kämpften (gegen)	→ They fought apartheid. *oder* They fought against apartheid.
university [juːnɪ'vɜːsəti]	Universität	
law [lɔː]	Jura, Rechtswissenschaft; Recht, Gesetz	**Ein Wort, zwei Bedeutungen:** *You must go to school. It's the law! She's studying law at university.*
law firm ['lɔː fɜːm]	Anwaltskanzlei	

(his) studies ['stʌdiz]	(sein) Studium	
p. 21 **political** [pə'lɪtɪkl]	politisch	→ The old political system in South Africa was called apartheid.
fighter ['faɪtə]	Kämpfer/in	*fight – fighter*
ANC (=African National Congress) [ei en 'siː, æfrɪkən næʃnəl 'kɒŋgres]	Afrikanischer Nationalkongress *(südafr. Partei und Interessenvertretung der Schwarzen)*	
unfair [ʌn'feə]	unfair	
government ['gʌvnmənt]	Regierung	**Beachte die Schreibweise!** Stummes n: *government*
peaceful ['piːsfl]	friedlich	
he **was sent** [wəz 'sent]	er wurde geschickt	
for life	*hier:* lebenslänglich *(Haftstrafe)*	→ He killed three people, so they sent him to prison for life. 
biography [baɪ'ɒgrəfi]	Biographie, Lebensbeschreibung	
not ... any more	nicht mehr, keine/n ... mehr	→ Jim isn't here any more. He left at 3.30.
join [dʒɔɪn]	mitmachen (bei), sich anschließen	→ We want to play football. Come and join us! 
he must **be freed**	er muss freigelassen werden	
he **was freed**	er wurde freigelassen	
peace [piːs] 	Friede(n)	*peace – peaceful*
Nobel Peace Prize [nəʊbel 'piːs praɪz]	Friedensnobelpreis	
skin [skɪn]	Haut	→ It doesn't matter what colour your skin is!
he has shown → **show** [ʃəʊn]	er hat gezeigt	

Irregular verbs

Infinitive	Simple past	Present perfect
fight [faɪt]	I fought [fɔːt]	I've fought [fɔːt]
hear [hɪə]	I heard [hɜːd]	I've heard [hɜːd]
keep [kiːp]	I kept [kept]	I've kept [kept]
show [ʃəʊ]	I showed [ʃəʊd]	I've shown [ʃəʊn]

æ scratch, matter ʌ gulf, sunshine

Unit 2

TIPP

Viele englische Wörter benutzen wir im Deutschen auch. Diese hier haben mit Technik oder Computern zu tun:

audio guide – MP3 player – click – download – email – attachment – print – computer – software – hardware – subject – re – video podcast – DVD – online banking – airbag

Kennst du noch mehr?

We aren't Americans!

p. 22	**Canadian** [kə'neɪdiən]	kanadisch; Kanadier/in
	prairie ['preəri]	Prärie
	ice [aɪs]	Eis *(gefrorenes Wasser)*
	ice hockey ['aɪs hɒki]	Eishockey
	Inuit people ['ɪnjuɪt]	Inuit *(arktisches Volk)*
	polar bear ['pəʊlə beə]	Eisbär
	maple leaf ['meɪpl li:f]	Ahornblatt
	grassland ['grɑ:slænd]	Grasland
	royal ['rɔɪəl]	königlich
	the Royal Canadian Mounted Police ['maʊntəd]	die königliche kanadische berittene Polizei
	province ['prɒvɪns]	Provinz, Distrikt
	aboriginal people [æbə'rɪdʒənl]	Ureinwohner/innen
	the Arctic ['ɑ:ktɪk]	die Arktis *(Gebiet um den Nordpol)*
	territory ['terətri]	Gebiet, Territorium
p. 23	**time zone** [zəʊn]	Zeitzone
	continental USA [kɒntɪ'nentl]	USA-Festland
	immigration [ɪmɪ'greɪʃn]	Einwanderung
	immigration **rate** [reɪt]	Einwanderungsquote
	Thanksgiving Day [θæŋks'gɪvɪŋ]	Thanksgiving Day *(Erntedankfest in den USA und in Kanada)*
	gas [gæs]	Gas
	uranium [ju'reɪniəm]	Uran
	electricity [ɪlek'trɪsəti]	Strom
	First Nations	indianische Völker in Kanada
	the Métis [meɪ'ti:]	*Nachfahren von Siedlern und kanad. Ureinwohnern*
	welcome ['welkəm]	willkommen heißen
	immigrant ['ɪmɪgrənt]	Einwanderer/Einwanderin
	large [lɑ:dʒ]	groß
	population [pɒpju'leɪʃn]	Bevölkerung
	distance ['dɪstəns]	Entfernung

→ Canadian winters are cold. Canadians are nice people.

Ice und ice cream
I love ice cream on hot days!
Ice on the roads is dangerous.

In der Sprache der Inuit bedeutet *Inuk* = Mensch. Der Plural ist *Inuit*.

→ The aboriginal people lived in Canada long before the Europeans came.

Thanksgiving wird in den USA im November, in Kanada im Oktober gefeiert. Die Familien treffen sich zu einem Festmahl.

Europäische Pelzhändler heirateten indianische Frauen. Die Kinder waren die ersten Métis. Der Name geht zurück auf das lateinische *mixtus* = gemischt.

Vergleiche!

large	big
area	*boy/girl*
numbers	*problem*
family	*surprise*

j **u**seful, **y**ou ʃ **s**ugar, ca**sh**

Presentation

p. 24	**I guess** [ges]	ich glaube, ich denke
	for years	seit Jahren
	my **folks** *(informal)* [fəʊks]	meine Leute, meine Familie
	religious [rɪ'lɪdʒəs]	religiös, Religions-
	freedom ['fri:dəm]	Freiheit
	scientist ['saɪəntɪst]	Wissenschaftler/in
	web designer ['web dɪzaɪnə]	Webdesigner/in
p. 25	**since** 1980 [sɪns]	seit 1980
	settler ['setlə]	Siedler/in
	century ['sentʃəri]	Jahrhundert
	reserve [rɪ'zɜ:v]	Reservat(ion) *(den Ureinwohnern vorbehaltenes Gebiet)*
	they were made	sie wurden errichtet
	mixture ['mɪkstʃə]	Mischung
	Arctic ['ɑ:ktɪk]	arktisch
	create [kri:'eɪt]	(er)schaffen
	it was created	es wurde geschaffen
	schools were started	Schulen wurden eröffnet
	traditional [trə'dɪʃənl]	traditionell
	dog **sled** [sled]	Hundeschlitten
	snowmobile ['snəʊməbi:l]	Schneemobil
	it has become → **become** [bɪ'kʌm]	es ist geworden
	climate ['klaɪmət]	Klima
	change [tʃeindʒ]	Veränderung, Wechsel
	climate change	Klimaveränderung(en)
	social ['səʊʃl]	sozial, gesellschaftlich
	medical ['medɪkl]	medizinisch

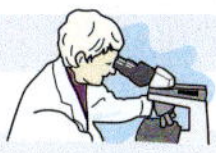

Achtung: *for* hat mehrere Bedeutungen
a present for you – für dich
for some time – seit einiger Zeit
for example – zum Beispiel

free – freedom

→ the 20th century = from 1901 to 2000

→ Polar bears live in the Arctic. The Arctic ice is disappearing.

tradition – traditional

→ What a change! Sarah has short green hair now.

Skills

p. 26	**outside the museum** [aʊt'saɪd]	außerhalb des Museums
	audio guide ['ɔ:dɪəʊ gaɪd]	Audioguide *(elektronischer Museumsführer)*
p. 28	**lively** ['laɪvli]	lebendig, lebhaft
p. 29	**presentation** [prezn'teɪʃn]	Präsentation; Referat
	indoor ['ɪndɔ:]	für drinnen, Innen-
	bone [bəʊn]	Knochen
	walk round the museum	im Museum umhergehen, durch das Museum gehen
	outdoor museum	Freilichtmuseum
	hoodoo ['hu:du:]	Hoodoo *(Gesteinsformation aus Kalkstein)*
	slide [slaɪd]	Dia; Folie *(Computer-Präsentation)*

→ Max is a very lively little dog.

Übersetzungen von *indoor*:
indoor swimming pool = Hallenbad
indoor market = überdachter Markt
indoor games/sport = Spiele/Sport für drinnen

Practice and Revision

p. 30	**snowshoes** ['snəʊʃu:z]	Schneeschuhe
	Calgary Stampede [stæm'pi:d]	*landwirtschaftliche Ausstellung in Calgary*
p. 31	**subject** ['sʌbdʒɪkt]	Betreff *(E-Mail)*

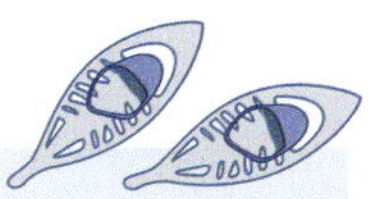

Calgary Stampede ist die größte Freiluft-Ausstellung der Welt und findet jährlich im Juli statt.

θ **s**ou**th**, pan**th**er ɑ: l**a**st, pl**a**nt

	bison (*pl.*: **bison**) ['baisn]	Bison (*nordamerik. Wildrind*)
	email **attachment** [ə'tætʃmənt]	Anhang an eine E-Mail
	happy listening!	viel Spaß beim Zuhören!
	gang (*informal*) [gæŋ]	Truppe, Clique
	re [ri']	AW = Antwort (*E-Mail*)

Story 2 – Just another day in the life of Étienne Brûlé

p. 34	**colony** ['kɒləni]	Kolonie →
	governor ['gʌvənə]]	Gouverneur/in
	expedition [ekspə'diʃn]	Expedition
	explore [ɪk'splɔ:]	erforschen, erkunden
	way of life [weɪ əv 'laɪf]	Lebensweise
	capture ['kæptʃə]	einnehmen, erobern
p. 35	**paddle** ['pædl]	paddeln
	current ['kʌrənt]	Strömung
	pelt [pelt]	Pelz, Fell
	trade for [treɪd]	(ein)tauschen gegen →
	gun [gʌn]	Waffe
	fortress ['fɔ:trəs]	Festung
	it **would** take [wʊd]	es würde dauern
	pass [pɑ:s]	vorbeifahren an
	they paddled as **hard** as they could [hɑ:d]	sie paddelten so kräftig sie konnten
	close [kləʊs]	dicht, nah →
	gunshot ['gʌnʃɒt]	Schuss
	he knew → **know** [nju:]	er kannte; er wusste
	rapids ['ræpɪdz]	Stromschnellen
	flow [fləʊ]	fließen
	point a gun at [pɔɪnt]	eine Waffe richten auf
	shoot [ʃu:t]	schießen
	signal ['sɪgnəl]	Zeichen, Signal
	calm [kɑ:m]	ruhig
	succeed [sək'si:d]	Erfolg haben
	be alive [ə'laɪv]	am Leben sein, leben
	death [deθ]	Tod →

→ **Vorsicht Betonung!**
<u>co</u>*lony* (Engl.)
Kolo<u>nie</u> (Dt.)

→ **Verben + *for***
trade for = tauschen <u>gegen</u>
wait for = warten <u>auf</u>
look for = suchen <u>nach</u>

→ **Beachte die Aussprache!**
***close** the door* mit weichem s [z]
*it's not far, it's **close*** mit scharfem s [s]

→ The sheriff pointed his gun at the man and said, "Leave this town. Now."

→ **Leben und Tod**
live – die
alive – dead
life – death

Canada Magazine

p. 36	*national anthem* ['ænθəm]	Nationalhymne
	native land [neɪtiv]	Heimatland
	patriot love ['peɪtrɪət]	Vaterlandsliebe
	thy (altes Englisch) [ðai]	dein/e
	command [kə'mɑ:nd]	*hier:* erwecken
	glowing hearts [gləʊɪŋ 'hɑ:ts]	glühende Herzen
	thee (altes Englisch) [ði:]	dich/dir
	rise [raiz]	*hier:* wachsen, stark werden
	stand on guard [stænd ɒn 'gɑ:d]	Wache halten
	God [gɒd]	Gott
	glorious [glɔ:rias]	ruhmreich
	raw [rɔ:]	roh
	meat [mi:t]	Fleisch
	for fun [fə 'fʌn]	aus Spaß, zum Spaß

ə liber**ty**, sys**tem** l memoria**l**, **l**iberty

highway ['haɪweɪ]	Autobahn *(US + Kanada)*
motorway ['məʊtəweɪ]	Autobahn *(Großbritannien)*
freeway ['fri:weɪ]	Autobahn *(US)*
railway ['reɪlweɪ]	Eisenbahn
railroad (AE) ['reɪlrəʊd]	Eisenbahn
pop [pɒp]	*hier:* Brause, Limonade
soda (pop) (AE) ['səʊdə]	Brause, Limonade
by your accent	aufgrund Ihres/deines Akzents
S. 37 *Parlez-vous français? (französisch)* [paʀle'vu fʀɑ̃'sɛ]	Sprechen Sie Französisch?
independent [ɪndɪ'pendənt]	unabhängig
mainly ['meɪnli]	hauptsächlich
(sense of) humour [sens əv 'hju:mə]	(Sinn für) Humor
take it seriously ['sɪəriəsli]	es ernst nehmen
Canada's really big	Kanada ist echt groß
economy [ɪ'kɒnəmi]	(Volks-)Wirtschaft
lousy ['laʊzi]	lausig, mies
barely ['beəli]	kaum
army ['ɑ:mi]	Armee
'cause [kɔ:z] = *because*	weil
planet ['plænɪt]	Planet
earth [ɜ:θ]	(die) Erde
Russia ['rʌʃə]	Russland
keeps on shrinking ['ʃrɪŋkɪŋ]	schrumpft immer weiter
tank [tæŋk]	Panzer
Switzerland ['swɪtsələnd]	die Schweiz
they don't amount [ə'maunt]	*etwa:* sie sind nicht viel wert
when you get down to it	*etwa:* wenn man mal genau hinschaut
truth [tru:θ]	Wahrheit
pretty large ['prɪti]	ziemlich groß
this land of ours ['lænd əv aʊəz]	unser Land
whole [həʊl]	ganz →
a whole lotta work (informal) = a whole lot of work	*etwa:* ein Riesenhaufen Arbeit
seldom ['seldəm]	selten
bother to go ['bɒðə]	sich die Mühe machen, zu gehen/fahren
go see (informal)	besuchen
pointy ['pɔɪnti]	spitz
kinda bumpy = kind of bumpy [kaɪndə 'bʌmpi]	irgendwie uneben, irgendwie huckelig
we gotta lot of ... = we've got a lot of ...	wir haben viel ...
a whole lot of land	*etwa:* enorm viel Land/Fläche
stand out from	hervorstechen aus

→ **Beachte die Schreibweise!**
Stummes w: ***w**hole*
hole = Loch

Irregular verbs

Infinitive form	Simple past form	Present perfect form
become [bɪ'kʌm]	I became [bɪ'keɪm]	I've become [bɪ'kʌm]
know [nəʊ]	I knew [nju:]	I've known [nəʊn]
shoot [ʃu:t]	I shot [ʃɒt]	I've shot [ʃɒt]

Unit 3

TIPP Wortarten-Zauberei mit Endungen

An der Endung eines Wortes kannst du oft sehen, ob es sich um ein Nomen, ein Verb oder ein Adjektiv handelt.

Nomen können von Verben stammen und haben dann verschiedene Endungen:
mix** these things → you'll get a nice **mixture**; they'll **free** him → he'll love his **freedom
*they **organise** things → it's an ...*

Bei Nomen mit ***-er*** kann es sich um Wörter für Menschen handeln.
*I **fight** → I'm a **fighter**; she **travels** → she's a **traveller***
*you **skate** well → you're a good ...; he can **dance** → he's a ...*

Manche Nomen haben gar keine Endung und sehen aus wie das Verb.
Hier erkennst du nur im Zusammenhang, ob es ein Verb oder ein Nomen ist.
*let's **dance** → this is a new **dance**; they **report** on music → it's an interesting ...*
*I can **help** you → do you need ...?*

Auch Adjektive entstehen oft aus anderen Wörtern und einer Endung:
*there's **peace** → we're **peaceful**; you **help** others → you're ...*
*it's an old **tradition** → **traditional** music; it's in the **centre** → it's ...*

Living in Calgary

p. 38	**railway** ['reɪlweɪ]	Eisenbahn →	
	oil was found	Öl wurde gefunden	
	clear [klɪə]	*hier:* (Schnee) fegen	→ Please clear the snow from the path.
p. 39	a big dump of snow *(informal)* [dʌmp əv 'snəʊ]	starker Schneefall	
	probationary driver's license *(CanE/AE)* [prə'beɪʃnri draɪvəz laɪsns]	Führerschein auf Probe →	
	after **bad** snow	wenn viel Schnee gefallen ist	
	the roads are cleared	die Straßen werden geräumt *(bei Schnee)*	
	snowshoeing ['snəʊʃuːɪŋ]	Snowshoeing *(mit speziellen Schuhen über Schnee und Eis wandern)*	
	skate [skeɪt]	*hier:* Schlittschuh laufen, Eis laufen	
	chore [tʃɔː]	(lästige) Arbeit, Pflicht	→ A chore is work which you don't like very much.
	sidewalk *(CanE/AE)* ['saɪdwɔːk]	Bürgersteig	
	Yuk! [jʌk]	Igitt!	
	out front [aʊt 'frʌnt]	draußen vor dem Haus	
	Chinook [tʃɪ'nuːk]	Chinook *(warmer Wind)* →	
	ski [ski]	Ski fahren	
	cottage ['kɒtɪdʒ]	Häuschen, Ferienhaus	
	grandparents ['grænpeərənts]	Großeltern	
	resort [rɪ'zɔːt]	Urlaubsort, Ferien- und Freizeitort	

Achtung:
the railway system, a railway station
aber: *I'm going by train.*

CanE/AE: Diese Wörter hörst du eher in Kanada und in den USA, nicht so häufig in Großbritannien.

Der Chinook ist ein Fallwind an der Ostseite der Rocky Mountains, ähnlich dem Föhn in den Alpen.

eɪ **na**tion, th**ey** dʒ **j**unior, ran**g**er

Presentation

p. 40	**skates** [skeɪts]	Schlittschuhe	
	quite [kwaɪt]	ziemlich →	
	she held → hold [held]	sie hielt	
	fall over [fɔːl 'əʊvə]	hinfallen	
	over and over again	immer und immer wieder	
	hold out a hand	eine Hand ausstrecken	
	cute [kjuːt]	süß, niedlich	→ What a cute little cat!
	pick up [pɪk 'ʌp]	hochheben	
	skater ['skeɪtə]	*hier:* Eisläufer/in	
p. 41	**date** [deɪt]	Verabredung	
	dinner ['dɪnə]	Abendessen	
	anniversary [ænɪ'vɜːsəri]	Jahrestag, Feiertag	
	hire ['haɪə]	mieten, (aus)leihen	→ You don't have skates? No problem. You can hire them here!
	graduation, grad *(informal)* *(CanE/AE)* [grædʒu'eɪʃn, græd]	Schulabschlussfeier *(mit feierlicher Überreichung der Zeugnisse)*	
	dress [dres]	Kleid	
	dinner dance ['dɪnə dɑːns]	Festessen mit anschließendem Tanz	
	pyjamas *(pl)* [pə'dʒɑːməz]	Schlafanzug	→ Where are my pink pyjamas?
	stay up	aufbleiben, nicht schlafen gehen	
	pancake ['pænkeɪk]	Pfannkuchen	
	awake [ə'weɪk]	wach	
	valentine card ['væləntaɪnz kɑːd]	Valentinskarte →	

Vorsicht Verwechlungsgefahr!
Adverb *quite*:
***quite** good* = ziemlich gut
Adjektiv *quiet*:
*it's **quiet*** = es ist ruhig

Am 14. Februar, dem Valentinstag, schicken Verliebte einander Karten oder kleine Geschenke.

Skills

p. 42	**online banking** ['ɒnlaɪn bæŋkɪŋ]	Onlinebanking, Bankgeschäfte abwickeln über das Internet	
p. 44	**chat** [tʃæt]	plaudern, sich unterhalten	
	active ['æktɪv]	aktiv →	
	chill out [tʃil 'aʊt] *(informal)*	sich entspannen, „relaxen"	
	reason ['riːzn]	Grund	→ There must be a reason why he's so sad.
	dirt biking ['dɜːt baɪkiŋ]	Offroad-Motorradfahren	
	dirt bike ['dɜːt baɪk]	Offroad-Motorrad	
	dirt track ['dɜːt træk]	Offroad-Strecke	

Vorsicht Betonung!
<u>ac</u>*tive* (Engl.)
ak<u>tiv</u> (Dt.)

Story 3 – Mallory gets the gold!

p. 50	**report on** [rɪ'pɔːt]	berichten über →	
	how long **have you been learning** it?	seit wann lernst du es?	
	I've been doing it for five years now	ich mache es jetzt seit fünf Jahren	
	I was scared [skeəd]	ich hatte Angst	→ Are you scared of mice?
	it's about being strong	es geht darum, stark zu sein	
	class [klɑːs]	Kurs	
	help out with	(aus)helfen bei	
	a bit [bɪt]	ein bisschen	→ You're a bit too late!
p. 51	**except for** [ɪ'ksept fə]	bis auf, abgesehen von	
	countryside ['kʌntrisaɪd]	Landschaft	
	neighbourhood ['neɪbəhʊd]	Gegend	

*a TV **report** about the competition = they **reported** on the competition*

z sci**ss**ors, gri**zz**ly s **s**oap, **s**un

huge [hjuːdʒ]	riesig	→ This is a huge building.
mostly [ˈməʊstli]	hauptsächlich	

Irregular verbs

Infinitive form	Simple past form	Present perfect form
hold [həʊld]	I held [held]	I've held [held]
fall over [fɔːl ˈəʊvə]	I fell [fel]	I've fallen [ˈfɔːlən]

Unit 4

TIPP Texte markieren

- **Wieso überhaupt?** Um in einem längeren Text wichtige Fakten hervorzuheben, damit du sie schnell wiederfindest oder weil du darüber berichten sollst.
- **Wo?** Nur auf Fotokopien oder in eigenen Materialien!
- **Was?** Nur Wörter oder Zahlen, die für dich und dein Thema wichtig sind. Das können ein oder zwei Wörter pro Satz sein oder sogar weniger.
- **Wie?** Durch Unterstreichen, Hervorheben mit einem Textmarker oder Einkreisen.

Koalas live in Australia. They look like small bears, but their closest relatives are in fact animals like kangaroos. They can live up to 13 years. They live in trees and eat leaves.

Koalas live in Australia. They look like small bears, but their closest relatives are in fact animals like kangaroos. They can live up to 13 years. They live in trees and eat leaves.

Koalas live in Australia. They look like small bears, but their closest relatives are in fact animals like kangaroos. They can live up to 13 years. They live in trees and eat leaves.

Down under

p. 52	**opera house** [ˈɒprə haʊs]	Opernhaus	→ Sydney has a very famous opera house.
	kookaburra [ˈkʊkəbʌrə]	Rieseneisvogel, „lachender Hans"	
	koala (bear) [kəʊˈɑːlə]	Koala(bär)	
	emu [ˈiːmjuː]	Emu *(großer Laufvogel)*	
	Australian rules football	Football nach australischen Regeln, australischer Football →	
	Aboriginal people [æbəˈridʒənl]	australische Ureinwohner/innen →	
	didgeridoo [dɪdʒəriˈduː]	Didgeridoo *(Blasinstrument der austr. Ureinwohner)*	
	boomerang [ˈbuːməræŋ]	Bumerang	
	kangaroo [kæŋgəˈruː]	Känguru	
	Australian [ɒˈstreɪliən]	australisch	→ Kangaroos are *Australian* animals.

→ Bei *Australian rules football* wird ein ovaler Ball mit Füßen und Händen gespielt.

→ *Aboriginal people* leben schon seit ca. 50.000 Jahren in Australien. Es gibt viele verschiedene Völker.

Presentation

p. 54	**Australian** [ɒˈstreɪliən]	Australier/in	→ *Australians* love sport.
	harm [hɑːm]	schaden, Schaden zufügen	→ Viruses can harm your computer.
	environment [ɪnˈvaɪrənmənt]	Umwelt	
	settlement [ˈsetlmənt]	Siedlung	

tʃ **ch**ip, **ch**eer iː pr**e**-, scr**ee**n

	criminal ['krɪmɪnl]	Verbrecher/in	→ Two criminals with masks and guns came into the bank.

	punishment ['pʌnɪʃmənt]	Strafe	
	land [lænd]	Land, Grund und Boden ➔	
	pom *(AustE)* [pɒm]	Engländer/in ➔	
	since (...) **they've been coming ...**	seit (...) kommen sie ...	

> ➔ **Vergleiche:** Zwei Wörter für **Land**!
> *Canada is a big **country**.*
> *They bought a piece of **land**.*

	wealthy ['welθi]	wohlhabend	→ another word for *rich*
p. 55	**G'day!** *(AustE)* [gə'deɪ]	Guten Tag!	
	Oz *(informal)* [ɒz]	Australien	
	I'll **introduce** myself [ɪntrə'djuːs]	ich werde mich vorstellen	→ Let me introduce my wife to you.

> ➔ ⚠ In Australien und Neuseeland ist *poms* oder *pommies* ein abwertendes Wort für Briten.

	they **enjoy themselves**	sie haben Spaß	
	spoil [spɔɪl]	verwöhnen	
	build [bɪld]	bauen ➔	
	it was built [bɪlt]	es wurde gebaut	
	stairs [steəz]	(Treppen-)Stufen	
	certificate [sə'tɪfɪkət]	Urkunde, Bescheinigung	
	climber ['klaɪmə]	Kletterer, Kletterin	

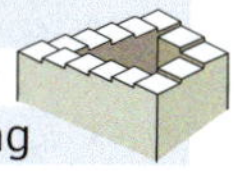

> ➔ **Beachte die Schreibweise!**
> Stummes u: *build*

	grey [greɪ]	grau	→ Mice and elephants are grey.
	mention ['menʃn]	erwähnen	
	attach to [ə'tætʃ]	befestigen an ➔	
	line [laɪn]	*hier:* Seil	
	she likes the photo of **herself** [hɜː'self]	sie mag das Foto von sich	
	FAQ = frequently asked questions [ef eɪ 'kjuː, friːkwəntli ɑːskt 'kwestʃnz]	häufig gestellte Fragen	

> ➔ **Vorsicht!**
> *Attach yourself to the line.* =
> Mach dich an dem Seil fest.

Skills

p. 56	**Aboriginal** life [æbə'ridʒənl]	Leben der australischen Ureinwohner/innen	
	drum [drʌm]	Trommel	→ *she plays (the) drums* = sie spielt Schlagzeug
	bullroarer ['bʊlrɔːrə]	Schwirrholz *(Musikinstrument der Aboriginal people)*	
	ceremony ['serəməni]	Zeremonie	
	Uluru [uːlʊ'ruː]	Ayers Rock *(berühmter Berg in Australien)* ➔	

> ➔ Der Uluru ist für die *Aboriginal people* ein Heiligtum. Sie dulden es zwar, sehen es aber nicht gern, dass Touristen ihn besteigen.

p. 58	**general** ['dʒenrəl]	allgemein	
	nationality [næʃə'næləti]	Nationalität	
	tall [tɔːl]	groß *(bei Menschen)*; hoch ➔	
	short [ʃɔːt]	klein *(bei Menschen)*	→ She's not very tall, she's short.
	fair [feə]	blond	
	glasses *(pl.)* ['glɑːsɪz]	(eine) Brille ➔	
	serious ['sɪəriəs]	ernst(haft)	
	laid-back [leɪd 'bæk]	gelassen, cool	
	guess [ges]	(er)raten	
	(a) guess [ges]	(einmal) Raten	
p. 59	**get on well** with	sich gut verstehen mit	
	specially ['speʃəli]	besonders	
	humour ['hjuːmə]	Humor	
	sense of humour [sens əv 'hjuːmə]	Sinn für Humor ➔	
	meet up	sich treffen	

> ➔ *a **tall** man; a **tall**/**high** building*

> ➔ **Achtung!**
> Englisch: Plural, Deutsch: Singular
> *glasses* = (eine) Brille
> *trousers* = (eine) Hose
> *pyjamas* = (ein) Schlafanzug

> ➔ **Vorsicht!**
> *He has a good sense of humour.*
> = einen guten Sinn für Humor.

eɪ late, raise   ʌ culture, stuck

Practice and Revision

p. 60	**comparison** [kəm'pærɪsən]	Vergleich	→ Trains are slow in comparison with planes.
	make comparisons!	vergleiche!	

Story 4 – Don't feed the dingoes!

p. 64	**dingo, pl. dingoes** ['dɪŋgəʊ]	Dingo, australischer Wildhund	
	bush [bʊʃ]	Buschlandschaft	
	hometown ['həʊmtaʊn]	Heimatstadt	
	mainland ['meɪnlænd]	Festland	
	put up (a tent)	(Zelt) aufbauen	
	throw [θrəʊ]	werfen	→ I'll throw these old comics away.
	scraps [skræps]	Reste	
	he fell **asleep** [ə'sli:p]	er schlief ein	→ The lesson was so boring that I fell asleep.
p. 65	**it woke him up → wake up** [wəʊk]	es weckte ihn auf	
	he was **asleep**	er schlief	
	put on	*(Kleidung)* anziehen	
	Land Rover ['lænd rəʊvə]	Landrover *(geländegängiges Auto)*	
	panic ['pænɪk]	Panik bekommen	→ Don't panic! Stay cool.
	they **had killed**	sie hatten getötet	
	stick [stɪk]	Stock	
	he threw → throw [θru:]	er warf	
	shoulder ['ʃəʊldə]	Schulter	

Vorsicht!
put up = aufbauen
put on = anziehen

Irregular verbs

Infinitive form	Simple past form	Present perfect form
build [bɪld]	I built [bɪlt]	I've built [bɪlt]
wake up [weɪk 'ʌp]	I woke up [wəʊk]	I've woken up ['wəʊkən]
throw [θrəʊ]	I threw [θru:]	I've thrown [θrəʊn]

Oz! Australia Magazine

p. 66	**the outback** ['aʊtbæk]	das Hinterland, der Busch (Australiens)	
	live [laɪv]	live, direkt (übertragen)	
	satellite technology ['sætəlaɪt teknɒlədʒi]	Satellitentechnik	
	so far	bisher	
	danger ['deɪndʒə]	Gefahr	
	a long way from	weit entfernt von	→ it's a long way from here = it's far from here
	a plane **is called**	ein Flugzeug wird gerufen	
	by **radio**	über Funk	
	patient ['peɪʃnt]	Patient/in	
	she **is taken**	sie wird gebracht	
	bend [bend]	*(hier:)* eine Kurve machen	→ The road goes down a hill and bends to the right.
	it **was finished**	es/sie wurde fertiggestellt	
	Afghan camel ['æfgæn 'kæml]	afghanisches Kamel	

Beachte die Aussprache!
live music mit [ai]
I live here mit [i]

Ein Wort, zwei Bedeutungen:
by radio = Funk
listen to the radio = Radio

w **working, wine**   aɪ **myself, design**

	slang [slæŋ]	Slang, Umgangssprache	
	sheila (AustE) ['ʃi:lə]	Frau	
	tinny (AustE) ['tɪni]	Dose Bier	
	no worries! (AustE) ['wʌriz]	*(etwa)* kein Problem!	
	barbie (AustE) ['bɑ:bi]	Grillfest	
	this arvo (AustE) ['ɑ:vəʊ]	heute Nachmittag	
	scratchie (AustE) ['skrætʃi]	Rubellos	
	lottery scratchcard ['lɒtəri 'skrætʃkɑ:d]	Rubellos	
	sunnies (AustE) ['sʌni:z]	Sonnenbrille	
p. 67	**western** ['westən]	westlich	
	musician [mju'zɪʃn]	Musiker/in	
	abroad [ə'brɔ:d]	im Ausland	
	several ['sevrəl]	mehrere	
	treaty ['tri:ti]	Vertrag	
	promise ['prɒmɪs]	Versprechen	→ You should always keep your promises!
	television ['telɪvɪʒn]	Fernsehen	
	politician [pɒlə'tɪʃn]	Politiker/in	
	priceless ['praɪsles]	unbezahlbar	
	it was given up	es wurde aufgegeben	
	it was bought	es wurde gekauft	
	it was sold	es wurde verkauft	
	the planting ['plɑ:ntiŋ]	*(etwa:)* das Aufstellen	
	Union Jack [ju:niən 'dʒæk]	die britische Flagge	
	separated ['sepəreɪtɪd]	getrennt	
	dream	träumen	
	bright [braɪt]	hell	
	destiny ['destəni]	Schicksal	
	promises can be broken	Versprechen werden manchmal nicht gehalten	
	writing in the sand	Schrift im Sand	

Unit 5

TIPP

Stell dir vor, du hörst einen englischen Text und sollst später den Inhalt wiedergeben. Hier sind einige Tipps.

- Gibt es vor dem Hören Hinweise, worum es geht (Bilder, Überschriften)?
- Konzentriere dich auf den gesamten Inhalt. Nicht aufgeben, wenn du manche Wörter nicht verstehst. Oft werden wichtige Informationen wiederholt.
- Klingt die Person, die spricht, ernst, fröhlich oder traurig? Was wird besonders betont? Solche Dinge können dir beim Verständnis helfen.
- Notiere dir die wichtigsten Fakten. Mach aber kurze Notizen oder verwende Symbole. Du kannst sie vielleicht später ergänzen.

A better life

p. 68	one **in** four	eine/r von vier(en)	→ 25 per cent of the students = one in four students
	emigrate ['emɪgreɪt]	auswandern	

ɔ: talk, yours e dead, met

	because of	wegen	→ Let's stay indoors because of the rain.
	lifestyle ['laɪfstaɪl]	Lebensstil	
	opportunity [ɒpə'ju:nəti]	Möglichkeit	
	member ['membə]	Mitglied	
p. 69	**for** different reasons	aus unterschiedlichen Gründen	

Presentation

p. 70	**new year**	Neujahr(stag)	
	decision [dɪ'sɪʒn]	Entscheidung	
	make a decision	eine Entscheidung treffen, sich entscheiden	
	exhibition [eksɪ'bɪʃn]	Ausstellung	→ Do you like art exhibitions?
	apply [ə'plaɪ]	einen Antrag stellen	
	medical ['medɪkl]	(ärztliche) Untersuchung	
	visa ['vi:zə] 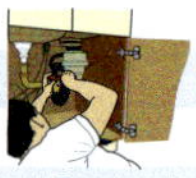	Visum →	
	plumber ['plʌmə]	Installateur/in	
	savings *(pl.)* ['seivɪŋz]	Ersparnisse	
	visa points	*Punkte, die man braucht, damit der Einwanderungsantrag genehmigt wird* →	
	send off	wegschicken	
	we chose → **choose** [tʃəʊz]	wir wählten (aus)	
	for our new home	als (unsere) neue Heimat	
	furniture *(sing.)* ['fɜ:nɪtʃə]	Möbel → 	
	seat [si:t]	Sitzplatz	
	one way	*(Fahrkarte)* einfache Strecke, ohne Rückfahrkarte	
	cry [kraɪ]	weinen	→ When you're sad, you cry. 
	we cried → **cry** [kraɪd]	wir weinten	
	settle in [setl 'ɪn]	sich einleben	
	papers *(pl.)* ['peɪpəz]	Papiere, Unterlagen	
p. 71	**even** ['i:vn]	sogar	
	complain [kəm'pleɪn]	sich beschweren	→ Don't complain about the weather! I can't change it.
	skin **cancer** ['kænsə]	Hautkrebs 	
	hat [hæt]	Hut; Mütze	
	sunscreen ['sʌnskri:n]	Sonnencreme	→ *BE* sun cream
	unpleasant [ʌn'pleznt] 	unangenehm	
	lizard ['lɪzəd]	Eidechse	
	spider ['spaɪdə] 	Spinne 	
	fly [flaɪ]	Fliege	
	annoying [ə'nɔɪɪŋ]	ärgerlich, lästig	
	midges ['mɪdʒɪz]	Kriebelmücken →	
	Slip, slop, slap! ['slɪp slɒp slæp]	Slogan in Australien zur Erinnerung an Sonnenschutzmaßnahmen	
	slip on ['slɪp ɒn]	schnell anziehen, überziehen	
	slop on sunscreen *(infml.)* ['slɒp ɒn]	sich mit reichlich Sonnencreme eincremen	
	slap on *(infml.)* ['slæp ɒn]	draufklatschen	
	relaxed [rɪ'lækst]	entspannt	
	hang out	herumhängen	
	make (new) friends	(neue) Freunde/Freundinnen finden	→ She's a nice person and makes friends easily.

→ **Vorsicht Verwechlungsgefahr!**
Englisch: *one visa, two visas*
Deutsch: ein Visum, zwei Visa

→ Zum Einwandern nach Australien muss man einen „Punktetest" bestehen. Punkte bekommt man z.B. für Beruf, Alter und Englischkenntnisse.

→ **Vorsicht! Im Englischen Singular!**
your furniture is nice =
eure Möbel sind schön

→ Diese kleinen schottischen Mücken sehen aus wie Obstfliegen, sind aber sehr beißfreudig und treten in großen Schwärmen auf.

ɑ won, lost ð **th**e, mo**th**er

	on the coast	an der Küste
	houses like **ours** ['aʊəz]	Häuser wie unseres

Skills

p. 72	**pilot** ['paɪlət]	Pilot/in
p. 74	**visit** ['vɪzɪt]	Besuch
	dry boat race	*etwa:* Trockenbootrennen →
	charity ['tʃærəti]	Wohltätigkeit(sorganisation), wohltätige Zwecke
p. 75	**mainly** ['meɪnli]	hauptsächlich
	alcohol ['ælkəhɒl]	Alkohol →
	snake [sneɪk]	Schlange
	Western Brown	Westliche Braunschlange *(hochgiftige Schlangenart)*

→ Bei dieser jährlichen „Scherz-Regatta" tragen die Teilnehmer ihre Boote durch ein ausgetrocknetes Flussbett. Bei Regen fällt die Regatta aus!

→ **Vorsicht Betonung!**
alcohol (Engl.)
Alkohol (Dt.)

Practice and Revision

p. 76	**it meant** → **mean** [ment]	es bedeutete
	hunter ['hʌntə]	Jäger/in
p. 77	**application** [æplɪ'keɪʃn]	Bewerbung (auf eine Arbeitsstelle)
	barista [bə'ri:stə]	Barista *(Spezialist/in an der Espressomaschine, der/die Kaffee zubereitet und serviert)*
	head barista	Chef-Barista
	senior job ['si:niə]	leitende Position
	application form	Bewerbungsformular
	resume ['rezjumeɪ]	Lebenslauf →
	by email	per E-Mail
	job **advertisement**, job **advert** [əd'vɜ:tɪsmənt, 'ædvɜ:t]	Stellenanzeige

→ Have you sent off your application for the job?

→ Im britischen Englisch heißt es *CV*, das steht für *curriculum vitae*, lateinisch für „Lebenslauf".

Irregular verbs

Infinitive form	Simple past form	Present perfect form
mean [mi:n]	I meant [ment]	I've meant [ment]
choose [tʃu:z]	I chose [tʃəʊz]	I've chosen ['tʃəʊzn]

Alphabetische Liste der Wörter aus Band 1–5 (Englisch–Deutsch)
Die Angaben nach den Einträgen verweisen auf das Vorkommen der Wörter:
U = Unit
Verwendete Abkürzungen:
AE = American English — CanE/AE = Canadian/American English
AustE = Australian English — BE = British English
sb. = somebody — sth. = something
jdn. = jemanden — jdm. = jemandem
ugs. = umgangssprachlich
pl. = Plural — no pl. = kein Plural
Die Auszeichnungen (**fett**, normal, *kursiv*) verweisen auf den Lernstatus:
U2: 35 = produktives Wort in Unit 2 auf Seite 35,
U1: 11 = rezeptives Wort auf Seite 11,
U1: 13 = fakultatives Wort in Unit 1 auf Seite 13.

A

a [ə] ein/eine; **an** ein/eine; **a (day)** pro (Tag)
a.m. [eɪ'em] vormittags, morgens
aboriginal [æbə'rɪdʒənl]: **Aboriginal life** Leben der australischen Ureinwohner/innen **U4:** 56; **Aboriginal people** australische Ureinwohner/innen **U4:** 52; **aboriginal people** Ureinwohner/innen **U2:** 22
about [ə'baʊt] ungefähr; über; **... the story is about ...** ... die Geschichte handelt von ...; **ask a partner about** eine(n) Partner/in fragen über/nach; **at about** gegen; (um) zirka; **it's about being strong** es geht darum, stark zu sein **U3:** 50; **mad about** verrückt nach; **talk about** sprechen über; **What about ...?** Wie wäre es mit ...?
above [ə'bʌv] über
abroad [ə'brɔːd] im Ausland **U4:** 67
abseil ['æbseɪl] abseilen
accent ['æksent] Akzent; *by your accent* aufgrund Ihres/deines Akzents *U2: 36*
access ['ækses]: *Internet access* Internetzugang *U1: 13*
accident ['æksɪdənt] Unfall
accurate ['ækjərət] genau, präzise *U5: 73*
across [ə'krɒs] (quer) über
act [ækt] **1** Aufführung, Auftritt; **2** darstellen, vorspielen
action ['ækʃn] Action; Handlung, Aktion, Aktivität
activity [æk'tɪvəti] Aktivität
address [ə'dres] Adresse, Anschrift
admire [əd'maɪə] bewundern, verehren
adult ['ædʌlt] Erwachsene/r
advance: in advance [ɪn əd'vɑːns] im Voraus
adventure [əd'ventʃə] Abenteuer
advert ['ædvɜːt] Anzeige; **job advert** Stellenanzeige **U5:** 77
advertisement [əd'vɜːtɪsmənt]: **job advertisement** Stellenanzeige **U5:** 77
Afghan camel ['æfgæn 'kæml] afghanisches Kamel *U4: 66*
African ['æfrɪkən] Afrikaner/in; afrikanisch
African National Congress (= ANC) [æfrɪkən næʃnəl 'kɒŋgres] Afrikanischer Nationalkongress *(südafr. Partei und Interessenvertretung der Schwarzen)* U1: 21
Afrikaans [æfrɪ'kɑːns] Afrikaans *(Sprache in Südafrika)* **U1:** 11
after ['ɑːftə] nach *(zeitlich)*
afternoon: Good afternoon. [gʊd ɑːftə'nuːn] Guten Tag. *(nachmittags)*
again [ə'gen] wieder; noch einmal; **over and over again** immer und immer wieder **U3:** 40
against [ə'geɪnst] gegen; **race against** um die Wette laufen
age [eɪdʒ] Alter
aggressive [ə'gresɪv] aggressiv
ago [ə'gəʊ] vor
agree [ə'griː] übereinstimmen, zustimmen
AIDS [eɪdz] Aids *(gefährliche Infektionskrankheit)* **U1:** 10
air [eə] Luft; **air-conditioning** Klimatisierung, Klimaanlage
airfield ['eəfiːld] Flugplatz *U5: 73*
airport ['eəpɔːt] Flughafen; **airport desk** Flugschalter
alarm clock [ə'lɑːm klɒk] Wecker
album ['ælbəm] Album
alcohol ['ælkəhɒl] Alkohol **U5:** 75
alien ['eɪliən] Außerirdischer
alive [ə'laɪv]: **be alive** am Leben sein, leben **U2:** 35
all [ɔːl] der/die/das ganze; alle; **all over** überall; **all right** in Ordnung
alligator ['ælɪgeɪtə] Alligator
allowed [ə'laʊd]: **they weren't allowed to** sie durften nicht **U1:** 20
almost ['ɔːlməʊst] fast, beinahe
alone [ə'ləʊn] allein
along [ə'lɒŋ] entlang; **go along** entlanggehen
alphabetical order [ælfə'betɪkl 'ɔːdə] alphabetische Reihenfolge
already [ɔːl'redi] schon, bereits
also ['ɔːlsəʊ] auch
always ['ɔːlweɪz] immer
amazed: he was amazed [hiː wɒz ə'meɪzd] er war erstaunt
America [ə'merɪkə] Amerika
American [ə'merɪkən] amerikanisch; Amerikaner/in; **Native American** ['neɪtɪv ə'merɪkən] amerikanische/r Ureinwohner/in

amount [ə'maunt]: *they don't amount* *etwa:* sie sind nicht viel wert *U2: 37*
ANC (= African National Congress) [ei en 'si] Afrikanischer Nationalkongress *(südafr. Partei und Interessenvertretung der Schwarzen)* U1: 21
and [ænd] und
angrily ['æŋgrili] ärgerlich
angry ['æŋgri] böse, wütend
animal ['ænıml] Tier; **animal home** Tierheim
anniversary [ænı'vɜ:səri] Jahrestag, Feiertag **U3:** 41
annoying [ə'nɔıŋ] ärgerlich, lästig **U5:** 71
another [ə'nʌðə] ein/e andere(r, s), ein/e weitere(r, s)
answer ['ɑ:nsə] **1** Antwort; **2** antworten; beantworten
antenna [æn'tenə] Antenne
anthem ['ænθəm]: *national anthem* Nationalhymne *U2: 36*
any ['eni] irgendein/e, jede/s, irgendwelche; **not any** kein/e; **not ... any more** nicht mehr, keine/n ... mehr **U1:** 21
anybody ['enibɒdi] jede(r) (beliebige); (irgend)jemand
anything ['eniθıŋ] (irgend)etwas; **Anything else?** Sonst noch etwas?
anywhere ['eniweə] irgendwo(hin)
apart from [ə'pɑ:t frəm] außer, abgesehen von
apartheid [ə'pɑ:thaıt] Apartheid *(früheres System der Trennung zwischen Weißen und Farbigen in Südafrika)* **U1:** 20
apartment *(AE)* [ə'pɑ:tmənt] Wohnung
applaud [ə'plɔ:d] Beifall klatschen *U5: 73*
apple ['æpl] Apfel
application [æplı'keıʃn] Bewerbung (auf eine Arbeitsstelle) **U5:** 77; **application form** Bewerbungsformular **U5:** 77
apply [ə'plaı] einen Antrag stellen **U5:** 70
April ['eıprəl] April
Arctic ['ɑ:ktık] arktisch **U2:** 25; **the Arctic** die Arktis *(Gebiet um den Nordpol)* **U2:** 22
are [ɑ: ðeı]: **Are they ...?** Sind sie ...?; **aren't (= are not)** sind nicht

area ['eəriə] Gebiet
arm [ɑ:m] Arm
army ['ɑ:mi] Armee **U2:** 37
around [ə'raʊnd] umher, herum; **get around** herumkommen
arrest [ə'rest] verhaften
arrive [ə'raıv] ankommen, eintreffen
arrogant ['ærəgənt] arrogant
art [ɑ:t] Kunst; **pop art** Pop-Art *(Kunstrichtung, die ihre Motive den Massenmedien, der Werbung usw. entnimmt)*; **art gallery** Kunstgalerie
article ['ɑ:tıkl] (Zeitungs-)Artikel
artist ['ɑ:tıst] Künstler/in
arvo ['ɑ:vəʊ]: *this arvo* *(AustE)* heute Nachmittag *U4: 66*
as [æz] als; **the same as** genauso wie; dasselbe wie; **not so popular as ...** nicht so beliebt wie ...; **as friendly as** (genau)so freundlich wie; **as long as** solange
Asian ['eıʃn] Asiate/Asiatin; asiatisch
ask [ɑ:sk] fragen; **ask a partner about** eine(n) Partner/in fragen über/nach; **she's asking about** sie fragt nach
asleep [ə'sli:p]: **he fell asleep** er schlief ein **U4:** 64; **he was asleep** er schlief **U4:** 65
assistant: shop assistant ['ʃɒp ə'sıstənt] Verkäufer/in
astronaut ['æstrənɔ:t] Astronaut/in
at [æt] an, in; bei; **at ... house** bei ... zu Hause; **at last** endlich; **at school** in der Schule; **at the moment** jetzt, in diesem Moment; **at the seaside** am Meer
ate → eat [eıt] *simple past* von **eat**
attach [ə'tætʃ]: **attach to** befestigen an **U4:** 55
attachment [ə'tætʃmənt]: **email attachment** Anhang an eine E-Mail **U2:** 31
attack [ə'tæk] Angriff, Attacke *U4: 57*
attraction [ə'trækʃn] Attraktion, Anziehungspunkt
audio guide ['ɔ:dıəʊ gaıd] Audioguide *(elektronischer Museumsführer)* **U2:** 26
August ['ɔ:gəst] August
aunt [ɑ:nt] Tante

Australian [ɒ'streıliən] australisch **U4:** 54; Australier/in **U4:** 52; **Australian rules football** Football nach australischen Regeln, australischer Football U4: 52
Austria ['ɒstriə] Österreich
autograph ['ɔ:təgrɑ:f] Autogramm
autumn ['ɔ:təm] Herbst
avenue ['ævənju:] Allee, Boulevard
awake [ə'weık] wach **U3:** 41
away [ə'weı] verreist; weg
Ayers Rock [eəz 'rɒk] *engl. Name für* Uluru *U4: 57*

B

B&B (Bed & Breakfast) [bed ənd 'brekfəst] Frühstückspension, Zimmer mit Frühstück
baby ['beıbi] Baby
babysitter ['beıbısıtə] Babysitter
back [bæk] zurück; *back yard* [bæk 'jɑ:d] Hinterhof *U2: 27*; **get back** zurückkommen/-finden
backcountry ['bækkʌntri] Hinterland, Wildnis
background ['bækgraʊnd] Hintergrund, Herkunft
backpack ['bækpæk] Rucksack
backpacker ['bækpækə] Rucksacktourist/in **U1:** 9
backpacking ['bækpækıŋ] Rucksackreisen; Wandern
backwards ['bækwədz] rückwärts
bad [bæd]: **bad at** schlecht in; **not bad** nicht schlecht (es geht/ging so); **That's too bad.** *(ugs.)* Das ist schade.; **after bad snow** wenn viel Schnee gefallen ist U3: 39
badge [bædʒ] Abzeichen, Button
bag [bæg] (Schul-)Tasche; Beutel, Tüte, Sack; **sleeping bag** Schlafsack
bagel *(AE)* ['beıgl] Bagel *(weiches, ringförmiges Brötchen)*
baked [beıkt 'bi:nz]: **baked beans** gebackene Bohnen (in Tomatensoße); **baked potato** gebackene Kartoffel
ball [bɔ:l] Ball
banana [bə'nɑ:nə] Banane
band [bænd] Band, (Musik-)Gruppe; **rock band** Rockband
bank [bæŋk] Bank, Sparkasse

banking: online banking ['ɒnlaɪn bæŋkɪŋ] Onlinebanking, Bankgeschäfte über das Internet abwickeln **U3:** 42
barbecue ['bɑ:bɪkju:] Grillparty
barbie (AustE) ['bɑ:bi] Grillfest *U4: 66*
barely ['beəli] kaum *U2: 37*
barista [bə'ri:stə] Barista *(Spezialist/in an der Espressomaschine, der/die Kaffee zubereitet und serviert)* U5: 77; **head barista** Chef-Barista U5: 77
base [beɪs] Basis(station) *U5: 73*
baseball ['beɪsbɔ:l] Baseball
based [beɪst]: *based (near Ottawa)* mit Sitz (nahe Ottawa) *U2: 27*
basement *(AE)* ['beɪsmənt] Keller
basic reading [beɪsɪk 'ri:dɪŋ] Basiswissen: Lesen
basket ['bɑ:skɪt] Korb
basketball ['bɑ:skɪtbɔ:l] Basketball
bathroom ['bɑ:θru:m] Badezimmer
battery (*pl.*: **batteries**) ['bætərɪ] Batterie, Batterien
battle ['bætl] Schlacht *U4: 57*
Bavaria [bə'veəriə] Bayern; **Bavarian** bayerisch; Bayer/in
bay [beɪ] Bucht *U2: 27*
BBC [bi: bi: 'si:] British Broadcasting Corporation *(öffentlich-rechtliche Rundfunk- und Fernsehanstalt Großbritanniens)*
be [bi] sein; **be fed up** die Nase voll haben; **be frightened** verängstigt sein; Angst haben
beach [bi:tʃ] Strand
bean [bi:n] Bohne; **baked beans** gebackene Bohnen (in Tomatensoße)
bear [beə] Bär; **grizzly bear** Grislibär; **polar bear** ['pəʊlə beə] Eisbär **U2:** 22; **teddy bear** Teddybär
beat: the beat of the street [bi:t əv ðə 'stri:t] der Rhythmus der Straße **U1:** 10
beautician [bju:'tɪʃn] Kosmetiker/in
beautiful ['bju:tɪfəl] (wunder) schön
became → become [bɪ'keɪm] *simple past* von **become**
because [bɪ'kɒz] weil; **because of** wegen **U5:** 68
become [bɪ'kʌm] werden
become → become [bɪ'kʌm]: **become → become** *present perfect* von **become** **U2:** 25
bed [bed] Bett; **Bed & Breakfast (B&B)** Frühstückspension, Zimmer mit Frühstück
bedroom ['bedru:m] Schlafzimmer
been → be [bɪn] *present perfect* von **be**
before [bɪ'fɔ:] vor, bevor; schon einmal
began → begin [bɪ'gæn] *simple past* von **begin**
beginning [bɪ'gɪnɪŋ] Anfang *U4: 57*
behave [bɪ'heɪv] sich benehmen
behind [bɪ'haɪnd] hinter
believe [bɪ'li:v] glauben
bell [bel] Glocke
belong to [bɪ'lɒŋ tə] gehören (zu)
below [bɪ'ləʊ] unter, unterhalb (von); unten; **below 0°C** unter null Grad Celsius
bend [bend] eine Kurve machen **U4:** 66; Kurve *U5: 73*
best [best] bester/beste/bestes
bestseller [best'selə] Bestseller *U3: 43*
better ['betə] besser; **Better late than never.** Lieber spät als gar nicht.
between [bɪ'twi:n] zwischen
big [bɪg] groß; **bigger** größer; **bigger than** größer als
bike [baɪk] Fahrrad; **dirt bike** Offroad-Motorrad **U3:** 44; **mountain bike** Mountainbike fahren; **mountain bike** Mountainbike; **ride a bike** Rad fahren
biking ['baɪkiŋ]: **dirt biking** Offroad-Motorradfahren **U3:** 44
biography [baɪ'ɒgrəfi] Biographie, Lebensbeschreibung **U1:** 21
bird [bɜ:d] Vogel
biro ['baɪrəʊ] Kugelschreiber
birthday ['bɜ:θdeɪ] Geburtstag
biscuit ['bɪskɪt] Keks
bison ['baisn] Bison *(nordamerik. Wildrind)* **U2:** 31
bit [bɪt]: **a bit** ein bisschen **U3:** 50
black [blæk] **1** schwarz; **2** Schwarze/r
blog [blɒg] Internet-Tagebuch
blood [blʌd] Blut *U4: 57*
blow up [bləʊ 'ʌp] in die Luft jagen
blue [blu:] blau
board [bɔ:d] Tafel; Brett; Skateboard
boarder ['bɔ:də] Skateboardfahrer/in
boarding ['bɔ:dɪŋ] Einsteigen; **boarding card** Bordkarte
boat [bəʊt] Boot, Schiff; **dry boat race** *etwa:* Trockenbootrennen U5: 74
bone [bəʊn] Knochen **U2:** 29
book [bʊk] **1** Buch; **guide book** Reiseführer; **phone book** Telefonbuch; **2** buchen, reservieren
booking ['bʊkɪŋ] Buchung, Reservierung
boom [bu:m] Wachstum, Boom
boomerang ['bu:məræŋ] Bumerang **U4:** 52
boot [bu:t] Stiefel, Wanderschuh; Kofferraum
bored [bɔ:d] gelangweilt; you're bored; **you're bored** du langweilst dich, dir ist langweilig; **I'm bored.** Ich langweile mich.
boring ['bɔ:rɪŋ] langweilig
born: I was born in ... [aɪ wəz 'bɔ:n ɪn] Ich bin ... geboren.; **When were you born?** Wann bist du geboren?
both [bəʊθ] beide
bother to go ['bɒðə] sich die Mühe machen, zu gehen/fahren *U2: 37*
bottle: a bottle of ... [ə 'bɒtl əv] eine Flasche ...
bought → buy [bɔ:t] *simple past* und *present perfect* von **buy**; *it was bought* es wurde gekauft *U4: 67*
box: lunch box ['lʌntʃ bɒks] Butterbrotdose
boy [bɔɪ] Junge
braai [braɪ] Grillfest *(südafrikanisch)* U1: 11
branch [brɑ:ntʃ] Ast *U5: 73*
brand [brænd] Marke, Sorte; **brand name** Markenzeichen, -name; *branded (toys)* Marken-(Spielwaren) *U3: 43*
brave [breɪv] tapfer, mutig
bread [bred] Brot
break [breɪk] **1** Pause; **2** (zer)brechen, kaputtmachen
breakdance ['breɪkdɑ:ns] Breakdance
breakfast ['brekfəst] Frühstück; **have breakfast** frühstücken; **Bed & Breakfast (B&B)** Frühstückspension, Zimmer mit Frühstück
breath [breθ]: *he held his breath* er hielt den Atem an *U5: 73*
bridge [brɪdʒ] Brücke; Kommandobrücke (Schiff) *U2: 27*

[ʊə] **s**ure	[b] **b**ike	[p] **p**en	[d] **d**ay	[t] **t**en	[k] **b**oo**k**	[g] **g**o	[ŋ] morni**ng**	[l] **l**ike	[r] **r**uler

bright [braɪt] hell *U4: 67*
bring [brɪŋ] bringen, mitbringen
Britain ['brɪtn] Großbritannien
British ['brɪtɪʃ] britisch; Brite/Britin
broccoli ['brɒkəli] Brokkoli
brochure ['brəʊʃə] Broschüre, Prospekt
broke → break [brəʊk] *simple past* von **break**
broken ['brəʊkən] gebrochen, zerbrochen; kaputt, defekt; *promises can be broken* Versprechen werden manchmal nicht gehalten *U4: 67*
brother ['brʌðə] Bruder
brought → bring [brɔːt] *simple past* und *present perfect* von **bring**
brown [braʊn] braun; **Western Brown** Westliche Braunschlange *(hochgiftige Schlangenart)* U5: 75
brush [brʌʃ] **1** Pinsel; **2** bürsten; putzen
bubble ['bʌbl] Blase
buck *(AE) (ugs.)* [bʌk] Dollar
buffalo (*pl.:* **buffalo**) ['bʌfələʊ] Büffel
build [bɪld] bauen **U4:** 55
building ['bɪldɪŋ] Gebäude
built → build [bɪlt] *simple past* und *present perfect* von **build** **U4:** 55; **it was built** sie/es wurde gebaut **U4:** 55
bullroarer ['bʊlrɔːrə] Schwirrholz *(Musikinstrument der Aboriginal people)* U4: 56
bumpy: kinda bumpy = kind of bumpy (ugs.) [kaɪndə 'bʌmpi] irgendwie uneben, irgendwie huckelig *U2: 37*
burger ['bɜːgə] Hamburger
bus [bʌs] Bus; **bus driver** Busfahrer/in; **bus stop** Bushaltestelle; **bus tour** Bus(rund)reise; **on the bus/train/...** im Zug/Bus/...
bush [bʊʃ] Buschlandschaft **U4:** 64
business: for business [fə 'bɪznəs] geschäftlich
busy ['bɪzi] beschäftigt; **busy shop** gut besuchter Laden; **keep him busy** ihn beschäftigen, ihm Arbeit machen **U1:** 11
but [bʌt] aber
button ['bʌtn] Knopf
buy [baɪ] kaufen
by [baɪ]**: by email** per E-Mail **U5:** 77; **by radio** über Funk **U4:** 66; **by the way** [baɪ ðə 'weɪ] übrigens **U1:** 11; *by your accent* aufgrund Ihres/deines Akzents *U2: 36*; *pay by the hour* Bezahlung stundenweise *U1: 13*; **written by** geschrieben von
Bye(-bye). [baɪ, bə 'baɪ] Tschüs.

C

C = Celsius: below 0° C = Celsius [bɪ'ləʊ 'zɪərəʊ dɪ'griːz 'selsiəs] unter null Grad Celsius
café ['kæfeɪ] Café
cage [keɪdʒ] Käfig; **shark cage diving** Hai-Tauchen mit Käfigen U1: 15
cake [keɪk] Kuchen
calculator ['kælkjuleɪtə] Taschenrechner
calendar ['kælɪndə] Kalender
Californian [kælɪ'fɔːniən] Kalifornier/in; kalifornisch
call [kɔːl]**: (phone) call** **1** (Telefon-)Anruf, (An-)Ruf; **call centre** Call-Center; **2** anrufen; nennen
called → call [kɔːld]**: it's called** es wird genannt **U1:** 10; **it was called** [wəz 'kɔːld] es wurde genannt **U1:** 20; **a plane is called** ein Flugzeug wird gerufen **U4:** 66
calm [kɑːm] ruhig **U2:** 35
came → come [keɪm] *simple past* von **come**
camel ['kæml]*: Afghan camel* afghanisches Kamel *U4: 66*
camera ['kæmərə] Kamera; Fotoapparat
camp [kæmp] **1** zelten; **2** Zeltlager, Camp
campaign [kæm'peɪn] Aktion; Kampagne
camping holiday ['kæmpɪŋ hɒlədeɪ] Camping-Urlaub
campsite ['kæmpsaɪt] Campingplatz
can [kæn] **1** Dose, Büchse; **2** können; **Can I have a ...?** Kann ich eine(n)/ein ... haben?; **Can you spell ...?** Kannst du ... buchstabieren?; **can't** nicht können; **What can you ...?** Was kannst du ...?
Canadian [kə'neɪdiən] kanadisch; Kanadier/in **U2:** 22; **the Royal Canadian Mounted Police** ['maʊntəd] die königliche kanadische berittene Polizei U2: 22
cancer ['kɑːnsə]**: skin cancer** Hautkrebs **U5:** 71
candy *(AE)* ['kændi] Bonbon, Süßigkeiten
canoe [kə'nuː] Kanu fahren
capital ['kæpɪtl] Hauptstadt
captain ['kæptɪn] Kapitän/in *U5: 73*
capture ['kæptʃə] einnehmen, erobern **U2:** 34
car [kɑː] Auto; **stock car** Stockcar *(für den Motorsport hergerichtetes Serienauto)*; **car park** Parkhaus, Parkplatz; **car-boot sale** (eine Art) Trödelmarkt
caravan park ['kærəvæn pɑːk] Caravan-Campingplatz, Wohnwagen-Campingplatz
card [kɑːd] (Spiel-, Gruß-)Karte; **boarding card** Bordkarte; **credit card** Kreditkarte
care [keə]**: care home** Pflegeheim; **care worker** Pfleger/in
career [kə'rɪə] Karriere; Beruf
careful ['keəfl] vorsichtig, sorgfältig
carnival ['kɑːnɪvəl] Karneval
carrot ['kærət] Karotte, Möhre
carry ['kæri] tragen
carton: a carton of ... [ə 'kɑːtn əv] ein Karton ...
case: pencil case ['pensl keɪs] Federmäppchen
cash machine [kæʃ mə'ʃiːn] Geldautomat
castle ['kɑːsl] Burg, Schloss
cat [kæt] Katze, Kater; **It's raining cats and dogs!** Es gießt wie aus Kübeln! **U1:** 19
catch [kætʃ] fangen, erwischen
caught → catch [kɔːt] *simple past* von **catch**
cause [kɔːz] verursachen; *'cause (ugs.)* = because *U2: 37*
CD [siː'diː] CD; **CD player** CD-Player
celebrate ['selɪbreɪt] feiern
cellphone *(AE)* ['selfəʊn] Handy
cent [sent] Cent
center *(AE)* ['sentə] Center, Zentrum
central ['sentrəl] zentral, Zentral-
centre ['sentə] Zentrum, Mittelpunkt

century ['sentʃəri] Jahrhundert **U2:** 25
ceremony ['serəməni] Zeremonie **U4:** 56
certificate [sə'tɪfɪkət] Urkunde, Bescheinigung **U4:** 55
chain [tʃeɪn] Kette *U3: 43*
chainsaw ['tʃeɪnsɔ:] Kettensäge *U5: 73*
chair [tʃeə] Stuhl
championship ['tʃæmpiənʃɪp] Meisterschaft
chance [tʃɑ:ns] Chance, Gelegenheit
change [tʃeɪndʒ] verändern, wechseln; Veränderung, Wechsel **U2:** 25; **climate change** ['klaɪmət] Klimaveränderung(en) **U2:** 25
charity ['tʃærəti] Wohltätigkeit (sorganisation), wohltätige Zwecke **U5:** 74
chat [tʃæt] plaudern, sich unterhalten **U3:** 44
cheap [tʃi:p] billig; **the cheapest** am billigsten
check [tʃek] (über)prüfen, kontrollieren; *check out* *(ugs.)* [tʃek 'aʊt] ansehen, mehr herausfinden über *U1: 13*
checklist ['tʃeklɪst] Checkliste
checkout ['tʃekaʊt] Kasse
cheer [tʃɪə] jubeln
cheerleader ['tʃɪəli:də] Anfeuerer/in
Cheers! [tʃɪəz] Tschüs!; *(ugs.)* Danke! *U1: 13*
cheese [tʃi:z] Käse; **cheeseburger** Cheeseburger
chewing gum ['tʃu:ɪŋ gʌm] Kaugummi
chicken ['tʃɪkɪn] Huhn; **roast chicken** Brathähnchen
chief pilot [tʃi:f] leitende/r Pilot/in *U5: 73*
children ['tʃɪldrən] Kinder
chill out *(ugs.)* [tʃil 'aʊt] sich entspannen, „relaxen" **U3:** 44; **Chill out!** Bleib(t) cool!
Chinese [tʃaɪ'ni:z] chinesisch; Chinese/Chinesin
Chinook [tʃɪ'nu:k] Chinook *(warmer Wind)* U3: 39
chips: chip shop ['tʃɪp ʃɒp] Pommes-frites-Bude, Imbiss-Bude; **fish and chips** Fisch und Pommes frites
chocolate ['tʃɒklət] Schokolade; **hot chocolate** heiße Schokolade
choice [tʃɔɪs] (Aus-)Wahl *U3: 42*
choose [tʃu:z] (aus)wählen
chore [tʃɔ:] (lästige) Arbeit, Pflicht **U3:** 39
chose → choose [tʃəʊz] *simple past* von **choose** **U5:** 70
Christmas ['krɪsməs] Weihnachten; **Christmas Day** der 1. Weihnachtstag
church [tʃɜ:tʃ] Kirche
cinema ['sɪnəmə] Kino
city ['sɪti] Stadt, Großstadt
class [klɑ:s] (Schul-)Klasse; Kurs **U3:** 50
classroom ['klɑ:sru:m] Klassenzimmer
clean [kli:n] **1** putzen; **cleaning** (das) Saubermachen; **2** sauber
clear [klɪə] aufräumen, ausräumen; (Schnee) fegen **U3:** 38
cleared → clear: the roads are cleared die Straßen werden geräumt (bei Schnee) **U3:** 39
clever ['klevə] schlau, klug
click [klɪk] (an-, hin-)klicken
cliff [klɪf] Klippe
climate ['klaɪmət] Klima **U2:** 25; **climate change** [tʃeɪndʒ] Klimaveränderung(en) **U2:** 25
climb [klaɪm] klettern
climber ['klaɪmə] Kletterer, Kletterin **U4:** 55
clock [klɒk] Uhr; **alarm clock** Wecker
close [kləʊz] schließen, zumachen; **closed** [kləʊzd] geschlossen, zu; [kləʊs] dicht, nah **U2:** 35
clothes [kləʊðz] Kleidung, Kleider
cloudy ['klaʊdi] bewölkt, wolkig
club [klʌb] Klub; Verein; **youth club** Jugendclub, -zentrum
coal [kəʊl] Kohle
coast [kəʊst] Küste; **on the coast** an der Küste **U5:** 71
cocktail ['kɒkteɪl] Cocktail *(Mischgetränk mit oder ohne Alkohol)* **U1:** 11
code: dialling code ['daɪəlɪŋ kəʊd] Vorwahl
coffee ['kɒfi] Kaffee
cola ['kəʊlə] Cola
cold [kəʊld] kalt
collect [kə'lekt] (ein)sammeln
colony ['kɒləni] Kolonie **U2:** 34
color *(AE)* ['kʌlə] Farbe
colour ['kʌlə] Farbe
come [kʌm] kommen; **Come to ...** Komm(t) nach ...; **come with us** komm(t) mit uns; **since (...) they've been coming ...** seit (...) kommen sie ... **U4:** 54
come → come [kʌm] *present perfect* von **come**
comfortable ['kʌmftəbl] bequem
comic ['kɒmɪk] Comic(heft)
command [kə'mɑ:nd] erwecken *U2: 36*
commission [kə'mɪʃən] Gebühren
company ['kʌmpəni] Firma, Unternehmen
comparison [kəm'pærɪsən] Vergleich **U4:** 60; Steigerung(sform) *U4: 60*; **make comparisons!** vergleiche! **U4:** 60
competition [kɒmpə'tɪʃn] Wettbewerb
complain [kəm'pleɪn] sich beschweren **U5:** 71
computer [kəm'pju:tə] Computer
concert ['kɒnsət] Konzert **U1:** 10
condition [kən'dɪʃn]: *working conditions* Arbeitsbedingungen *U3: 43*
Congratulations! [kɒngrætʃʊ'leɪʃnz] Herzlichen Glückwunsch!
console [kən'səʊl]: **(games) console** (Spiel-)Konsole
construction worker [kən'strʌkʃn wɜ:kə] Bauarbeiter/in
contact ['kɒntækt] sich in Verbindung setzen mit
continent ['kɒntɪnənt] Kontinent **U1:** 12
continental [kɒntɪ'nentl]: **continental USA** USA-Festland **U2:** 23
control: remote control [rɪ'məʊt kən'trəʊl] Fernbedienung
convenient [kən'vi:niənt] günstig (gelegen), praktisch *U1: 12*
cook ['kʊk] kochen; **cooking** (das) Kochen
cool [ku:l] kühl; cool, scharf, stark; **cool off** [ku:l 'ɒf] (sich) abkühlen **U1:** 11
copy ['kɒpi] kopieren, abschreiben
cornflakes ['kɔ:nfleɪks] Cornflakes
corporation [kɔ:pə'reɪʃn] Gesellschaft *U2: 27*
cost [kɒst] kosten
cost → cost [kɒst] *simple past* von **cost**
cottage ['kɒtɪdʒ] Häuschen, Ferienhaus **U3:** 39
cotton ['kɒtn] Baumwolle
couch [kaʊtʃ] Couch, Sofa

[i:] **he** [ɑ:] **car** [ɔ:] **or** [u:] **too** [ɜ:] **girl** [i] **sorry** [u] **July** [ɪ] **big** [e] **yes** [æ] **cat** [ʌ] **bus**

could → can [kʊd] *simple past* von **can**; **couldn't** konnte/n nicht
count [kaʊnt] zählen
country ['kʌntri] Land; **in the country** auf dem Land
countryside ['kʌntrisaɪd] Landschaft **U3:** 51
couple ['kʌpl] Paar **U1:** 15
course: of course [əf 'kɔːs] natürlich, selbstverständlich
coursework ['kɔːswɜːk] schriftliche Arbeit
cousin ['kʌzn] Cousin, Cousine/Kusine
cow [kaʊ] Kuh
cowboy ['kaʊbɔɪ] Cowboy **U2:** 30
cowgirl ['kaʊgɜːl] Cowgirl *(berittene amerik. Rinderhirtin)* **U3:** 38
crash (into) [kræʃ] aufprallen (auf)
crazy about sport ['kreɪzi] verrückt nach Sport
cream [kriːm] Creme; **ice cream** (Speise-)Eis; **sun cream** Sonnencreme
create [kriː'eɪt] (er)schaffen **U2:** 25
created → create: it was created es wurde geschaffen **U2:** 25
credit card ['kredɪt kɑːd] Kreditkarte
cried → cry [kraɪd] *simple past* von **cry** **U5:** 70
crime [kraɪm] Verbrechen, Kriminalität
criminal ['krɪmɪnl] Verbrecher/in **U4:** 54
crisps *(pl.)* [krɪsps] Kartoffelchips
critical of ['krɪtɪkl] kritisch gegenüber *U3: 43*
crocodile ['krɒkədaɪl] Krokodil
cross [krɒs] überqueren, kreuzen; **fingers crossed** Ich drücke die Daumen.
crowd [kraʊd] (Menschen-)Menge
cry [kraɪ] weinen **U5:** 70
culture ['kʌltʃə] Kultur
cup [kʌp] Tasse
cupboard ['kʌbəd] Schrank
current ['kʌrənt] Strömung U2: 35
curriculum vitae = CV (BE) [kərɪkjəltʃəm 'viːtaɪ] Lebenslauf *U5: 77*
curtain ['kɜːtn] Vorhang, Gardine
cushion ['kʊʃn] Kissen
customer ['kʌstəmə] Kunde/Kundin
cut [kʌt]**: Cut!** Schnitt!; **cut ... in pieces** in Stücke schneiden
cute [kjuːt] süß, niedlich **U3:** 40
CV = curriculum vitae (BE) [siː 'viː] Lebenslauf *U5: 77*

D

dad [dæd] Papa, Vati
dance [dɑːns] tanzen; **dinner dance** ['dɪnə dɑːns] Festessen mit anschließendem Tanz **U3:** 41
dancer ['dɑːnsə] Tänzer/in
dancing ['dɑːnsɪŋ] (das) Tanzen
danger ['deɪndʒə] Gefahr **U4:** 66
dangerous ['deɪndʒərəs] gefährlich
dark [dɑːk] dunkel
database ['deɪtəbeɪs] Datenbank
date [deɪt] Datum; Verabredung **U3:** 41
daughter ['dɔːtə] Tochter
day [deɪ] Tag; **every day** jeden Tag; **special day** besonderer Tag; **day out** (Tages-)Ausflug; **have a day out** einen Tagesausflug machen
dead [ded] tot
Dear ..., [dɪə] Liebe(r, s) ...,
death [deθ] Tod **U2:** 35
December [dɪ'sembə] Dezember
decide [dɪ'saɪd] (sich) entscheiden, beschließen **U1:** 20
decision [dɪ'sɪʒn] Entscheidung **U5:** 70; **make a decision** eine Entscheidung treffen, sich entscheiden **U5:** 70
deep [diːp] tief
degrees *(pl.)* [dɪ'griːz] Grad
deli *(AE)* ['deli] (Feinkost-)Imbiss
deliver [dɪ'lɪvə] liefern
deodorant [di'əʊdərənt] Deo, Deodorant
department store [dɪ'pɑːtmənt stɔː] Kaufhaus
dependent on [dɪ'pendənt] abhängig von *U3: 43*
describe [dɪ'skraɪb] beschreiben
design [dɪ'zaɪn] entwerfen, konstruieren
designer: web designer ['web dɪzaɪnə] Webdesigner/in **U2:** 24
desk [desk] Schreibtisch; Empfang, Anmeldung; **airport desk** Flugschalter
destiny ['destəni] Schicksal *U4: 67*
detail ['diːteɪl] Detail, Einzelheit
developing countries [dɪ'veləpɪŋ] Entwicklungsländer *U3: 43*
dialling code ['daɪəlɪŋ kəʊd] Vorwahl
dialogue ['daɪəlɒg] Dialog
diary ['daɪəri] Tagebuch
dictionary ['dɪkʃənri] Wörterbuch
did → do [dɪd] *simple past* von **do**; **No, I didn't (= did not).** Nein (habe ich nicht).
didgeridoo [dɪdʒəri'duː] Didgeridoo *(Blasinstrument der austr. Ureinwohner)* **U4:** 52
die [daɪ] sterben
died → die [daɪd] *simple past* von **die**
difference: (time) difference ['taɪm dɪfrəns] (Zeit-)Unterschied
different ['dɪfrənt] anderer/andere/anderes; verschieden
difficult ['dɪfɪkəlt] schwierig, schwer
digital ['dɪdʒɪtl] Digital-
diner *(AE)* ['daɪnə] einfaches Restaurant mit Theke und Tischen
dingo ['dɪŋgəʊ] Dingo, australischer Wildhund **U4:** 64
dinner ['dɪnə] Abendessen **U3:** 41; **dinner dance** ['dɪnə dɑːns] Festessen mit anschließendem Tanz **U3:** 41
dinosaur ['daɪnəsɔː] Dinosaurier
direction [də'rekʃn] Richtung *U5: 73*
director [də'rektə] Regisseur
dirt bike ['dɜːt baɪk] Offroad-Motorrad **U3:** 44
dirt biking ['dɜːt baɪkiŋ] Offroad-Motorradfahren **U3:** 44
dirt track ['dɜːt træk] Offroad-Strecke **U3:** 44
disappear [dɪsə'pɪə] verschwinden
disappointed [dɪsə'pɔɪntɪd] enttäuscht
dishwasher ['dɪʃwɒʃə] Geschirrspülmaschine
dislike [dɪs'laɪk] nicht mögen
disposable [dɪ'spəʊzəbl] Wegwerf-, Einmal-
distance ['dɪstəns] Entfernung **U2:** 23
dive [daɪv] tauchen; **shark cage diving** Hai-Tauchen mit Käfigen U1: 15
divorce [dɪ'vɔːs] sich scheiden lassen

do [du:] tun, machen; **I've been doing it for five years now** ich mache es jetzt seit fünf Jahren U3: 50
dock [dɒk] Hafen, Dock
doctor ['dɒktə] Arzt/Ärztin
does: Does your cousin live...? [dʌz jʊə kʌzn 'lɪv] Wohnt dein Cousin/deine Kusine ...?; **No, she doesn't.** Nein (tut sie nicht).; **Yes, she does.** Ja (tut sie).
dog [dɒg] Hund; **dog sled** [sled] Hundeschlitten U2: 25; **It's raining cats and dogs!** Es gießt wie aus Kübeln! U1: 19; **take the dog for a walk** mit dem Hund rausgehen/spazierengehen
doll [dɒl] Puppe
dollar ($) ['dɒlə] Dollar *(US-Währung)*
dolphin ['dɒlfɪn] Delfin
done → do [dʌn] *present perfect* von **do**; **Well done!** Gut gemacht!
door [dɔ:] Tür; *door-to-door (bus service)* [dɔ: tə 'dɔ:] (Busverbindung) von Haus zu Haus *U1: 13*
double ['dʌbl] doppelt, Doppel-
down [daʊn] herunter, hinunter; *computers are down* Rechner sind heruntergefahren/funktionieren nicht *U1: 88*; *when you get down to it* *etwa:* wenn man mal genau hinschaut *U2: 37*
download ['daʊnləʊd] (Daten) herunterladen, downloaden
downtown *(AE)* ['daʊntaʊn] Innenstadt, Stadtzentrum
drank → drink [dræŋk] *simple past* von **drink**
dream [dri:m] träumen *U4: 67*; Traum
dress [dres] Kleid U3: 41
drink [drɪŋk] **1** Getränk; **2** trinken
drive [draɪv] fahren *(ein Auto, Bus usw.)*
driver: bus driver ['bʌs draɪvə] Busfahrer/in; **probationary driver's license** *(CanE/AE)* [prə'beɪʃnri draɪvəz laɪsns] Führerschein auf Probe U3: 39
driving ['draɪvɪŋ] (das) Autofahren
drop off [drɒp] absetzen, aussteigen lassen *U1: 13*
dropped → drop [drɒpt]: *you are dropped off* du wirst abgesetzt *U1: 13*
drove → drive [drəʊv] *simple past* von **drive**
drugs [drʌgz] Drogen; Medikamente U1: 10
drum [drʌm] Trommel U4: 56
drummer ['drʌmə] Schlagzeuger/in
drums *(pl.)* [drʌmz] Schlagzeug
dry [draɪ] trocken; **dry boat race** *etwa:* Trockenbootrennen U5: 74
dump [dʌmp]**: a big dump of snow** *(ugs.)* [dʌmp əv 'snəʊ] starker Schneefall U3: 39
during ['djʊərɪŋ] während
dustman ['dʌstmən] Müllmann
DVD [di: vi: 'di:] DVD (= Digital Versatile Disk); **DVD player** DVD-Spieler

E

each [i:tʃ] jede(r, s)
early ['ɜ:li] früh, frühzeitig
earn [ɜ:n] verdienen
earth [ɜ:θ] (die) Erde *U2: 37*
earthquake ['ɜ:θkweɪk] Erdbeben
east [i:st] Ost
easy ['i:zi] leicht, einfach
eat [i:t] essen; **eat fire** Feuer schlucken/speien
ecard ['i:kɑ:d] elektronische Postkarte *U2: 30*
economy [ɪ'kɒnəmi] (Volks-)Wirtschaft *U2: 37*
ecosystem ['i:kəʊsɪstəm] Ökosystem *U2: 27*
egg [eg] Ei
eight [eɪt] acht
eighteen [eɪ'ti:n] achtzehn
eighteenth [eɪ'ti:nθ] achzehnte(r, s)
eighth [eɪtθ] achte(r, s)
eighty ['eɪti] achtzig
electrician [ɪlek'trɪʃn] Elektriker/in
electricity [ɪlek'trɪsəti] Strom U2: 23
electronic gadget [ɪlek'trɒnɪk 'gædʒɪt] Elektrogerät, -apparat
elephant ['elɪfənt] Elefant U1: 15
eleven [ɪ'levn] elf
eleventh [ɪ'levnθ] elfte(r, s)
elk [elk] Elch
else: Anything else? [eniθɪŋ 'els] Sonst noch etwas?
email ['i:meɪl] **1** E-Mail; **by email** per E-Mail U5: 77; **email attachment** [ə'tætʃmənt] Anhang an eine E-Mail U2: 31; **2** als E-Mail verschicken, mailen
emigrate ['emɪgreɪt] auswandern U5: 68
empty ['empti] leer
emu ['i:mju:] Emu *(großer Laufvogel)* U4: 52
en route *(Französisch)* [ã 'ʀut] unterwegs, auf dem Weg *U1: 13*
end [end] Ende; *in the end* schließlich, am Ende *U3: 42*
England ['ɪŋglənd] England
English ['ɪŋglɪʃ] englisch; **in English** auf Englisch
enjoy [ɪn'dʒɔɪ] genießen; **they enjoy themselves** sie haben Spaß U4: 55
enormous [ɪ'nɔ:məs] ungeheuer groß
enough [ɪ'nʌf] genug
environment [ɪn'vaɪrənmənt] Umwelt U4: 54
equipment *(no pl.)* [ɪ'kwɪpmənt] Ausrüstung
escape [ɪ'skeɪp] (ent)fliehen
espresso [e'spresəʊ] Espresso *(starkes Kaffeegetränk aus spezieller Maschine)* U5: 77
ethnic ['eθnɪk] ethnisch
euro ['jʊərəʊ] Euro
Europe ['jʊərəp] Europa
European [jʊərə'pi:ən] Europäer/in
even ['i:vn] sogar U5: 71
evening: in the evening [ɪn ði 'i:vnɪŋ] abends; **Good evening.** Guten Abend.
ever ['evə] je, jemals; **Have you ever been ...?** Bist du jemals ... gewesen?
every ['evri] jede/jeder/jedes; **every day** jeden Tag
everybody ['evribɒdi] jede(r, s), alle
everyone ['evriwʌn] jede(r, s), alle
everything ['evriθɪŋ] alles
everywhere ['evriweə] überall
example: for example [fər ɪg'zɑ:mpl] zum Beispiel
except [ɪ'ksept] außer; **except for** [ɪ'ksept fə] bis auf, abgesehen von U3: 51
excited [ɪk'saɪtɪd] aufgeregt
exciting [ɪk'saɪtɪŋ] aufregend, spannend
Excuse me. [ɪk'skju:z mi] Entschuldigung./Entschuldigen Sie.

[ʊə] s**ure** [b] **b**ike [p] **p**en [d] **d**ay [t] **t**en [k] boo**k** [g] **g**o [ŋ] morni**ng** [l] **l**ike [r] **r**uler

exercise ['eksəsaɪz] Übung
exhibition [eksɪ'bɪʃn] Ausstellung U5: 70
expect [ɪk'spekt] erwarten, annehmen, vermuten
expedition [ekspə'diʃn] Expedition U2: 34
expensive: too expensive [tu: ɪk'spensɪv] zu teuer
experience [ɪk'spɪəriəns] Erfahrung *U4: 57*; **work experience** ['wɜ:k ɪk'spɪəriəns] Arbeitserfahrung; Praktikum
experiment [ɪk'sperɪmənt] Experiment, Versuch
expert ['ekspɜ:t] Experte/Expertin, Fachmann/Fachfrau
explain [ɪk'spleɪn] erklären
explore [ɪk'splɔ:] erforschen, erkunden U2: 34
extra (pocket money) ['ekstrə] zusätzliches (Taschengeld) *U1: 13*
eye [aɪ] Auge

F

face [feɪs] Gesicht
fact [fækt] Fakt, Tatsache
factory ['fæktəri] Fabrik
fair [feə] **1** Jahrmarkt; **2** fair, gerecht; blond U4: 58
fall *(AE)* [fɔ:l] **1** Herbst; **2** fallen, stürzen; **fall over** [fɔ:l 'əʊvə] hinfallen U3: 40
false [fɔ:ls] falsch U1: 12
family ['fæməli] Familie
famous ['feɪməs] berühmt
fan [fæn] Fan
fantastic [fæn'tæstɪk] fantastisch, toll
FAQ (= frequently asked questions) [ef eɪ 'kju] häufig gestellte Fragen U4: 55
far [fɑ:] weit; **so far** bisher U4: 66
farm [fɑ:m] Bauernhof, Farm
fashion ['fæʃn] Mode U1: 10
fast [fɑ:st] schnell
father ['fɑ:ðə] Vater
favorite *(AE)* ['feɪvərɪt] bevorzugt, Lieblings-
favourite ['feɪvərɪt] Lieblings-
February ['februəri] Februar
fed up: be fed up [bi fed 'ʌp] die Nase voll haben; **Asif was fed up.** Asif hatte die Nase voll.
feed [fi:d] füttern, zu fressen geben
feel [fi:l] (sich) fühlen, sich anfühlen; **feel sorry for somebody (sb.)** jemanden (jdn.) bedauern, Mitleid mit jemandem (jdm.) haben
fell → fall [fell] *simple past* von **fall**
felt → feel [felt] *simple past* von **feel**
felt-tip ['felttɪp] Filzstift
fence [fens] Zaun
ferry ['feri] Fähre
festival ['festɪvl] Festival
few [fju:] wenige; **a few** ein paar, einige
field [fi:ld] Feld, Wiese; **football field** Fußballplatz
fifteen [fɪf'ti:n] fünfzehn
fifteenth [fɪf'ti:nθ] fünfzehnte(r, s)
fifth [fɪfθ] fünfte(r, s)
fifty ['fɪfti] fünfzig
fight [faɪt] kämpfen (gegen) U1: 20
fighter ['faɪtə] Kämpfer/in U1: 21
fill (in) [fɪl 'ɪn] füllen, auffüllen, ausfüllen
film [fɪlm] Film
film guide ['fɪlm gaɪd] Filmführer, Filmprogrammheft
find [faɪnd] finden; **find out** herausfinden; entdecken
fine [faɪn] gut
finger ['fɪŋgə] Finger; **fish fingers** Fischstäbchen; **fingers crossed** Ich drücke die Daumen.
finish ['fɪnɪʃ] beenden, zu Ende machen
finished → finish ['fɪnɪʃt]**: it was finished** es/sie wurde fertiggestellt U4: 66
fire: eat fire [i:t 'faɪə] Feuer schlucken/speien
firefighter ['faɪəfaɪtə] Feuerwehrmann/Feuerwehrfrau
firework ['faɪəwɜ:k] Feuerwerkskörper
firm [fɜ:m] Firma
first [fɜ:st] **1** erste(r, s); **First Nations** *indianische Völker in Kanada* U2: 23; **May the first (= 1st May)** der erste Mai (1. Mai); **2** zuerst, zum ersten Mal; **at first** zuerst
fish: fish and chips [fɪʃ ənd 'tʃɪps] Fisch und Pommes frites; **fish fingers** Fischstäbchen
fishing ['fɪʃɪŋ] (das) Angeln
fit [fɪt] montieren U1: 11
fitness ['fɪtnəs] Fitness
five [faɪv] fünf
flag [flæg] Flagge, Fahne
flashlight *(AE)* ['flæʃlaɪt] Taschenlampe
flat [flæt] **1** Wohnung; **2** flach, eben
flew → fly [flu:] *simple past* von **fly**
flexible ['fleksəbl] flexibel *U1: 13*
flight [flaɪt] Flug
floor: ground floor ['graʊnd flɔ:] Erdgeschoss
flow [fləʊ] fließen U2: 35
flower ['flaʊə] Blume, Blüte; **flower-bed** Blumenbeet
flute [flu:t] (Quer-)Flöte
fly [flaɪ] fliegen; Fliege U5: 71
flyer ['flaɪə] Flyer, Handzettel *U1: 13*
foggy ['fɒgi] neblig
folks [fəʊks]**: my folks** *(ugs.)* meine Leute, meine Familie U2: 24
follow ['fɒləʊ] folgen
food [fu:d] Essen, Lebensmittel
foot [fʊt] Fuß
football ['fʊtbɔ:l] Fußball; **Australian rules football** Football nach australischen Regeln, australischer Football U4: 52; **football field** Fußballplatz
for [fɔ:] für; **for different reasons** aus unterschiedlichen Gründen U5: 69; **for example** zum Beispiel; *for fun* aus Spaß, zum Spaß *U2: 36*; **for life** lebenslänglich *(Haftstrafe)* U1: 21; **for our new home** als (unsere) neue Heimat U5: 70; **for years** seit Jahren U2: 24
foreign language [fɒrən 'læŋgwɪdʒ] Fremdsprache
foreigner ['fɒrənə] Ausländer/in U1: 9
forest ['fɒrəst] Wald
forget [fə'get] vergessen; **Don't forget!** Vergesst/Vergiss nicht!
forgot → forget [fə'gɒt] *simple past* von **forget**
forgotten → forget [fə'gɒtn] *present perfect* von **forget**
form [fɔ:m] **1** Form; Formular; **application form** [æplɪ'keɪʃn] Bewerbungsformular U5: 77; **2** bilden *U4: 57*
formed → form [fɔ:md]*: it was formed* es wurde gebildet *U4: 57*
fortress ['fɔ:trəs] Festung U2: 35
forty ['fɔ:ti] vierzig

[v] seven [w] **w**e [s] **s**ix [z] hi**s** [ʃ] **sh**e [tʃ] tea**ch**er [dʒ] **j**eans [j] **y**es [θ] **th**ing [ð] **th**e

forward: look forward to sth. [lʊk 'fɔːwəd tʊ] sich auf etwas freuen
fought → fight [fɔːt] *simple past* und *present perfect* von **fight** **U1:** 20
found → find [faʊnd] *simple past* und *present perfect* von **find**; **oil was found** Öl wurde gefunden **U3:** 38
four [fɔː] vier
fourteen [fɔː'tiːn] vierzehn
fourteenth [fɔː'tiːnθ] vierzehnte(r, s)
fourth (= 4th) [fɔːθ] vierte(r, s)
France [frɑːns] Frankreich
freak [friːk] Freak, Fanatiker/in
free [friː] **1** befreien; **he must be freed → free** er muss freigelassen werden **U1:** 21; **he was freed → free** er wurde freigelassen **U1:** 21; **2** frei, kostenlos; **free time** Freizeit
freed → free [friːd] *simple past* und *present perfect* von **free**; **he must be freed** er muss freigelassen werden **U1:** 21; **he was freed** er wurde freigelassen **U1:** 21
freedom ['friːdəm] Freiheit **U2:** 24
freeway ['friːweɪ] Autobahn *(US)* *U2: 36*
French [frentʃ] Französisch, französisch
frequently asked questions ['friːkwəntli ɑːskt 'kwestʃnz] häufig gestellte Fragen **U4:** 55
fresh [freʃ] frisch
Friday ['fraɪdeɪ] Freitag
fridge [frɪdʒ] Kühlschrank
friend [frend] Freund/in; **make (new) friends** (neue) Freunde/ Freundinnen finden **U5:** 71
friendly ['frendli] freundlich, nett; **as friendly as** (genau)so freundlich wie
frightened: be frightened [bi 'fraɪtnd] verängstigt sein; Angst haben; **They were frightened.** Sie hatten Angst.
from [frɒm] von, aus; **from ... till** von ... bis; **from ... to** von ... bis; **Where are you from?** Wo kommst du her?
front: in front of [ɪn 'frʌnt əv] vor; **out front** draußen vor dem Haus **U3:** 39
fruit [fruːt] Obst; **fruit juice** (Frucht-)Saft
full of ['fʊl əv] voll (mit, von)

fun [fʌn] Spaß; **be fun** Spaß machen; *for fun* aus Spaß, zum Spaß *U2: 36*
funny ['fʌni] lustig, witzig; komisch, merkwürdig
furniture ['fɜːnɪtʃə] Möbel **U5:** 70
future ['fjuːtʃə] Zukunft
fuzzy ['fʌzi] unscharf, verschwommen

G

gadget: electronic gadget [ɪlek'trɒnɪk 'gædʒɪt] Elektrogerät, -apparat
gallery: art gallery [ɑːt 'gæləri] Kunstgalerie
game [geɪm] Spiel; **games console** Spielkonsole; **video game** Videospiel
gameboy ['geɪmbɔɪ] Gameboy
gang [gæŋ] Truppe, Clique **U2:** 31
gangster *(ugs.)* ['gæŋstə] Gangster/in, Verbrecher/in
garage ['gærɑːʒ] Garage; Werkstatt; Tankstelle
garbage *(AE)* ['gɑːbɪdʒ] Abfall
garden ['gɑːdn] Garten
gas [gæs] Gas **U2:** 23
gate [geɪt] Tor, Pforte; Gate, Flugsteig
gave → give [geɪv] *simple past* von **give**
G'day! *(AustE)* [gə'deɪ] Guten Tag! **U4:** 55
general ['dʒenrəl] allgemein **U4:** 58
geography [dʒi'ɒgrəfi] Geographie, Erdkunde
geologist [dʒi'ɒlədʒɪst] Geologe/ Geologin *U4: 57*
German ['dʒɜːmən] deutsch; **in German** auf Deutsch
Germany ['dʒɜːməni] Deutschland
get [get] gelangen, hinkommen; holen; erreichen; bekommen; **get around** herumkommen; **get back** zurückkommen/ -finden; **get on** aufsteigen, einsteigen; **get on well with** sich gut verstehen mit **U4:** 59; **get out (of)** aussteigen (aus); **get up** aufstehen; *when you get down to it* *etwa:* wenn man mal genau hinschaut *U2: 37*; *you get to see ...* du kannst ... sehen *U2: 27*
ghetto ['getəʊ] Getto
girl [gɜːl] Mädchen

girlfriend ['gɜːlfrend] (feste) Freundin
give [gɪv] geben; **give a talk** einen Vortrag halten; **Give my greetings to ...** Grüße mir ...; *give up* aufgeben *U4: 67*
given → give ['gɪvn] *present perfect* von **give** *U4: 67*; *it was given up* es wurde aufgegeben *U4: 67*
glad [glæd] froh
glass [glɑːs] Glas; **glasses** *(pl.)* ['glɑːsɪz] (eine) Brille **U4:** 58
global warming [gləʊbl 'wɔːmɪŋ] Erwärmung der Erdatmosphäre *U2: 27*
glorious ['glɔːriəs] ruhmreich *U2: 36*
glow [gləʊ]: *glowing hearts* [gləʊɪŋ 'hɑːts] glühende Herzen *U2: 36*
go [gəʊ] gehen, fahren; **go along** entlanggehen; **go away** verreisen; **go by ...** mit dem/der ... fahren; **go on holiday** in Urlaub gehen/fahren; **go out for a meal** essen gehen; **go out in the car** eine Spazierfahrt machen; *go see* *(ugs.)* besuchen *U2: 37*; **Go straight on.** geradeaus (weiter)gehen; **go to the shops** einen Einkaufsbummel machen; einkaufen gehen; **go to town** in die (Innen-)Stadt fahren
goal [gəʊl] Tor
God [gɒd] Gott *U2: 36*
gold [gəʊld] Gold; **gold rush** Goldrausch
golf [gɒlf] Golf
gone [gɒn] weg, verschwunden
good [gʊd]: **good (at)** gut (in); **Good afternoon.** Guten Tag. *(nachmittags)*; **Good evening.** Guten Abend.; **good luck** (viel) Glück; **Good morning.** Guten Morgen.; **good value** preisgünstig; **good-looking** gut aussehend, attraktiv
Goodbye. ['gʊdbaɪ] Auf Wiedersehen.
goods [gʊdz] Waren, Güter
got → get [gɒt] *simple past* und *present perfect* von **get**
gotta: we gotta lot of = we've got a lot of *(ugs.)* ['gɒtə] wir haben viel *U2: 37*
government ['gʌvnmənt] Regierung **U1:** 21

[iː] he [ɑː] car [ɔː] or [uː] too [ɜː] girl [i] sorry [u] July [ɪ] big [e] yes [æ] cat [ʌ] bus

governor ['gʌvənə] Gouverneur/in *(jemand, der eine Kolonie regiert)* U2: 34
grad (= graduation) *(CanE/AE)* *(ugs.)* [græd] Schulabschlussfeier *(mit feierlicher Überreichung der Zeugnisse)* **U3:** 41
grade *(AE)* [greɪd] Klasse(nstufe)
graduation *(CanE/AE)* [grædʒu'eɪʃn] Schulabschlussfeier *(mit feierlicher Überreichung der Zeugnisse)* **U3:** 41
graffiti [grə'fi:ti] Graffiti
gram [græm] Gramm
grandad *(ugs.)* ['grændæd] Opa
grandfather ['grænfɑ:ðə] Großvater
grandma ['grænmɑ:] Oma
grandmother ['grænmʌðə] Großmutter
grandparents ['grænpeərənts] Großeltern **U3:** 39
grass [grɑ:s] Gras
grassland ['grɑ:slænd] Grasland **U2:** 22
great [greɪt] groß, großartig; toll; **great at** super/großartig in
green [gri:n] grün
greeter ['gri:tə] jmd., der Gäste oder Kunden begrüßt
greetings: Give my greetings to ... [gɪv maɪ 'gri:tɪŋz tə] Grüße mir ...
grey [greɪ] grau **U4:** 55
grizzly bear ['grɪzli beə] Grislibär
ground [graʊnd] Erde, Boden; **ground floor** Erdgeschoss
Ground Zero [graʊnd 'zɪərəʊ] Ground Zero *(Ort der Anschläge vom 11. Sept. 2001 in NY)*
group [gru:p] Gruppe
grow [grəʊ] anbauen; wachsen; **Grow up!** Sei(d) mal vernünftig!
grumpy ['grʌmpi] mürrisch, brummig
guard [gɑ:d]*: stand on guard* [stænd ɒn 'gɑ:d] Wache halten *U2: 36*
guess [ges] (er)raten **U4:** 58; **(a) guess** (einmal) Raten **U4:** 58; **I guess** ich glaube, ich denke **U2:** 24; *guess what!* stell dir vor! *U2: 27*
guest [gest] Gast *U1: 13*
guide: guide book Reiseführer; **audio guide** ['ɔ:diəʊ] gaɪd Audioguide *(elektronischer Museumsführer)* **U2:** 26; **tour guide** ['tʊə gaɪd] Reiseführer/in
gum: chewing gum ['tʃu:ɪŋ gʌm] Kaugummi
gun [gʌn] Waffe **U2:** 35; **point a gun at** eine Waffe richten auf **U2:** 35
gunshot ['gʌnʃɒt] Schuss **U2:** 35
guys [gaɪz]**: hi there, guys!** *(ugs.)* hallo Leute! **U1:** 15
gym [dʒɪm] Turnhalle, Sporthalle

H

had → have [hæd] *simple past* und *present perfect* von **have**
hair [heə] Haar(e)
hairdresser ['heədresə] Friseur/in
half *(pl.:* **halves***)* [hɑ:f, hɑ:vz] Hälfte; **half-brother** Halbbruder; **half past** halb *(Uhrzeit)*; **half-time** Halbzeit
Halloween [hæləʊ'i:n] Halloween
hamburger ['hæmbɜ:gə] Hamburger
hamster ['hæmstə] Hamster
hand [hænd] Hand; **hold out a hand** eine Hand ausstrecken **U3:** 40
handbook ['hændbʊk] Gebrauchsanweisung
hang [hæŋ] hängen, aufhängen; **hang out** herumhängen **U5:** 71
happen ['hæpən] passieren, geschehen; **What's happening?** Was ist los?/Was geht hier vor?
happy ['hæpi] glücklich, froh; **happy listening!** viel Spaß beim Zuhören! **U2:** 31
harbor *(AE)* ['hɑ:bə] Hafen
hard [hɑ:d] hart; schwierig; **as hard as they could** so kräftig sie konnten **U2:** 35
hardware ['hɑ:dweə] Hardware
harm [hɑ:m] schaden, Schaden zufügen **U4:** 54
hat [hæt] Hut; Mütze **U5:** 71
hate [heɪt] hassen, gar nicht mögen
have [hæv] haben; essen, trinken; **I don't have** Ich habe keinen/keine/kein; **he doesn't have** er hat keinen/keine/kein; **Can I have a ...?** Kann ich eine(n)/ein ... haben?; **have a day out** einen Tagesausflug machen; **have a good time** sich gut amüsieren; **have a race** um die Wette laufen; **have a wash** sich waschen; **have breakfast** frühstücken;
have to müssen; **Have you ever been ...?** Bist du jemals ... gewesen?
he's (= he is) [hi:z] er ist
head [hed] Kopf; **head barista** Chef-Barista U5: 77
headline ['hedlaɪn] Überschrift, Schlagzeile
headphones ['hedfəʊnz] Kopfhörer
healthy ['helθi] gesund
hear [hɪə] hören; **heard → hear** [hɜ:d] *present perfect* von **hear** **U1:** 9
heard → hear [hɜ:d] *simple past* und *present perfect* von **hear** **U1:** 9
heart: glowing hearts [gləʊɪŋ 'hɑ:ts] glühende Herzen *U2: 36*
held → hold [held] *simple past* von **hold** **U3:** 40; *he held his breath* er hielt den Atem an *U5: 73*
helicopter ['helɪkɒptə] Hubschrauber
helmet ['helmɪt] Helm
help [help] helfen; **help out with** (aus)helfen bei **U3:** 50; **Help yourselves.** Bedient euch! Nehmt euch!
helpful ['helpfəl] hilfreich, behilflich
her [hɜ:] ihr/ihre
here [hɪə] hier; **here are** hier sind; **Here you are.** (hier) Bitte.; **here's (= here is)** hier ist
hero ['hɪərəʊ] Held/in **U1:** 20
herself [hɜ:'self]**: she likes the photo of herself** sie mag das Foto von sich **U4:** 55
Hey! [heɪ] Hey!
Hi. [haɪ] Hallo.
high [haɪ] hoch; **high school** (US) Gesamtschule für 13- bis 18-Jährige
highway ['haɪweɪ] Autobahn *(US + Kanada) U2: 36*
hike [haɪk] wandern; **hiker** Wanderer/Wandererin
hill [hɪl] Hügel, Berg
him [hɪm] ihn; ihm
himself [hɪm'self] (er/ihm/ihn) selbst, selber
hire ['haɪə] mieten, (aus)leihen **U3:** 41
his [hɪz] sein/seine
Hispanic [hɪ'spænɪk] Hispano-Amerikaner/in *(Einwanderer aus Lateinamerika und Nachkommen)*
historical [hɪ'stɒrɪkl] historisch

[ɒ] dog [ʊ] put [ə] again [eɪ] name [aɪ] time [ɔɪ] boy [əʊ] no [aʊ] house [ɪə] here [eə] chair

history ['hɪstri] Geschichte, Vergangenheit
hit ['hɪt] **1** Hit, Schlager; **2** treffen, schlagen, stoßen
hit → hit [hɪt] *simple past* und *present perfect* von **hit**
hi-tech ['haɪ tek] Hightech-
hobby ['hɒbi] Hobby; **What's your hobby?** Welches Hobby hast du?
hockey ['hɒki] Hockey; **ice hockey** ['aɪs hɒki] Eishockey **U2:** 22
hold [həʊld] (fest)halten; **hold out a hand** eine Hand ausstrecken **U3:** 40
hole [həʊl] Loch; *watering hole* Wasserstelle *U4: 57*
holiday ['hɒlədeɪ] Urlaub, Urlaubs-; Ferien; **public holiday** gesetzlicher Feiertag; **on holiday** im Urlaub; **go on holiday** in Urlaub gehen/fahren
home [həʊm] **1** Zuhause, Heim, Heimat; **animal home** Tierheim; **care home** Pflegeheim; **2** nach Hause; **at home** zu Hause
home page ['həʊm peɪdʒ] Homepage, Startseite
homesick: be/get homesick [bɪ, get 'həʊmsɪk] Heimweh haben/bekommen
hometown ['həʊmtaʊn] Heimatstadt **U4:** 64
homework ['həʊmwɜːk] Hausaufgabe(n)
hoodoo ['huːduː] Hoodoo *(Gesteinsformation aus Kalkstein)* U2: 29
hop: hop-on hop-off (bus service) [hɒp ɒn hɒp 'ɒf] (Busverbindung) zum Zu- und Aussteigen *U1: 13*
hope [həʊp] hoffen
horse [hɔːs] Pferd
hospital ['hɒspɪtl] Krankenhaus
hostel: youth hostel ['juːθ hɒstl] Jugendherberge
hot [hɒt] heiß; **hot chocolate** heiße Schokolade; **hot dog** Hotdog
hotel [həʊ'tel] Hotel
hour ['aʊə] Stunde
house [haʊs] Haus; **at ... house** bei ... zu Hause; **leave the house** das Haus verlassen

how [haʊ] wie; *how about ...?* wie wär's mit ...? *U2: 27*; **How are things?** *(ugs.)* Wie geht's?, Wie läuft's?; **How are you?** Wie geht es dir/euch/Ihnen?; **how many?** wie viele?; **How much is it?** Was kostet das?; **how much?** wie viel?; **How old are you?** Wie alt bist du?
huge [hjuːdʒ] riesig **U3:** 51
human ['hjuːmən] menschlich, Menschen-
humour ['hjuːmə]: **(sense of) humour** [sens əv 'hjuːmə] (Sinn für) Humor **U4:** 59
hundred ['hʌndrəd] hundert
hung → hang [hʌŋ] *simple past* und *present perfect* von **hang**
hungry: I'm hungry. [aɪm 'hʌŋgri] Ich habe Hunger.
hunt [hʌnt] jagen
hunter ['hʌntə] Jäger/in **U5:** 76
Hurry! ['hʌri] Beeilt euch!/Beeil dich!
hurt [hɜːt] **1** schmerzen; **2** verletzt
hurt → hurt [hɜːt] *simple past* und *present perfect* von **hurt** *U4: 55*

I

I [aɪ] ich; **I'm (= I am)** ich bin
ice [aɪs] Eis *(gefrorenes Wasser)* **U2:** 22; *ice-breaker* ['aɪs breɪkə] Eisbrecher *U2: 27*; **ice cream** [aɪs 'kriːm] (Speise-)Eis; **ice hockey** ['aɪs hɒki] Eishockey **U2:** 22; **iced tea** Eistee
idea [aɪ'dɪə] Idee, Gedanke; Vorstellung, Ahnung, Meinung; **have no idea** keine Ahnung haben
ideal [aɪ'dɪəl] ideal
idol ['aɪdl] Idol, Star
if [ɪf] wenn
ill [ɪl] krank
illness ['ɪlnəs] Krankheit **U1:** 10
immigrant ['ɪmɪgrənt] Einwanderer/Einwanderin **U2:** 23
immigration [ɪmɪ'greɪʃn] Einwanderung **U2:** 23; **immigration rate** [reɪt] Einwanderungsquote **U2:** 23
impact ['ɪmpækt] (Aus-)Wirkung *U2: 27*
important [ɪm'pɔːtnt] wichtig

in [ɪn] in, auf; **in advance** im Voraus; **in English** auf Englisch; **in German** auf Deutsch; **in the country** auf dem Land; **in the morning** morgens; **one in four** eine/r von vier(en) **U5:** 68
included [ɪn'kluːdɪd] mitgerechnet, einschließlich
independence [ɪndɪ'pendəns] Unabhängigkeit; **Independence Day** Unabhängigkeitstag der USA *(4. Juli)*
independent [ɪndɪ'pendənt] unabhängig *U2: 37*
Indian ['ɪndiən] indisch; Inder/in
indoor ['ɪndɔː] für drinnen, Innen- **U2:** 29
indoors [ɪn'dɔːz] drinnen, im Haus
Industrial Revolution [ɪndʌstriəl revə'luːʃn] industrielle Revolution
industry ['ɪndəstri] Industrie
information [ɪnfə'meɪʃn] Information(en); **information technology (IT)** Informationstechnologie
injure ['ɪndʒə] verletzen; **injured** verletzt
inline skating ['ɪnlaɪn skeɪtɪŋ] Inlineskating
insect ['ɪnsekt] Insekt; **insect spray** Insektenspray
instrument: play an instrument [pleɪ ən 'ɪnstrəmənt] ein Instrument spielen
interest ['ɪntrəst] Interesse; Hobby
interested in ['ɪntrəstɪd ɪn] interessiert an
interesting ['ɪntrəstɪŋ] interessant; **more interesting than** interessanter als
international [ɪntə'næʃənl] international
Internet ['ɪntənet] Internet; *Internet access* ['ækses] Internetzugang *U1: 13*; *Internet rates* [reɪts] Internet-Gebühren *U1: 13*; **surf the Internet** im Internet surfen
interpret [ɪn'tɜːprɪt] übersetzen, dolmetschen **U1:** 15
interview ['ɪntəvjuː] **1** Interview; **2** befragen, interviewen
into ['ɪntə] in ... (hinein)
intonation [ɪntə'neɪʃn] Intonation, Tonfall
introduce [ɪntrə'djuːs]: **I'll introduce myself** ich werde mich vorstellen **U4:** 55

[ʊə] sure [b] **b**ike [p] **p**en [d] **d**ay [t] **t**en [k] boo**k** [g] **g**o [ŋ] morni**ng** [l] **l**ike [r] **r**uler

introduction [ɪntrə'dʌkʃn] Einleitung, Einführung
Inuit ['ɪnjuɪt]: **Inuit people** Inuit *(arktisches Volk)* **U2:** 22
invitation [ɪnvɪ'teɪʃn] Einladung
Ireland: Northern Ireland [nɔːðən 'aɪələnd] Nordirland
is [ɪz] ist; **Is it ...?** Ist es ...?; **Is that ...?** Ist das ...?; **isn't (= is not)** ist nicht
island ['aɪlənd] Insel
it's (= it is) [ɪts] es ist, er ist, sie ist *(nicht Personen)*
its [ɪts] sein/seine, ihr/ihr
itself [ɪt'self] (es) selbst, selber *U4: 63*

J

jack: union jack [juːniən 'dʒæk] die britische Flagge *U4: 67*
January ['dʒænjuəri] Januar
jazz [dʒæz] Jazz
jeans *(pl.)* [dʒiːnz] Jeans
jet lag ['dʒet læg] Jetlag *(wenn die innere Uhr nach einer Flugreise „falsch" geht)*
job [dʒɒb] Arbeit, Arbeitsplatz, Stelle; Aufgabe; **job advertisement, job advert** [əd'vɜːtɪsmənt, 'ædvɜːt] Stellenanzeige **U5:** 77; **part-time job** Teilzeitstelle
jogging ['dʒɒgɪŋ] (das) Joggen, Jogging
join [dʒɔɪn] verknüpfen; mitmachen (bei), sich anschließen **U1:** 21
joke [dʒəʊk] Witz, Scherz
journalist ['dʒɜːnəlɪst] Journalist/in *U3: 43*
journey ['dʒɜːni] (lange) Reise, Fahrt
juggle ['dʒʌgl] jonglieren
juggler ['dʒʌglə] Jongleur/in, Gaukler/in
juice: fruit juice ['fruːt dʒuːs] (Frucht-)Saft
July [dʒu'laɪ] Juli
jump off [dʒʌmp 'ɒf] herunter-/hinunterspringen von, herunter-/hinunterhüpfen von
jumper ['dʒʌmpə] Pullover
June [dʒuːn] Juni
Junior (Jr.) ['dʒuːniə] Junior *(Bezeichnung für den Sohn)*
junk [dʒʌŋk] Gerümpel, altes Zeug, Müll
jury ['dʒʊəri] Jury

just [dʒʌst] **1** nur; **Just a minute.** Einen Augenblick.; **Just phone me.** Ruf(t) mich einfach an.; **2** gerade

K

kaffir ['kæfə] Kaffer *(abwertendes Wort für Farbige/n in Südafrika)* **U1:** 16
kangaroo [kæŋgə'ruː] Känguru **U4:** 52
keep [kiːp] (be)halten **U1:** 11; **keep him busy** ihn beschäftigen, ihm Arbeit machen **U1:** 11; *keeps on shrinking* ['ʃrɪŋkɪŋ] schrumpft immer weiter *U2: 37*
kept → keep [kept] *simple past* von **keep** **U1:** 11
ketchup ['ketʃəp] Ketschup
key [kiː] Schlüssel
kick [kɪk] treten, kicken
kid [kɪd] Kind, Jugendliche(r)
kill [kɪl] töten, umbringen
killed → kill: the young boy who had been killed der Junge, der getötet worden war **U4:** 65
kilometre [kɪ'lɒmɪtə] Kilometer
kinda ['kaində]: *kinda bumpy = kind of bumpy* *(ugs.)* ['bʌmpi] irgendwie uneben, irgendwie huckelig *U2: 37*
kinds of [kaɪndz əv] Arten (von) *(Tiere und Pflanzen)*
king ['kɪŋ] König
kingdom: United Kingdom (UK) [junaɪtɪd 'kɪŋdəm] Vereinigtes Königreich
kiosk ['kiːɒsk] Kiosk **U1:** 16
kitchen ['kɪtʃɪn] Küche
kite [kaɪt] Drachen
knew → know [njuː] *simple past* von **know** **U2:** 35
know [nəʊ] wissen; kennen; **know the way** den Weg kennen
koala (bear) [kəʊ'ɑːlə] Koala(bär) **U4:** 52
kookaburra ['kʊkəbʌrə] Riesen-eisvogel, „lachender Hans" **U4:** 52

L

laid-back [leɪd 'bæk] gelassen, cool **U4:** 58
lake [leɪk] (Binnen-)See

land [lænd] landen; Land, Grund und Boden **U4:** 54; *native land* Heimatland *U2: 36*; *this land of ours* ['lænd əv aʊəz] unser Land *U2: 37*
Land Rover ['lænd rəʊvə] Landrover *(geländegängiges Auto)* U4: 65
landing ['lændɪŋ] Landung *U5: 73*; *landing strip* Landebahn *U5: 73*
language ['læŋgwɪdʒ] Sprache; **foreign language** Fremdsprache
laptop ['læptɒp] Laptop
large [lɑːdʒ] groß **U2:** 23
last [lɑːst] **1** dauern; **2** letzte(r, s); **at last** endlich
late [leɪt] spät; **till late** bis spät; **he is late** er kommt zu spät, er verspätet sich; **run late** sich verspäten, Verspätung haben; **late parking** das Überziehen der Parkzeit; **Better late than never.** Lieber spät als gar nicht.; **See you later.** Bis später.; **latest** neueste(r, s)
laugh [lɑːf] lachen
law [lɔː] Jura, Rechtswissenschaft; Recht, Gesetz **U1:** 20
law firm ['lɔː fɜːm] Anwaltskanzlei **U1:** 20
lay → lie [laɪ] *simple past* von **lie**
lazy ['leɪzi] faul
lead singer [liːd 'sɪŋə] Leadsänger/in
leaf *(pl.:* **leaves**) [liːf, liːvz] Blatt; **maple leaf** ['meɪpl liːf] Ahornblatt **U2:** 22
leaflet ['liːflet] Flugblatt, Werbeprospekt, Handzettel
leafy ['liːfi] grün, belaubt *U5: 73*
learn [lɜːn] lernen; **learn about** etwas erfahren über; **how long have you been learning it?** seit wann lernst du es? **U3:** 50
leave [liːv] (stehen) lassen; lassen, verlassen; abfahren; **leave the house** das Haus verlassen
left: take a left links abbiegen *U1: 88*; **to the left** [tə ðə 'left] links
left → leave [left] *simple past* und *present perfect* von **leave**
leg [leg] Bein
legend ['ledʒənd] Legende, Sage
lemonade [lemə'neɪd] Limonade
lend [lend] leihen
less [les] weniger
lesson ['lesn] (Unterrichts-)Stunde

[v] seven [w] we [s] six [z] his [ʃ] she [tʃ] teacher [dʒ] jeans [j] yes [θ] thing [ð] the

Let's ... [lets] Lass(t) uns ...
letter ['letə] Brief; Buchstabe
lettuce ['letɪs] (Kopf-)Salat
level ['levl] Ebene, Höhe
library ['laɪbrəri] Bibliothek, Bücherei
license: probationary driver's license *(CanE/AE)* [prə'beɪʃnri draɪvəz laɪsns] Führerschein auf Probe U3: 39
lie (on) [laɪ] liegen (auf)
life [laɪf] Leben; **for life** lebenslänglich *(Haftstrafe)* **U1:** 21; **Run for your life!** Renn/t um dein/euer Leben!; **way of life** [weɪ əv 'laɪf] Lebensweise **U2:** 34
lifestyle ['laɪfstaɪl] Lebensstil **U5:** 68
lift [lɪft] Fahrstuhl, Aufzug
light [laɪt] **1** Licht, Lampe; **2** hell
like [laɪk] **1** mögen; **I don't like ...** Ich mag ... nicht.; **I'd like ... (= I would like)** Ich hätte gern .../Ich möchte ...; **What would you like ...?** Was würdest du gern ...?; **2** wie; **be like** (sein/aussehen) wie; **What is/was/were ... like?** Wie ist/war/waren ...?
line [laɪn] Linie, Strecke; Seil **U4:** 55
link [lɪŋk] Link; Verbindung
lion ['laɪən] Löwe **U1:** 12
list [lɪst] Liste; **make a list** eine Liste schreiben
listen (to) ['lɪsn tə] hören, sich anhören; **happy listening!** viel Spaß beim Zuhören! **U2:** 31
literature ['lɪtrətʃə] Literatur
little: a little [ə 'lɪtl] ein bisschen, ein wenig
live [lɪv] leben, wohnen; **Does your cousin live ...?** Wohnt dein Cousin/deine Kusine ...?; [laɪv] live, direkt (übertragen) **U4:** 66
lively ['laɪvli] lebendig, lebhaft **U2:** 28
living room ['lɪvɪŋru:m] Wohnzimmer
lizard ['lɪzəd] Eidechse **U5:** 71
local ['ləʊkl] örtlich, am/vom Ort
logo ['ləʊgəʊ] Logo, Firmenzeichen **U3:** 42
Londoner ['lʌndənə] Londoner/in
long [lɒŋ] lang; **a long way from** weit entfernt von **U4:** 66; **as long as** solange
look [lʊk] gucken, schauen; (nach)schauen; aussehen; **look after** sich kümmern um; betreuen; **look at** anschauen; **look for** suchen; **look forward to sth.** sich auf etwas freuen; **look up** nachschauen; **look up** hochschauen
lose [lu:z] verlieren
lost → lose [lɒst] *simple past* und *present perfect* on **lose**; **Lost in the maze.** Verloren im Irrgarten.
lot: a lot of [ə 'lɒt əv] eine Menge, viel, viele; **lots of** viel, viele; eine Menge; *a whole lot of (land)* *etwa:* enorm viel (Land) *U2: 37*
lotta: a whole lotta (work) *(ugs.)* ['lɒtə] *etwa:* ein Riesenhaufen (Arbeit) *U2: 37*
lottery scratchcard ['lɒtəri 'skrætʃkɑ:d] Rubellos *U4: 66*
loud [laʊd] laut
loudspeaker ['laʊdspi:kə] Lautsprecher
lounge [laʊndʒ]: *TV lounge* Fernsehraum *(Hotel, Jugendherberge etc.)* *U1: 13*
lousy ['laʊzi] lausig, mies *U2: 37*
love [lʌv] **1** Liebe; *patriot love* Vaterlandsliebe *U2: 36*; **2** lieben, sehr mögen
lovely ['lʌvli] wunderschön **U1:** 11
lover ['lʌvə] Liebhaber/in
low [ləʊ] niedrig, tief *U5: 73*
luck: good luck [gʊd 'lʌk] (viel) Glück
lucky ['lʌki] glücklich, Glücks-; **we were lucky** wir hatten Glück; **You're lucky!** Du hast Glück!
lunch [lʌntʃ] Mittag(essen); **lunch box** Butterbrotdose
lunchtime ['lʌntʃtaɪm] Mittagszeit
lyrics *(pl.)* ['lɪrɪks] Gedicht, Liedtext

M

machine [mə'ʃi:n] Maschine, Gerät; **cash machine** Geldautomat
mad about ['mæd əbaʊt] verrückt nach
madam ['mædəm] Dame
made → make [meɪd] *simple past* und *present perfect* von **make**; *it was made* er/es wurde gemacht *U4: 57*; **they were made** sie wurden errichtet **U2:** 25
mag *(ugs.)* [mæg] Zeitschrift *U2: 27*
magazine [mægə'zi:n] Zeitschrift
magic show ['mædʒɪk ʃəʊ] Zaubershow
mainland ['meɪnlænd] Festland U4: 64
mainly ['meɪnli] hauptsächlich **U5:** 75
maize [meɪz] Mais
make [meɪk] machen; **we're making** wir machen (gerade); **make comparisons!** vergleiche! **U4:** 60; **make a decision** eine Entscheidung treffen, sich entscheiden **U5:** 70; **make (new) friends** (neue) Freunde/Freundinnen finden **U5:** 71; *make money* Geld verdienen *U3: 42*
mall [mɔ:l] Einkaufszentrum
man *(pl.:* **men**) [mæn, men] Mann
manager ['mænɪdʒə] Geschäftsleiter/in
manatee [mænə'ti:] Seekuh
many ['meni] viele; **how many?** wie viele?
map [mæp] Landkarte, Stadtplan
maple: maple leaf ['meɪpl li:f] Ahornblatt **U2:** 22
March [mɑ:tʃ] März
mark [mɑ:k] Abdruck, Spur *U4: 57*
market ['mɑ:kɪt] Markt; **market hall** Markthalle
marry ['mæri] heiraten
mask [mɑ:sk] Maske
mass [mæs] Masse *U4: 57*
match [mætʃ] Spiel, Wettkampf
mate *(ugs.)* [meɪt] Freund, Kumpel
maths [mæθs] Mathe(matik)
matter ['mætə]: **it doesn't matter** Das macht doch nichts.; **What's the matter?** Was ist denn (los)?
May [meɪ] Mai
maybe ['meɪbi] vielleicht
maze: Lost in the maze. [lɒst ɪn ðə 'meɪz] Verloren im Irrgarten.
me [mi:] mich, mir; **it's me** ich bin's

meal [mi:l] Mahlzeit, (zubereitetes) Essen; **go out for a meal** essen gehen; **pot-luck meal** Essen, zu dem alle Gäste etwas mitbringen
mean [mi:n] **1** bedeuten, meinen; **2** geizig, kleinlich
meant → mean [ment] *simple past* von **mean** **U5:** 76
meat [mi:t] Fleisch *U2: 36*
mechanic: (car) mechanic [mə'kænɪk] (Auto-)Mechaniker/in
medical ['medɪkl] medizinisch **U2:** 25; (ärztliche) Untersuchung **U5:** 70
meet [mi:t] treffen; sich treffen (mit); **I'll meet you at the station.** Ich hole dich vom Bahnhof ab.; **meet up** sich treffen **U4:** 59
member ['membə] Mitglied **U5:** 68
memorial [mə'mɔ:riəl] Denkmal, Ehrenmal
mention ['menʃn] erwähnen **U4:** 55
mess [mes] Durcheinander
message ['mesɪdʒ] Nachricht; *radio message* Funkmeldung *U5: 73*; **text message** SMS-Nachricht
met → meet [met] *simple past* und *present perfect* von **meet**
Métis [meɪ'ti:]**: the Métis** *Nachfahren von Siedlern und kanad. Ureinwohnern* **U2:** 23
metre ['mi:tə] Meter
middle ['mɪdl] Mitte; **middle school** Schule für 11- bis 14-Jährige
midges ['mɪdʒɪz] Kriebelmücken **U5:** 71
mile [maɪl] Meile
milk [mɪlk] Milch
milkman ['mɪlkmən] Milchmann
milkshake ['mɪlkʃeɪk] Shake
million ['mɪljən] Million
mind: never mind [nevə 'maɪnd] macht nichts
miner ['maɪnə] Bergarbeiter/in
mineral water ['mɪnərəl wɔ:tə] Mineralwasser
minigolf ['mɪnigɒlf] Minigolf
minority [maɪ'nɒrəti] Minderheit
minus ['maɪnəs] minus
minute ['mɪnɪt] Minute; **Just a minute.** Einen Augenblick.
miss [mɪs] verpassen; vermissen; **one word is missing** ein Wort fehlt
mix [mɪks] Mischung; **mix everything** alles miteinander vermischen
mixer ['mɪksə] Mixer
mixture ['mɪkstʃə] Mischung **U2:** 25
mobile ['məʊbaɪl] Handy, Mobiltelefon
model train [mɒdl 'treɪn] Modelleisenbahn
modern ['mɒdn] modern
mom *(AE)* [mɒm] Mutti, Mama
Monday ['mʌndeɪ] Montag
money ['mʌni] Geld; **no money** kein Geld; **pocket money** Taschengeld
monster ['mɒnstə] Monster, Ungeheuer
month [mʌnθ] Monat
more [mɔ:] mehr; **more interesting than** interessanter als; **not ... any more** nicht mehr, keine/n ... mehr **U1:** 21
morning: in the morning [ɪn ðə 'mɔ:nɪŋ] morgens; **Good morning.** Guten Morgen.
most [məʊst] die meisten; **most popular** beliebteste(r, s)
mostly ['məʊstli] hauptsächlich **U3:** 51
motel [məʊ'tel] Motel
mother ['mʌðə] Mutter
motor ['məʊtə] Motor
motorway ['məʊtəweɪ] Autobahn *(Großbritannien) U2: 36*
mountain ['maʊntən] Berg; **mountain bike** Mountainbike; Mountainbike fahren
mounted ['maʊntəd]**: the Royal Canadian Mounted Police** die königliche kanadische berittene Polizei U2: 22
mouse (*pl.*: **mice**) [maʊs, maɪs] Maus
move [mu:v] **1** (um)ziehen *(Wohnort)*; **their family has moved** ihre Familie ist umgezogen; **2** sich bewegen
movie *(AE)* ['mu:vi] Kinofilm
movie theater *(AE)* ['mu:vi 'θɪətə] Kino, Filmtheater
MP3 player [empi:'θri: 'pleɪə] MP3-Player, MP3-Spieler
Mr ['mɪstə] Herr *(Anrede)*
Mrs ['mɪsɪz] Frau *(Anrede)*
much [mʌtʃ] viel; **How much is it?** Was kostet das?; **how much?** wie viel?
mud [mʌd] Matsch, Schlamm *U2: 27*
multinational [mʌlti'næʃnəl] multinational *U3: 43*
mum *(BE)* [mʌm] Mutti, Mama
museum [mju'zi:əm] Museum; **outdoor museum** Freilichtmuseum **U2:** 29
music ['mju:zɪk] Musik
musician [mju'zɪʃn] Musiker/in **U4:** 67
must [mʌst] müssen; **you mustn't** du darfst/Sie dürfen nicht; **he must be freed** er muss freigelassen werden **U1:** 21
mustard ['mʌstəd] Senf **U1:** 14
my [maɪ] mein/meine
myself [maɪ'self] (ich/mir/mich) selbst, selber

N

name [neɪm] Name; **What's your name?** Wie heißt du?
narrow ['nærəʊ] schmal *U5: 73*
NASA ['næsə] NASA *(National Aeronautics and Space Administration, US-Weltraumbehörde)*
nation ['neɪʃn] Nation; **First Nations** *indianische Völker in Kanada* **U2:** 23
national ['næʃənl] national, National-, Landes-; *national anthem* Nationalhymne *U2: 36*
nationality [næʃə'næləti] Nationalität **U4:** 58
native: Native American ['neɪtɪv ə'merɪkən] amerikanische/r Ureinwohner/in; *native land* Heimatland *U2: 36*
near [nɪə] in der Nähe von, nahe; **Where's the nearest ...?** Wo ist der/die/das nächst(e) ...?
need [ni:d] brauchen
needed → need [ni:dɪd]**: English is needed** Englisch wird gebraucht **U1:** 9
neighbour ['neɪbə] Nachbar/in
neighbourhood ['neɪbəhʊd] Gegend **U3:** 51
nervous ['nɜ:vəs] nervös, aufgeregt
net [net] Netz
never ['nevə] nie, niemals; **never mind** macht nichts; **Better late than never.** Lieber spät als gar nicht.
new [nju:] neu; **new year** Neujahr(stag) **U5:** 70

[ɒ] dog [ʊ] put [ə] **a**gain [eɪ] name [aɪ] time [ɔɪ] boy [əʊ] no [aʊ] house [ɪə] here [eə] chair

New Yorker [nju: 'jɔ:kə] Einwohner/in von New York
newspaper ['nju:zpeɪpə] Zeitung
next [nekst] **1** nächster/nächste/nächstes; **2** als Nächstes; **next to** neben
nice [naɪs] nett; **will be very nice** wird sehr schön sein
nickname ['nɪkneɪm] Spitzname **U1:** 9
night [naɪt] Nacht, (später) Abend
nine [naɪn] neun
nineteen [naɪn'ti:n] neunzehn
nineteenth [naɪn'ti:nθ] neunzehnte(r, s)
ninety ['naɪnti] neunzig
ninth [naɪnθ] neunte(r, s)
no [nəʊ] nein; kein/e; **No, I didn't (= did not).** Nein (habe ich nicht).; **No, she doesn't.** Nein (tut sie nicht).
Nobel Peace Prize [nəʊbel 'pi:s praɪz] Friedensnobelpreis U1: 21
nobody ['nəʊbədi] niemand, keiner
noise [nɔɪz] Lärm, Geräusch
noisy ['nɔɪzi] laut, lärmend
normal ['nɔ:ml] normal
north [nɔ:θ] Norden; nördlich
Northern Ireland [nɔ:ðən 'aɪələnd] Nordirland
nose [nəʊz] Nase
not [nɒt] nicht; **not ... any more** nicht mehr, keine/n ... mehr **U1:** 21
note [nəʊt] Notiz, (kurzer) Brief
nothing ['nʌθɪŋ] nichts
notice ['nəʊtɪs] bemerken
November [nəʊ'vembə] November
now [naʊ] jetzt
nowhere ['nəʊweə] nirgendwo, nirgendwohin
number ['nʌmbə] Zahl, Nummer
nurse [nɜ:s] Pfleger/in

O

o'clock: two o'clock [tu: ə'klɒk] zwei Uhr; **at ... o'clock** um ... Uhr
October [ɒk'təʊbə] Oktober
of course [əf 'kɔ:s] natürlich, selbstverständlich
offer: special offer [speʃl 'ɒfə] Sonderangebot
office ['ɒfɪs] Büro, Amt; **post office** Postamt; **tourist office** Fremdenverkehrsamt; Auskunft
officer ['ɒfɪsə] (Polizei-)Beamter/Beamtin; **police officer** Polizeibeamter/Polizeibeamtin
official [ə'fɪʃl] offiziell
often ['ɒfn] oft
oil [ɔɪl] Öl
OK ['əʊkeɪ] O.K., in Ordnung
old [əʊld] alt; **How old are you?** Wie alt bist du?; **oldest** älteste
on [ɒn] auf; an; **on Sundays** sonntags, am Sonntag; **on the coast** an der Küste **U5:** 71; **on the train/bus/...** im Zug/Bus/...
once [wʌns] einmal
one [wʌn] ein(e/r), eins; **the small one/s** der/die/das kleine, die kleinen; **one way** *(Fahrkarte)* einfache Strecke, ohne Rückfahrkarte **U5:** 70
onion ['ʌnjən] Zwiebel **U1:** 14
online ['ɒnlaɪn] online *(in direkter Verbindung zum Internet)* **U1:** 12; **online banking** ['ɒnlaɪn bæŋkɪŋ] Onlinebanking, Bankgeschäfte über das Internet abwickeln **U3:** 42
only ['əʊnli] **1** nur, bloß; erst; **2** einzige(r/s) **U1:** 9
onto ['ɒntə] auf, darauf
open ['əʊpən] **1** öffnen, aufmachen; **2** geöffnet
opera house ['ɒprə haʊs] Opernhaus **U4:** 52
opinion [ə'pɪniən] Meinung
opportunity [ɒpə'ju:nəti] Möglichkeit **U5:** 68
opposite ['ɒpəzɪt] Gegenteil
or [ɔ:] oder
orange ['ɒrɪndʒ] Apfelsine, Orange
order ['ɔ:də] bestellen; **(alphabetical) order** (alphabetische) Reihenfolge
ordinary ['ɔ:dnəri] gewöhnlich, normal *U5: 73*
organisation [ɔ:gənaɪ'zeɪʃn] Organisation
organise ['ɔ:gənaɪz] organisieren, veranstalten
ostrich ['ɒstrɪtʃ] Strauß *(Vogel)* **U1:** 11
other ['ʌðə] andere, weitere; **some others** einige andere
our ['aʊə] unser/unsere
ours [aʊəz]: **houses like ours** Häuser wie unseres **U5:** 71; *this land of ours* ['lænd əv aʊəz] unser Land *U2: 37*
ourselves [aʊə'selvz] (wir/uns) selbst, selber
out: get out (of) [get 'aʊt] aussteigen (aus); **out front** draußen vor dem Haus **U3:** 39
outback ['aʊtbæk]: **the outback** das Hinterland, der Busch (Australiens) **U4:** 66
outdoor ['aʊtdɔ:] im Freien, Außen-; **outdoor museum** Freilichtmuseum **U2:** 29
outdoors [aʊt'dɔ:z] im Freien, draußen
outside [aʊt'saɪd] draußen; nach draußen; **outside (the museum)** außerhalb (des Museums) **U2:** 26
over ['əʊvə] über, mehr als; **over and over again** immer und immer wieder **U3:** 40; **over there** dort/da drüben; **fall over** [fɔ:l 'əʊvə] hinfallen **U3:** 40
overnight [əʊvə'naɪt] über Nacht
own [əʊn] eigen
owner ['əʊnə] Besitzer/in
Oz *(ugs.)* [ɒz] Australien **U4:** 55

P

p.m. [pi: 'em] nachmittags, abends
pack [pæk] packen
packet ['pækɪt] Schachtel; Paket, Päckchen
pad [pæd] Schützer
paddle ['pædl] paddeln **U2:** 35
paddler ['pædlə] Paddler/in *U2: 35*
page [peɪdʒ] Seite; **home page** Homepage, Startseite
paid → pay [peɪd] *simple past* von **pay** *U3: 43*
paint [peɪnt] malen
painting ['peɪntɪŋ] Bild, Gemälde *U4: 57*
pair [peə] Paar
Pakistan [pækɪ'stɑ:n] Pakistan
pancake ['pænkeɪk] Pfannkuchen **U3:** 41
panic ['pænɪk] Panik bekommen **U4:** 65
panther ['pænθə] Panther
papers ['peɪpəz] Papiere, Unterlagen **U5:** 70
Pardon? ['pɑ:dən] Wie bitte?
parents *(pl.)* ['peərənts] Eltern
park [pɑ:k] Park; **park ranger** Parkaufseher/in
parking: late parking [leɪt 'pɑ:kɪŋ] das Überziehen der Parkzeit; **parking lot** *(AE)* Parkplatz

[ʊə] s**u**re [b] **b**ike [p] **p**en [d] **d**ay [t] **t**en [k] boo**k** [g] **g**o [ŋ] morni**ng** [l] **l**ike [r] **r**uler

Parlez-vous français? (Französisch) [paʀle'vu fʀɑ̃'sɛ] Sprechen Sie Französisch? *U2: 37*
parliament ['pɑːləmənt] Parlament
part [pɑːt] Teil; **work part-time** halbtags arbeiten, (auch: Teilzeit); **part-time job** Teilzeitstelle
partner ['pɑːtnə] Partner-; **ask a partner about** eine(n) Partner/in fragen über/nach
party ['pɑːti] Party, Feier
pass [pɑːs] vorbeifahren an **U2:** 35
passenger ['pæsɪndʒə] Passagier/in **U1:** 17
passport ['pɑːspɔːt] Pass
past [pɑːst] **1** Vergangenheit; **2** an ... vorbei; **half past** halb; **quarter to/past** Viertel vor/nach ...
path [pɑːθ] Weg, Pfad
patient ['peɪʃnt] Patient/in **U4:** 66
patriot love ['peɪtrɪət] Vaterlandsliebe *U2: 36*
pay [peɪ]**: pay for** bezahlen, zahlen für; *pay by the hour* Bezahlung stundenweise *U1: 13*
peace [piːs] Friede(n) **U1:** 21; **Nobel Peace Prize** [nəʊbel 'piːs praɪz] Friedensnobelpreis U1: 21
peaceful ['piːsfl] friedlich **U1:** 21
pelt [pelt] Pelz, Fell **U2:** 35
pen [pen] Füller
pence *(pl.)* [pens] Pence
pencil ['pensl] Bleistift; **pencil case** ['pensl keɪs] Federmäppchen
people ['piːpl] Leute, Menschen
pepper ['pepə] Paprika(schote)
per cent (%) [pə 'sent] Prozent
perhaps [pə'hæps] vielleicht
period ['pɪərɪəd] Zeitraum *U4: 57*
permit ['pɜːmɪt] Genehmigung
person ['pɜːsn] Person
pet shop ['pet ʃɒp] Tierhandlung
phone [fəʊn] anrufen; **phone book** Telefonbuch; **(phone) call** (Telefon-)Anruf, (An-)Ruf; **Just phone me.** Ruf(t) mich einfach an.
photo ['fəʊtəʊ] Foto; **take photos (of)** Fotos von ... machen
photocopy ['fəʊtəkɒpi] fotokopieren
phrase [freɪz] (Rede-)Wendung, Ausdruck
pick up [pɪk 'ʌp] hochheben **U3:** 40; abholen *U1: 13*
picked up → pick up [pɪkt 'ʌp]: *you are picked up* du wirst abgeholt *U1: 13*
picnic ['pɪknɪk] Picknick
picture ['pɪktʃə] Bild
piece [piːs] Stück; **cut ... in pieces** in Stücke schneiden
pig [pɪg] Schwein
pilot ['paɪlət] Pilot/in **U5:** 72
pink [pɪŋk] rosa
pirate ['paɪrət] Pirat/in
pitch [pɪtʃ] aufstellen *(Zelt)*
pity: That's a pity. [ðæts ə 'pɪti] Das ist schade.
pizza ['piːtsə] Pizza
place [pleɪs] Ort, Stelle
plan [plæn] **1** Plan, Vorhaben; **2** planen
plane [pleɪn] Flugzeug
planet ['plænɪt] Planet *U2: 37*
plant [plɑːnt] Pflanze
planting ['plɑːntɪŋ]: *the planting etwa:* das Aufstellen *U4: 67*
plasma TV ['plæzmə tiː viː] Plasma-TV, -Fernseher
plate [pleɪt] Teller
play [pleɪ] spielen; **play a trick** einen Streich spielen; **play an instrument** ein Instrument spielen; **play sport** Sport treiben; **Did you play with ...?** Hast du mit ... gespielt?
player ['pleɪə] Spieler/in; **CD player** CD-Player; **DVD player** DVD-Spieler; **MP3 player** MP3-Player, MP3-Spieler
please [pliːz] bitte
plumber ['plʌmə] Installateur/in **U5:** 70
pocket ['pɒkɪt] Tasche; **pocket money** Taschengeld
podcast ['pɒdkɑːst]**: video podcast** ['pɒdkɑːst] (Video-) Podcast *(Videodatei aus dem Internet)* **U1:** 8
poem ['pəʊɪm] Gedicht
poet ['pəʊɪt] Dichter/in
poetry ['pəʊətri] Dichtung
point [pɔɪnt] Punkt; **point a gun at** eine Waffe richten auf **U2:** 35; **visa points** Punkte, die man braucht, damit der Einwanderungsantrag genehmigt wird **U5:** 70
pointy ['pɔɪnti] spitz *U2: 37*
polar bear ['pəʊlə beə] Eisbär **U2:** 22
police [pə'liːs] Polizei; **police officer** Polizeibeamter/Polizeibeamtin; **police station** Polizeiwache, Polizeirevier; **the Royal Canadian Mounted Police** ['maʊntəd] die königliche kanadische berittene Polizei U2: 22
political [pə'lɪtɪkl] politisch **U1:** 21
politician [pɒlə'tɪʃn] Politiker/in *U4: 67*
pollution [pə'luːʃn] (Umwelt-) Verschmutzung
pom *(AustE)* [pɒm] Engländer/in U4: 54
pool [puːl] Schwimmbad, Pool
poor [pʊə] arm; schwach, dürftig
pop [pɒp]**: pop art** ['pɒp ɑːt] Pop-Art *(Kunstrichtung, die ihre Motive den Massenmedien, der Werbung usw. entnimmt)*; **pop group** Popgruppe; **pop music** Popmusik; Brause, Limonade *U2: 36*; *soda pop (AE)* Brause, Limonade *U2: 36*
popular ['pɒpjələ] beliebt; **most popular** beliebteste(r, s); **popular with** beliebt bei
population [pɒpju'leɪʃn] Bevölkerung **U2:** 23
port [pɔːt] Hafen
portion ['pɔːʃn] Portion
post office ['pəʊst ɒfɪs] Postamt
postcard ['pəʊstkɑːd] Postkarte
postcode ['pəʊstkəʊd] Postleitzahl
poster ['pəʊstə] Poster
potato (*pl.*: **potatoes**) [pə'teɪtəʊ] Kartoffel; **baked potato** gebackene Kartoffel
pot-luck meal [pɒt lʌk 'miːl] Essen, zu dem alle Gäste etwas mitbringen
pound [paʊnd] Pfund *(britisches Geld)*
power ['paʊə] Kraft, Macht *U3: 43*
practice ['præktɪs] Übung
practise ['præktɪs] üben
prairie ['preəri] Prärie **U2:** 22
pre- [priː] vor-
prefer [prɪ'fɜː] bevorzugen, lieber haben/mögen *U1: 13*
preposition [prepə'zɪʃn] Präposition
present ['preznt] Gegenwart; Geschenk
presentation [prezn'teɪʃn] Präsentation; Referat **U2:** 29
president ['prezɪdənt] Präsident/in

[v] seven [w] we [s] six [z] his [ʃ] she [tʃ] teacher [dʒ] jeans [j] yes [θ] thing [ð] the [iː]

pretty (large) ['prɪti] ziemlich (groß) *U2: 37*
price [praɪs] (Kauf-)Preis
priceless ['praɪsles] unbezahlbar *U4: 67*
principal *(AE)* ['prɪnsɪpl] Schulleiter/in, Direktor/in
print [prɪnt] drucken
prison ['prɪzn] Gefängnis
prize [praɪz] Preis, Gewinn; **Nobel Peace Prize** [nəʊbel 'pi:s praɪz] Friedensnobelpreis U1: 21
probationary driver's license *(CanE/AE)* [prə'beɪʃnri draɪvəz laɪsns] Führerschein auf Probe U3: 39
problem ['prɒbləm] Problem
program *(AE)* ['prəʊgræm] Programm
programme ['prəʊgræm] (Fernseh-)Sendung; Programm
project ['prɒdʒekt] Projekt
promise ['prɒmɪs] Versprechen **U4:** 67; *promises can be broken* Versprechen werden manchmal nicht gehalten *U4: 67*
protect [prə'tekt] (be)schützen
protest ['prəʊtest] Protest
proud [praʊd] stolz
provider [prə'vaɪdə] Provider *(Anbieter eines Internetzugangs)* *U1: 88*
province ['prɒvɪns] Provinz, Distrikt **U2:** 22
PS ['pi: ɛs] PS/Postskript(um)
pub [pʌb] Kneipe, Lokal
public ['pʌblɪk] öffentlich; **public holiday** gesetzlicher Feiertag; **public transportation system** öffentliches Nahverkehrssystem
pull up [pʊl 'ʌp] hochziehen
punishment ['pʌnɪʃmənt] Strafe **U4:** 54
pupil ['pju:pl] Schüler/in
puppy ['pʌpi] Welpe, Hundejunges
purse [pɜ:s] Geldbeutel; *AE:* Handtasche
push [pʊʃ] schieben; drücken
put [pʊt]: **put (on)** (hin)stellen, legen (auf); **put in** hineintun, -stecken; **put on** *(Kleidung)* anziehen **U4:** 65; **put together** zusammensetzen; **put up (a tent)** (Zelt) aufbauen **U4:** 64
put → put [pʊt] *simple past* und *present perfect* von **put**
pyjamas *(pl.)* [pə'dʒɑ:məz] Schlafanzug **U3:** 41

Q

quality ['kwɒləti] Qualität; **quality time** *etwa:* schöne Zeit des Zusammenseins
quarter ['kwɔ:tə] Viertel; **quarter to/past** Viertel vor/nach ...
queen [kwi:n] Königin
question ['kwestʃən] Frage
quick [kwɪk] schnell; **quickly** schnell *(Adverb)*
quiet ['kwaɪət] ruhig, leise, still
quite [kwaɪt] ziemlich **U3:** 40
quiz [kwɪz] Quiz

R

race [reɪs] Wettlauf, Rennen; **have a race** um die Wette laufen; **race against** um die Wette laufen; **dry boat race** *etwa:* Trockenbootrennen *U5: 74*
radio ['reɪdiəʊ] Radio, Rundfunk; **by radio** über Funk **U4:** 66; *radio message* Funkmeldung *U5: 73*
raft [rɑ:ft] Floß
railroad *(AE)* ['reɪlrəʊd] Eisenbahn *U2: 36*
railway ['reɪlweɪ] Eisenbahn **U3:** 38
rain [reɪn] regnen; **it's raining cats and dogs** es gießt wie aus Kübeln **U1:** 19
rainy ['reɪni] regnerisch
ran → run [ræn] *simple past* von **run**
rand [rænd]: **eight rand = R8** acht Rand *(südafrikanische Währung)* **U1:** 15
rang → ring [ræŋ] *simple past* von **ring**
ranger ['reɪndʒə] Aufseher/in; **park ranger** Parkaufseher/in
rap [ræp] **1** Rap; **2** „rappen";
rapper Rapper/in
rapids ['ræpɪdz] Stromschnellen **U2:** 35
rare [reə] selten
rat [ræt] Ratte
rate [reɪt]: **immigration rate** Einwanderungsquote **U2:** 23; *Internet rates* Internet-Gebühren *U1: 13*
raw [rɔ:] roh *U2: 36*
re [ri:] AW = Antwort *(E-Mail)* **U2:** 31
reach [ri:tʃ] erreichen *U5: 73*

read [ri:d] lesen; **reading** (das) Lesen
read → read [red] *simple past* und *present perfect* von **read**
reader ['ri:də] Leser/in
ready ['redi] fertig
real [rɪəl] wirklich; **really** sehr, echt; **really** wirklich; **not really** eigentlich nicht
reason ['ri:zn] Grund **U3:** 44
reception [rɪ'sepʃn] Empfang *(Hotel, Jugendherberge etc.)* **U1:** 15
receptionist [rɪ'sepʃnɪst] Herr/Dame an der Anmeldung *(in Krankenhäusern)*
recognize ['rekəgnaɪz] erkennen
record [rɪ'kɔ:d] aufnehmen, aufzeichnen
recorder: video recorder ['vɪdiəʊ rɪ'kɔ:də] Videorekorder
red [red] rot
relative ['relətɪv] Verwandte/r
relaxed [rɪ'lækst] entspannt **U5:** 71
relieved [rɪ'li:vd] erleichtert *U5: 73*
religious [rɪ'lɪdʒəs] religiös, Religions- **U2:** 24
remember [rɪ'membə] sich erinnern; daran denken
remind [rɪ'maɪnd]: *it reminds us of ...* es erinnert uns an ... *U2: 27*
remote control [rɪ'məʊt kən'trəʊl] Fernbedienung
rent [rent] mieten, leihen
repair [rɪ'peə] reparieren
report [rɪ'pɔ:t] Bericht; Umfrage; **report on** berichten über **U3:** 50
reserve [rɪ'zɜ:v] Reservat(ion) *(den Ureinwohnern vorbehaltenes Gebiet)* **U2:** 25
resort [rɪ'zɔ:t] Urlaubsort, Ferien- und Freizeitort **U3:** 39
respect [rɪ'spekt] Respekt *U2: 27*
rest [rest] Rest
restaurant ['restrɒnt] Restaurant
result [rɪ'zʌlt] Ergebnis
résumé ['rezjumeɪ] Lebenslauf **U5:** 77
Revolution: Industrial Revolution [ɪndʌstriəl revə'lu:ʃn] industrielle Revolution
rhythm ['rɪðəm] Rhythmus
rhythmic ['rɪðmɪk] rhythmisch
rich [rɪtʃ] reich
ride [raɪd] **1** Fahrt; **2** reiten; **ride a bike** Rad fahren

he	[ɑ:] car	[ɔ:] or	[u:] too	[ɜ:] girl	[i] sorry	[u] July	[ɪ] big	[e] yes	[æ] cat	[ʌ] bus

right [raɪt] **1** Recht, Rechtsanspruch; **2** richtig, korrekt; **all right** in Ordnung; **Right or wrong?** Richtig oder falsch?; **You're right.** Du hast Recht./Stimmt.; **to the right** rechts
ring [rɪŋ] klingeln
rise [raiz] wachsen, stark werden *U2: 36*; nach oben steigen *U5: 73*
river ['rɪvə] Fluss
road [rəʊd] Straße
roast chicken [rəʊst 'tʃɪkɪn] Brathähnchen
rock [rɒk] Rock(musik) **U4:** 66; Fels, Stein; **rock band** Rockband
rode → ride [rəʊd] *simple past* von **ride** *U2: 28*
rodeo ['rəʊdiəʊ] Rodeo **U2:** 30
role-play ['rəʊlpleɪ] Rollenspiel
roll [rəʊl] Brötchen
room [ru:m] Zimmer, Raum; **living room** Wohnzimmer
rose → rise [rəʊz] *simple past* von **rise** *U5: 73*
round [raʊnd] um ... herum; **walk round the museum** im Museum umhergehen, durch das Museum gehen **U2:** 29
route [ru:t] Route, Strecke *U1: 13*; *en route* [ã 'ʀut] unterwegs, auf dem Weg *U1: 13*
royal ['rɔɪəl] königlich **U2:** 22; **the Royal Canadian Mounted Police** ['maʊntəd] die königliche kanadische berittene Polizei U2: 22
rubber ['rʌbə] Radiergummi
rubbish ['rʌbɪʃ] Abfall, Müll
rugby ['rʌgbi] Rugby
rule [ru:l] Regel, Vorschrift; **Australian rules football** Football nach australischen Regeln, australischer Football U4: 52
ruler ['ru:lə] Lineal
run [rʌn] rennen, laufen; **Run for your life!** Renn/t um dein/euer Leben!; **run late** sich verspäten, Verspätung haben
rush: gold rush ['gəʊld rʌʃ] Goldrausch
Russia ['rʌʃə] Russland *U2: 37*

S

sacred ['seɪkrɪd] heilig *U4: 57*
sad [sæd] traurig
safari [sə'fɑ:ri] Safari
safe [seɪf] sicher
said → say [sed] *simple past* und *present perfect* von **say**
sail [seɪl] segeln
salad ['sæləd] Salat *(Gericht)* **U1:** 11
sale: car-boot sale [kɑ: 'bu:t seɪl] (eine Art) Trödelmarkt
salsa ['sælsə] Salsa *(scharfe Sauce)*
same: the same as [ðə 'seɪm əz] genauso wie; dasselbe wie
sand [sænd] Sand
sandstone ['sændstəʊn] Sandstein *U4: 57*
sandwich ['sænwɪtʃ] Sandwich *(belegtes Brot)*
sandy ['sændi] sandig, Sand-
sat → sit [sæt] *simple past* von **sit**
satellite technology ['sætəlaɪt teknɒlədʒi] Satellitentechnik **U4:** 66
Saturday ['sætədeɪ] Samstag/Sonnabend; **on Saturday** am Samstag/Sonnabend
sauce [sɔ:s] Soße
sauna ['sɔ:nə] Sauna
sausage ['sɒsɪdʒ] Würstchen, Wurst
savings ['seivɪŋz] Ersparnisse **U5:** 70
saw → see [sɔ:] *simple past* von **see**
saxophone ['sæksəfəʊn] Saxophon
say [seɪ] sagen
scare [skeə] erschrecken
scared [skeəd]: **I was scared** ich hatte Angst **U3:** 50
scene [si:n] Szene; Ort
scenery ['si:nəri] Landschaft
schedule ['ʃedju:l] Zeitplan; (AE) Stundenplan, Fahrplan
school [sku:l] Schule; **at school** in der Schule; **middle school** Schule für 11- bis 14-Jährige; **high school** (US) Gesamtschule für 13- bis 18-Jährige
science ['saɪəns] (Natur-)Wissenschaft; **science fiction** [saɪəns 'fɪkʃn] Science-Fiction **U3:** 42
scientist ['saɪəntɪst] Wissenschaftler/in **U2:** 24
scissors *(pl.)* ['sɪzəz] Schere
score [skɔ:] Spielstand
Scotland ['skɒtlənd] Schottland
Scottish ['skɒtɪʃ] schottisch
scraps [skræps] Reste **U4:** 64
scratch [skrætʃ] kratzen
scratchcard ['skrætʃkɑ:d]: *lottery scratchcard* ['lɒtəri 'skrætʃkɑ:d] Rubellos *U4: 66*
scratchie (AustE) ['skrætʃi] Rubellos *U4: 66*
scream [skri:m] schreien
screen [skri:n] Bildschirm
sea [si:] Meer, die See
seal [si:l] Seehund *U2: 27*
search [sɜ:tʃ] (durch)suchen
seaside: at the seaside [ət ðə 'si:saɪd] am Meer
season ['si:zn] Jahreszeit
seat [si:t] Sitzplatz **U5:** 70
second ['sekənd] **1** Sekunde; **2** zweite(r, s) (= 2nd); **second-hand** gebraucht
security [sɪ'kjʊərəti] Sicherheit **U1:** 11
see [si:] sehen; *go see (ugs.)* besuchen *U2: 37*; **See you later.** Bis später.
seem [si:m] scheinen
seen → see [si:n] *present perfect* von **see**
seldom ['seldəm] selten *U2: 37*
select [sɪ'lekt] (aus)wählen *U1: 13*
sell [sel] verkaufen
send [send] senden, schicken; **send off** wegschicken **U5:** 70
senior ['si:niə]: **senior job** leitende Position **U5:** 77
sense of humour [sens əv 'hju:mə] Sinn für Humor *U2: 37*
sent → send [sent] *simple past* und *present perfect* von **send**; **he was sent** [wəz 'sent] er wurde geschickt **U1:** 21
sentence ['sentəns] Satz
separated ['sepəreɪtɪd] getrennt *U4: 67*
September [sep'tembə] September
serious ['sɪəriəs] ernst(haft) **U4:** 58; schlimm *U5: 73*
seriously ['sɪəriəsli]: *take it seriously* es ernst nehmen *U2: 37*
serve [sɜ:v] bedienen, servieren
service ['sɜ:vɪs] Dienst, Service
set [set] Bühnenbild, Drehort
settle in [setl 'ɪn] sich einleben **U5:** 70
settlement ['setlmənt] Siedlung **U4:** 54
settler ['setlə] Siedler/in **U2:** 25
seven ['sevn] sieben
seventeen [sevn'ti:n] siebzehn
seventeenth [sevn'ti:nθ] siebzehnte(r, s)
seventh ['sevnθ] siebte(r, s)

[ɒ] dog [ʊ] put [ə] again [eɪ] name [aɪ] time [ɔɪ] boy [əʊ] no [aʊ] house [ɪə] here [eə] chair

seventy ['sevnti] siebzig
several ['sevrəl] mehrere **U4:** 67
shadow ['ʃædəʊ] Schatten
shark [ʃa:k] Hai **U1:** 15; **shark cage diving** Hai-Tauchen mit Käfigen U1: 15
she [ʃi:] sie
she's (= she is) [ʃi:z] sie ist
sheep (*pl.:* **sheep**) [ʃi:p] Schaf, Schafe
sheila (AustE) ['ʃi:lə] Frau *U4: 66*
shelf (*pl.:* **shelves**) [ʃelf, ʃelvz] Regal
Sheriff ['ʃerɪf] Sheriff
shine: the sun is shining [ðə sʌn iz 'ʃaɪnɪŋ] die Sonne scheint; **shining** glänzend
ship [ʃɪp] Schiff
shirt [ʃɜ:t] Hemd; Fußballtrikot
shoe [ʃu:] Schuh
shoot [ʃu:t] schießen **U2:** 35
shop [ʃɒp] Laden, Geschäft; **busy shop** gut besuchter Laden; **chip shop** Pommes-frites-Bude, Imbiss-Bude; **shop assistant** Verkäufer/in; **shopping centre** Einkaufszentrum; **go to the shops** einen Einkaufsbummel machen; einkaufen gehen
shoplifter ['shɔplɪftə] Ladendieb/in
short [ʃɔ:t] klein *(bei Menschen)* **U4:** 58; kurz; **shorts** *(pl.)* Shorts, kurze Hosen; **too short** zu kurz
should [ʃʊd] sollte/solltest/sollten/solltet
shoulder ['ʃəʊldə] Schulter **U4:** 65
shout [ʃaʊt] rufen, schreien
show [ʃəʊ] **1** (Fernseh-, Radio-) Sendung; **2** zeigen; **Show me, please.** Zeig(t) es mir bitte.
shown → **show** [ʃəʊn] [ʃəʊn] *present perfect* von **show U1:** 21
shrink [ʃrɪŋk]*: keeps on shrinking* schrumpft immer weiter *U2: 37*
sick [sɪk] deprimiert; krank, übel
side [saɪd] Seite
sidewalk *(CanE/AE)* ['saɪdwɔ:k] Bürgersteig **U3:** 39
sight [saɪt] Sehenswürdigkeit
sightseeing ['saɪtsi:ɪŋ] Besichtigung, Besichtigung von Sehenswürdigkeiten
sign [saɪn] Schild
signal ['sɪgnəl] Zeichen, Signal **U2:** 35
silicon ['sɪlɪkən] Silizium, Silikon
silly ['sɪli] blöd, albern
simple ['sɪmpl] einfach
since [sins]**: since 1980** seit 1980 **U2:** 25; **since (...) they've been coming ...** seit (...) kommen sie ... **U4:** 54
sincerely: Yours sincerely [jɔ:z sɪn'sɪəli] mit freundlichen Grüßen
sing [sɪŋ] singen
singer ['sɪŋə] Sänger/in
sir [sɜ:] Herr
sister ['sɪstə] Schwester
sit [sɪt] sich setzen; sitzen; **sit down** sich hinsetzen; **Sit here.** Setz dich hierhin.
situation [sɪtʃu'eɪʃn] Situation
six [sɪks] sechs
sixteen [sɪk'sti:n] sechzehn
sixteenth [sɪks'ti:nθ] sechzehnte(r, s)
sixth [sɪksθ] sechste(r, s)
sixty ['sɪksti] sechzig
size [saɪz] Größe
skate [skeɪt] „skaten", Skateboard fahren; Schlittschuh laufen, Eis laufen **U3:** 39
skateboard ['skeɪtbɔ:d] Skateboard; **skateboarder** Skateboardfahrer/in; **go skateboarding** zum Skateboarden gehen
skateboarder ['skeɪtbɔ:də] Skateboarder/in **U3:** 40
skater ['skeɪtə] Eisläufer/in **U3:** 40
skates [skeɪts] Inlineskates, Rollschuhe; Schlittschuhe **U3:** 40
skating ['skeɪtɪŋ] Rollschuhlaufen, Schlittschuhlaufen
skiing ['ski:ɪŋ] (das) Skilaufen, Skisport; Ski fahren **U3:** 39
skill [skɪl] Fähigkeit
skin [skɪn] Haut **U1:** 21; **skin cancer** Hautkrebs **U5:** 71
skunk [skʌŋk] Stinktier
sky [skaɪ]*: in the sky* am Himmel *U4: 57*
skyscraper ['skaɪskreɪpə] Wolkenkratzer
slang [slæng] Slang, saloppe Umgangssprache **U4:** 66
slap on [slæp]**: slap on** *(ugs.)* draufklatschen U5: 71; **Slip, slop, slap!** ['slɪp slɒp slæp] Slogan in Australien zur Erinnerung an Sonnenschutzmaßnahmen U5: 71
slave [sleɪv] Sklave, Sklavin
sled [sled]**: dog sled** Hundeschlitten **U2:** 25
sleep [sli:p] schlafen
sleeping ['sli:pɪŋ] (das) Schlafen; **sleeping bag** Schlafsack
slept → **sleep** [slept] *simple past* von **sleep**
slide [slaɪd] Dia; Folie *(Computer-Präsentation)* **U2:** 29
slip on [slɪp] schnell anziehen, überziehen U5: 71; **Slip, slop, slap!** ['slɪp slɒp slæp] Slogan in Australien zur Erinnerung an Sonnenschutzmaßnahmen U5: 71
slogan ['sləʊgən] Slogan, Werbespruch
slop on sunscreen *(ugs.)* [slɒp] sich mit reichlich Sonnencreme eincremen U5: 71; **Slip, slop, slap!** ['slɪp slɒp slæp] Slogan in Australien zur Erinnerung an Sonnenschutzmaßnahmen U5: 71
slow [sləʊ] langsam; **slowly** langsam *(Adverb)*
small [smɔ:l] klein
smell [smel] **1** Geruch; **2** riechen
smile [smaɪl] **1** Lächeln; **2** lächeln; **smile at somebody (sb.)** jemanden (jdn.) anlächeln, jemandem (jdm.) zulächeln
smoky ['sməʊki] rauchend *U5: 73*
snack [snæk] Snack
snake [sneɪk] Schlange **U5:** 75
snow [snəʊ] **1** Schnee; **a big dump of snow** *(ugs.)* [dʌmp əv 'snəʊ] starker Schneefall U3: 39; **after bad snow** wenn viel Schnee gefallen ist U3: 39; **2** schneien
snowboarding ['snəʊbɔ:dɪŋ] Snowboard fahren, snowboarden
snowmobile ['snəʊməbi:l] Schneemobil **U2:** 25
snowshoeing ['snəuʃu:iŋ] Snowshoeing *(mit speziellen Schuhen über Schnee und Eis wandern)* **U3:** 39
snowshoes ['snəʊʃu:z] Schneeschuhe **U2:** 30
snowstorm ['snəʊstɔ:m] Schneesturm
snowy ['snəʊi] verschneit
so [səʊ] daher, deshalb; so; **not so popular as ...** nicht so beliebt wie ...; **so far** bisher **U4:** 66
soap [səʊp] Seife; TV-Seifenoper

social ['səʊʃl] sozial, gesellschaftlich **U2:** 25
sock [sɒk] Socke, Strumpf
soda ['səʊdə]: *soda (pop) (AE)* Brause, Limonade *U2: 36*
software ['sɒftweə] Software
sold → sell [səʊld] *simple past* und *present perfect* von **sell**; *it was sold* es wurde verkauft *U4: 67*
solo ['səʊləʊ] Solo
some [sʌm] einige, ein paar; **some others** einige andere
somebody ['sʌmbədi] jemand
something ['sʌmθɪŋ] etwas
sometimes ['sʌmtaɪmz] manchmal
somewhere ['sʌmweə] irgendwo
son [sʌn] Sohn
song [sɒŋ] Lied
soon [su:n] bald
sorry: I'm sorry. [aɪm 'sɒri] Es tut mir leid.; **feel sorry for somebody (sb.)** jemanden (jdn.) bedauern, Mitleid mit jemandem (jdm.) haben
sound [saʊnd] Klang, Geräusch; klingen **U1:** 9
soup [su:p] Suppe
south [saʊθ] Süden; **south (of)** südlich (von)
South African [saʊθ 'æfrɪkən] Südafrikaner/in; südafrikanisch **U1:** 16
souvenir [su:və'nɪə] Souvenir, Andenken
space [speɪs] Platz, Raum; Weltraum
spaghetti [spə'geti] Spaghetti
Spain [speɪn] Spanien
Spanish ['spænɪʃ] Spanisch
speak [spi:k] sprechen
special: special day ['speʃl deɪ] besonderer Tag; **special offer** Sonderangebot
specially ['speʃəli] besonders **U4:** 59
sped → speed [sped] *simple past* von **speed**
speech [spi:tʃ] Rede, Ansprache
speed [spi:d] rasen, schnell fahren
spell: Can you spell ...? [kən ju spel] Kannst du ... buchstabieren?
spelling ['spelɪŋ] (Recht-)Schreibung, Schreibweise
spend (time/money) [spend] verbringen *(Zeit)*; ausgeben *(Geld)*
spent → spend [spent] *simple past* von **spend**
spider ['spaɪdə] Spinne **U5:** 71
spirit ['spɪrɪt] Geist *U4: 57*
spoil [spɔɪl] verwöhnen **U4:** 55
spoke → speak [spəʊk] *simple past* von **speak**
spoken → speak ['spəʊkən] *present perfect* von **speak** **U1:** 9; **English is spoken** Englisch wird gesprochen **U1:** 9
sponsor ['spɒnsə] Sponsor/in, Geldgeber/in *U2: 27*
sport [spɔ:t] Sport; **play sport** Sport treiben; **sports centre** Sportzentrum
spray [spreɪ] Spray; **insect spray** Insektenspray
spring [sprɪŋ] Frühling; Quelle
square [skweə] Quadrat
stadium ['steɪdiəm] Stadion
stairs [steəz] (Treppen-)Stufen **U4:** 55
stall [stɔ:l] (Verkaufs-)Stand
stallholder ['stɔ:lhəʊldə] Standbesitzer/in
stamp [stæmp] Briefmarke
Stampede [stæm'pi:d]: **Calgary Stampede** *landwirtschaftliche Ausstellung in Calgary* **U2:** 30
stand [stænd] stehen; *stand on guard* [stænd ɒn 'gɑ:d] Wache halten *U2: 36*; *stand out from* hervorstechen aus *U2: 37*; **stand up** aufstehen, aufrecht stehen; **they're standing** sie stehen
star [stɑ:] Star; **the Stars and Stripes** die Nationalflagge der USA
start [stɑ:t] **1** Start; **2** beginnen, starten; **(they) started eating** (sie) fingen an zu essen
started → start ['stɑ:tɪd]: **schools were started** Schulen wurden eröffnet **U2:** 25
state [steɪt] (Bundes-)Staat, (Bundes-)Land
station ['steɪʃn] Bahnhof; **police station** Polizeiwache, Polizeirevier; **TV station** Fernsehsender; **I'll meet you at the station.** Ich hole dich vom Bahnhof ab.
Statue of Liberty ['stætʃu: əv 'lɪbəti] Freiheitsstatue
stay [steɪ] bleiben; **stay at (a hotel)** übernachten in (einem Hotel); **stay up** aufbleiben, nicht schlafen gehen **U3:** 41
stayed → stay [steɪd] *simple past* von **stay**
steak [steɪk] Steak **U1:** 11
steal [sti:l] stehlen
stepfather ['stepfɑ:ðə] Stiefvater
stepmother ['stepmʌðə] Stiefmutter
stick [stɪk] Stock **U4:** 65
sticker ['stɪkə] Sticker, Aufkleber
still [stɪl] **1** bewegungslos, still; **2** noch
stock car [stɒk kɑ:] Stockcar *(für den Motorsport hergerichtetes Serienauto)*
stole → steal [stəʊl] *simple past* von **steal**
stone [stəʊn] Stein *U4: 57*
stood → stand [stʊd] *simple past* von **stand**
stop [stɒp] anhalten; **bus stop** Bushaltestelle; **Stop it!** Hör(t) auf!
store *(AE)* [stɔ:] Geschäft; **department store** Kaufhaus
stork [stɔ:k] Storch
story ['stɔ:ri] Geschichte, Erzählung; **... the story is about ...** ... die Geschichte handelt von ...
straight: Go straight on. [gəʊ streɪt 'ɒn] geradeaus (weiter)gehen; *straight up* gerade nach oben *U5: 73*
strange [streɪndʒ] seltsam, sonderbar
street [stri:t] Straße; **the beat of the street** [bi:t əv ðə 'stri:t] der Rhythmus der Straße **U1:** 10
Strine *(ugs.)* [straɪn] australisches Englisch **U1:** 9
string [strɪŋ] Schnur, Bindfaden
strip [strɪp]: *landing strip* Landebahn *U5: 73*
strong [strɒŋ] stark; **it's about being strong** es geht darum, stark zu sein **U3:** 50
structure ['strʌktʃə] Struktur
student ['stju:dnt] Schüler/in; Student/in
studies ['stʌdiz]: **(his) studies** (sein) Studium **U1:** 20
studio ['stju:diəʊ] Studio
study ['stʌdi] lernen, studieren
stupid ['stju:pɪd] blöd, dämlich
style [staɪl] Stil
subject ['sʌbdʒɪkt] (Schul-)Fach; Betreff (E-Mail) **U2:** 31
suburb ['sʌbɜ:b] Vorort
subway *(AE)* ['sʌbweɪ] U-Bahn
succeed [sək'si:d] Erfolg haben **U2:** 35
successful [sə'ksesfl] erfolgreich

such [sʌtʃ] so, derartig
suddenly ['sʌdnli] plötzlich, auf einmal
suffer from [sʌfə] leiden an/unter **U1:** 10
sugar ['ʃʊgə] Zucker
suitcase ['su:tkeɪs] Koffer
summer ['sʌmə] Sommer
sun [sʌn] Sonne; **sun cream** Sonnencreme; **the sun is shining** die Sonne scheint
Sunday ['sʌndeɪ] Sonntag; **on Sundays** sonntags, am Sonntag
sunglasses *(pl.)* ['sʌnglɑ:sɪz] Sonnenbrille
sunnies (AustE) ['sʌni:z] Sonnenbrille *U4: 66*
sunny ['sʌni] sonnig
sunscreen ['sʌnskri:n] Sonnencreme **U5:** 71
sunshine ['sʌnʃaɪn] Sonnenschein
super ['su:pə] super, toll
Super Bowl ['su:pə bəʊl] Football-Pokalendspiel
supermarket ['su:pəmɑ:kɪt] Supermarkt
sure: be sure [bi 'ʃʊə] sicher sein
surf [sɜ:f] surfen; **surf the Internet** im Internet surfen
surprise [sə'praɪz] Überraschung; Überraschungs-; **surprised** überrascht
swam → swim [swæm] *simple past* von **swim** *U2: 27*
sweatshirt ['swetʃɜ:t] Sweatshirt
sweet [swi:t] **1** Süßigkeit, Bonbon; **2** süß, niedlich
swim [swɪm] schwimmen
swimming ['swɪmɪŋ] (das) Schwimmen; **swimming pool** Schwimmbad, Freibad; Schwimmbecken
swimsuit ['swɪmsu:t] Badeanzug, Badehose
Switzerland ['swɪtsələnd] die Schweiz *U2: 37*
symbol ['sɪmbl] Symbol
system ['sɪstəm] System; **public transportation system** öffentliches Nahverkehrssystem

T

table ['teɪbl] Tisch; **table tennis** Tischtennis
tae kwon do [tai kwɒn 'dəʊ] Taekwondo *(koreanischer Selbstverteidigungssport)* **U3:** 50
take [teɪk] aufnehmen; dauern, brauchen; hinfahren, bringen; nehmen; **take a trip** eine Fahrt machen, eine Reise machen; *take it seriously* ['sɪəriəsli] es ernst nehmen *U2: 37*; **take notes** Notizen machen; **take photos (of)** Fotos von ... machen; **take the dog for a walk** mit dem Hund rausgehen/spazierengehen; **take-away ...** ... zum Mitnehmen
taken → take ['teɪkən] *present perfect* von **take**; **she is taken** sie wird gebracht **U4:** 66
talk [tɔ:k]: **talk about** sprechen über; **she talked (to)** sie redete/sprach (mit); hat mit ... gesprochen/geredet; **give a talk** einen Vortrag halten
tall [tɔ:l] groß (bei Menschen); hoch **U4:** 58
tank [tæŋk] Panzer *U2: 37*
task [tɑ:sk] Aufgabe
taxi ['tæksi] Taxi
tea [ti:] Tee; **iced tea** Eistee
teacher ['ti:tʃə] Lehrer/in
team [ti:m] Team, Mannschaft
technology: information technology (IT) [ɪnfəmeɪʃn tek'nɒlədʒi] Informationstechnologie; **satellite technology** ['sætəlaɪt teknɒlədʒi] Satellitentechnik **U4:** 66
teddy bear ['tedi beə] Teddybär
teenage ['ti:neɪdʒ] Teenager-, für/von Teenager
teenager ['ti:neɪdʒə] Teenager
teeth [ti:θ] Zähne
telephone ['telɪfəʊn] Telefon
television ['telɪvɪʒn] Fernsehen *U4: 67*
tell [tel] erzählen, berichten; **tell about** erzählen, berichten über
temperature ['temprətʃə] Temperatur
ten [ten] zehn
tennis ['tenɪs] Tennis
tent [tent] Zelt; **put up a tent** ein Zelt aufbauen **U4:** 64
tenth [tenθ] zehnte/zehnter/zehntes
terrible ['terəbl] schrecklich, furchtbar
terrific [tə'rɪfɪk] fantastisch, toll; wunderbar, hervorragend
territory ['terətri] Gebiet, Territorium **U2:** 22
test [test] **1** Test, Prüfung, Klassenarbeit; **2** testen, prüfen
text [tekst] Text; **text message** SMS-Nachricht
than: bigger than ['bɪgə ðən] größer als; **more interesting than** interessanter als
thank [θæŋk] danken; **Thank you.** Danke (schön).; **Thanks.** Danke.
Thanksgiving Day *(CanE/AE)* [θæŋks'gɪvɪŋ] Thanksgiving Day *(Erntedankfest in den USA und in Kanada)* **U2:** 23
that [ðæt] welche/r/s; der, die, das; **an advert that was ...** eine Anzeige, die (auch: der, das) ...
that's (= that is) [ðæts] das ist; **That's too bad.** *(ugs.)* Das ist schade.; **That's tough.** Das ist hart.
the [ðə] der/die/das
theater *(AE)* ['θɪətə] Theater
theatre ['θɪətə] Theater
thee (veraltet) [ði:] dich/dir *U2: 36*
their [ðeə] ihr/ihre
them [ðem] sie, ihnen
theme park ['θi:m pɑ:k] Freizeitpark
themselves [ðəm'selvz] (sie/ihnen) selbst, selber
then [ðen] dann
there [ðeə] da, dort; **over there** dort/da drüben; **there is/are** es gibt
these [ði:z] diese
they [ðeɪ] sie; **they're (= they are)** sie sind
thing [θɪŋ] Ding, Sache; **How are things?** *(ugs.)* Wie geht's?, Wie läuft's?
think [θɪŋk] denken, glauben; **What do you think ...?** Was meinst/glaubst du ...?
third (= 3rd) [θɜ:d] dritte(r, s); **a third** ein Drittel
thirsty: I'm thirsty. [aɪm 'θɜ:sti] Ich habe Durst.
thirteen [θɜ:'ti:n] dreizehn
thirteenth [θɜ:'ti:nθ] dreizehnte(r, s)
thirtieth ['θɜ:tiəθ] dreißigste(r, s)
thirty ['θɜ:ti] dreißig
this [ðɪs] dies; *this land of ours* ['lænd əv aʊəz] unser Land *U2: 37*
those [ðəʊz] die (da), jene (dort)
though [ðəʊ] jedoch, aber; obwohl
thought → think [θɔ:t] *simple past* von **think**

he [ɑ:] car [ɔ:] or [u:] too [ɜ:] girl [i] sorry [u] July [ɪ] big [e] yes [æ] cat [ʌ] bus

thousand ['θaʊznd] tausend
three [θriː] drei
threw → throw [θruː] *simple past* von **throw** **U4:** 65
through [θruː] durch, hindurch
throw [θrəʊ] werfen **U4:** 64
Thursday ['θɜːzdeɪ] Donnerstag
thy (veraltet) [ðai] dein/e *U2: 36*
ticket ['tɪkɪt] Eintrittskarte; Fahrkarte
tidy ['taɪdi] aufräumen
till: from … till [frəm tɪl] von … bis; **till late** bis spät
time [taɪm] Zeit, Uhrzeit; **free time** Freizeit; **have a good time** sich gut amüsieren; **have time** Zeit haben; **quality time** *etwa:* schöne Zeit des Zusammenseins; **times** mal; **time zone** [zəʊn] Zeitzone **U2:** 23; **What time is it?** Wie spät ist es?
timetable ['taɪmteɪbl] Stundenplan, Tagesablauf
tin [tɪn] Dose, Büchse
tinny (AustE) ['tɪni] Dose Bier *U4: 66*
tip [tɪp] Hinweis, Tipp
tired ['taɪəd] müde
title ['taɪtl] Titel, Überschrift
to [tu] zu, nach; (um) zu **U1:** 11; **quarter to/past** Viertel vor/nach …
toast [təʊst] Toast
tobacco [tə'bækəʊ] Tabak
today [tə'deɪ] heute
together [tə'geðə] zusammen, gemeinsam
toilet ['tɔɪlət] Toilette
told → tell [təʊld] *simple past* von **tell**
tomato (*pl.:* **tomatoes**) [tə'mɑːtəʊ] Tomate
tomorrow [tə'mɒrəʊ] morgen
tonight [tə'naɪt] heute Nacht, heute Abend
too [tuː] auch; zu; **too expensive** zu teuer
took → take [tʊk] *simple past* von **take**
tool [tuːl] Werkzeug
top: at the top [æt ðə 'tɒp] oben, am oberen Ende, an der Spitze
topic ['tɒpɪk] Thema, Themenbereich
torch [tɔːtʃ] Taschenlampe
tortilla chip [tɔː'tiːə tʃɪp] Tortillachips *(kleine, meist dreieckig geformte Maismehl-Plätzchen)*
tough: That's tough. [ðæts 'tʌf] Das ist hart.
tour [tʊə] **1** Führung, Besichtigung; **tour guide** Reiseführer/in; **2** bereisen, durch etw. reisen
tourism ['tʊərɪzəm] Tourismus
tourist ['tʊərɪst] Tourist/in; **tourist office** Fremdenverkehrsamt; Auskunft
towards [tə'wɔːdz] entgegen, in Richtung auf, auf … zu
town [taʊn] Stadt
township ['taʊnʃɪp] Township *(von Farbigen bewohnte Siedlung)* **U1:** 10
toy [tɔɪ] Spielzeug
track [træk]**: dirt track** Offroad-Strecke **U3:** 44
trade [treɪd] Handel; **trade for** (ein)tauschen gegen **U2:** 35
tradition [trə'dɪʃn] Tradition
traditional [trə'dɪʃənl] traditionell **U2:** 25
traffic ['træfɪk] Verkehr
trail [treɪl] Pfad, Wanderweg
train [treɪn] Zug; **model train** Modelleisenbahn; **on the train/bus/…** im Zug/Bus/…
trainers *(pl.)* ['treɪnəz] Turnschuhe
tram [træm] Tram, Straßenbahn
transport *(no pl.)* ['trænspɔːt] Transport, Verkehr, Beförderung
transportation [trænspɔː'teɪʃn] Transport, Transportmittel; **public transportation system** öffentliches Nahverkehrssystem
travel ['trævl] **1** Reise; **2** reisen; fahren, gelangen, hinkommen
traveller ['trævələ] Reisende/r **U1:** 8
treaty ['triːti] Vertrag **U4:** 67
tree [triː] Baum
triangle ['traɪæŋgl] Dreieck
trick [trɪk] Trick, Kunststück; **play a trick** einen Streich spielen
tried → try [traɪ] *simple past* von **try**
trip: (school) trip [trɪp] (Schul-)Ausflug
trouble ['trʌbl] Ärger, Schwierigkeiten
truck *(AE)* [trʌk] Lastwagen
true [truː] WAHR
truth [truːθ] Wahrheit *U2: 37*
try [traɪ] versuchen, (aus)probieren
T-shirt ['tiːʃɜːt] T-Shirt
Tuesday ['tjuːzdeɪ] Dienstag
tunnel ['tʌnl] Tunnel
Turkey ['tɜːki] Türkei
turn [tɜːn] (sich) umdrehen, wenden; **turn (on, off)** (ab-, an-)drehen; *turn around* sich umdrehen *U2: 35*; **turn left/right** nach links/rechts abbiegen
turtle ['tɜːtl] Schildkröte
TV [tiː'viː] Fernseher, Fernsehapparat; *TV lounge* [laʊndʒ] Fernsehraum (Hotel, Jugendherberge etc.) *U1: 13*; **TV station** Fernsehsender; **watch TV** fernsehen
twelfth [twelθ] zwölfte(r, s)
twelve [twelv] zwölf
twentieth ['twentiəθ] zwanzigste(r, s)
twenty ['twenti] zwanzig
twice [twaɪs] zweimal
two [tuː] zwei
typical ['tɪpɪkl] typisch

U

Uluru [uːlʊ'ruː] Ayers Rock *(berühmter Berg in Australien)* U4: 56
uncle ['ʌŋkl] Onkel
under ['ʌndə] unter
underground ['ʌndəgraʊnd] U-Bahn
understand [ʌndə'stænd] verstehen
understood → understand [ʌndə'stʊd] *simple past* und *present perfect* von **understand** **U1:** 9; **English is understood** Englisch wird verstanden **U1:** 9
unfair [ʌn'feə] unfair **U1:** 21
unfriendly [ʌn'frendli] unfreundlich
unhappy [ʌn'hæpi] unglücklich
uniform ['juːnɪfɔːm] Uniform
Union Jack [juːniən 'dʒæk] die britische Flagge *U4: 67*
United Kingdom (UK) [junaɪtɪd 'kɪŋdəm, juː 'keɪ] Vereinigtes Königreich
United Nations (UN) [juː'naɪtɪd 'neɪʃnz, juː 'en] Vereinte Nationen (UNO)
university [juːnɪ'vɜːsəti] Universität **U1:** 20
unlucky [ʌn'lʌki] glücklos, unglücklich
unpleasant [ʌn'pleznt] unangenehm **U5:** 71

until [ən'tɪl] bis
up [ʌp] (hin/her)auf, nach oben
update ['ʌpdeɪt] Aktualisierung
uranium [ju'reɪniəm] Uran U2: 23
us [ʌs] uns
USA [juː es 'eɪ] USA, die Vereinigten Staaten
use [juːz] verwenden, benutzen
useful ['juːsfl] nützlich
usually ['juːʒuəli] normalerweise

V

vacation *(AE)* [və'keɪʃn] Ferien, Urlaub
vacuum cleaner ['vækjuəm kliːnə] Staubsauger
valentine card ['væləntaɪnz kɑːd] Valentinskarte **U3:** 41
valley ['væli] Tal
value: good value [gʊd 'væljuː] preisgünstig
vegetables ['vedʒtəblz] Gemüse
verb [vɜːb] Verb
very ['veri] sehr
video ['vɪdiəʊ] Video; **video clip** Videoclip (kurzer Videofilm zu einem Popmusikstück) **U3:** 44; **video game** Videospiel; **video podcast** ['pɒdkɑːst] (Video-) Podcast *(Videodatei aus dem Internet)* **U1:** 8; **video recorder** Videorekorder
view [vjuː] ansehen, betrachten **U1:** 11; **view (of)** Aussicht, Blick (auf/über)
village ['vɪlɪdʒ] Dorf
violence ['vaɪələns] Gewalt(tätigkeit) **U1:** 10
violent ['vaɪələnt] gewalttätig, gewaltsam
visa ['viːzə] Visum **U5:** 70; **visa points** *Punkte, die man braucht, damit der Einwanderungsantrag genehmigt wird* **U5:** 70
visit ['vɪzɪt] Besuch **U5:** 74; besuchen
visitor ['vɪzɪtə] Besucher/in
voice [vɔɪs] Stimme
voicemail ['vɔɪsmeɪl] Voicemail *(Nachricht auf der Mailbox)*
volleyball ['vɒlibɔːl] Volleyball
vote [vəʊt] abstimmen, wählen *(bei einer politischen Wahl)* **U1:** 20

W

wait [weɪt] warten
wake [weɪk] wecken; **wake up** (auf)wecken, aufwachen **U4:** 65
walk [wɔːk] **1** Spaziergang; **take the dog for a walk** mit dem Hund rausgehen/spazierengehen; **2** (spazieren) gehen; **walk round the museum** im Museum umhergehen, durch das Museum gehen **U2:** 29; **we've walked** wir sind gegangen, wir gingen
Walkman ['wɔːkmən] Walkman
wall [wɔːl] Mauer
wallpaper ['wɔːlpeɪpə] Tapete
want [wɒnt] wollen; **want a word** sich unterhalten wollen, ein Wort wechseln wollen
war [wɔː] Krieg
warden ['wɔːdən] Aufsicht, Aufseher/in
warehouse ['weəhaʊs] Lager
warm [wɔːm] warm
warning ['wɔːnɪŋ] Warnung
was [wɒz] war; **wasn't (= was not)** war nicht
wash [wɒʃ] waschen; **have a wash** sich waschen; **wash up** abwaschen, spülen
watch [wɒtʃ] zuschauen, sich ansehen; **watch TV** fernsehen
water ['wɔːtə] Wasser; **mineral water** Mineralwasser; **water sports** Wassersport; *watering hole* Wasserstelle *U4: 57*
wave at him [weɪv] ihm zuwinken *U5: 73*
way [weɪ] Art, Weise, Möglichkeit; **a long way from** weit entfernt von **U4:** 66; **by the way** [baɪ ðə 'weɪ] übrigens **U1:** 11; **Do it this way.** Mach(t) es so.; **know the way** den Weg kennen; **on the way** auf dem Weg, unterwegs; **one way** *(Fahrkarte)* einfache Strecke, ohne Rückfahrkarte **U5:** 70; **way of life** [weɪ əv 'laɪf] Lebensweise **U2:** 34
we [wiː] wir; **we're (= we are)** wir sind
wealthy ['welθi] wohlhabend **U4:** 54
wear [weə] tragen, anhaben *(Kleidung)*
weather ['weðə] Wetter
Web (= World Wide Web) [web] Netz *(= Internet)*; **web designer** ['web dɪzaɪnə] Webdesigner/in **U2:** 24
webcam ['webkæm] Webcam, Webcamera
website ['websaɪt] Website
Wednesday ['wenzdeɪ] Mittwoch
week [wiːk] Woche
weekday ['wiːkdeɪ] Wochentag
weekend [wiːk'end] Wochenende
welcome ['welkəm] willkommen heißen **U2:** 23; **Welcome!** Willkommen!
well [wel] nun, also; **get on well with** sich gut verstehen mit **U4:** 59; **Well done!** Gut gemacht!
Welsh [welʃ] walisisch; (die) Waliser
went → go [went] *simple past* von **go**
were [wɜː] waren; **weren't (= were not)** warst/wart/waren nicht
west [west] Westen
western ['westən] westlich **U4:** 67; **Western Brown** Westliche Braunschlange *(hochgiftige Schlangenart)* U5: 75
wet [wet] nass, feucht
whale [weɪl] Wal *U2: 27*
what [wɒt] welche/welcher/welches; **What a ...** Was für ein/eine ...; **What about ...?** Wie wäre es mit ...?; **What can you ...?** Was kannst du ...?; **What do you think ...?** Was meinst/glaubst du ...?; **What time is it?** Wie spät ist es?; **What's ...?** Was ist ...?; **What's your name?** Wie heißt du?
wheel [wiːl] Rad
wheelchair ['wiːltʃeə] Rollstuhl *U2: 27*
when [wen] als, wenn; wann; **When were you born?** Wann bist du geboren?; *when you get down to it* *etwa:* wenn man mal genau hinschaut *U2: 37*
where [weə] wo; **Where are you from?** Wo kommst du her?
which [wɪtʃ] welche(r, s); der, die, das; **which ...?** welche(r, s) ...?; **a form which you download** ein Formular, das du herunterlädst (auch: der, die, den)
while [waɪl] **1** Weile; **2** während
whisky ['wɪski] Whisky

[ʊə] **s**ure	[b] **b**ike	[p] **p**en	[d] **d**ay	[t] **t**en	[k] boo**k**	[g] **g**o	[ŋ] morni**ng**	[l] **l**ike	[r] **r**uler

white [waɪt] weiß
who [huː] **1** wer; **Who is it?** Wer ist es?; **who's (= who is)** wer ist; **2** welche(r, s); der, die, das; **lots of teenagers who ...** viele Teenager, die ... (auch: der, das)
whole [həʊl] ganz *U2: 37*; *a whole lot of (land)* *etwa:* enorm viel (Land) *U2: 37*; *a whole lotta (work)* *(ugs.)* ['lɒtə] *etwa:* ein Riesenhaufen (Arbeit) *U2: 37*
why [waɪ] warum; **that's why** deshalb, daher; **Why not?** Warum nicht?
wild [waɪld] wild
wilderness ['wɪldənəs] Wildnis
will [wɪl] werden; **will be very nice** wird sehr schön sein
win [wɪn] gewinnen, siegen
wind [wɪnd] Wind
window ['wɪndəʊ] Fenster
windy ['wɪndi] windig
wine [waɪn] Wein
winner ['wɪnə] Sieger/in
winning ['wɪnɪŋ] (das) Gewinnen
winter ['wɪntə] Winter
wish: Best wishes [best 'wɪʃɪz] Viele Grüße; **Wish you were here.** Ich wünschte, du wärst hier.
with [wɪð] mit; bei
without [wɪ'ðaʊt] ohne
woke → wake [wəʊk] *simple past* von **wake**; **it woke him up** es weckte ihn auf **U4:** 65
woman *(pl.:* **women**) ['wʊmən] Frau
won → win [wɒn] *simple past* von **win**
won't (= will not) [wəʊnt] werden/wird nicht; **We won't (= will not) have time.** Wir werden keine Zeit haben.
wood [wʊd] Holz; (kleinerer) Wald
word [wɜːd] Wort; **want a word** sich unterhalten wollen, ein Wort wechseln wollen; **one word is missing** ein Wort fehlt
wore → wear [wɔː] *simple past* von **wear**
work [wɜːk] **1** Arbeit; **work experience** Arbeitserfahrung; Praktikum; **2** arbeiten; **work out** trainieren; **work out** herausbekommen **U1:** 9; **work part-time** halbtags arbeiten, (auch: Teilzeit); *working conditions* Arbeitsbedingungen *U3: 43*
worker ['wɜːkə] Arbeiter/in; **care worker** Pfleger/in; **construction worker** Bauarbeiter/in
working out ['wɜːkɪŋ aʊt] Training
world [wɜːld] Welt
worry: Don't worry. ['dəʊnt wʌri] Mach dir keine Sorgen.; *no worries* *(AustE)* ['wʌriz] *etwa:* kein Problem! *U4: 66*
worse [wɜːs] schlimmer, schlechter
worst: the worst [ðə 'wɜːst] der/die/das schlimmste, der/die/das schlechteste
would [wʊd]**: I'd like ... (= I would like)** Ich hätte gern .../ich möchte ...; **What would you like ...?** Was würdest du gern ...?; **it would take** es würde dauern **U2:** 35
Wow! [waʊ] Krass!/Wahnsinn!
write [raɪt] schreiben; **write down** aufschreiben
writing ['raɪtɪŋ] Schreiben; *writing in the sand* Schrift im Sand *U4: 67*
written → write ['rɪtn] *present perfect* von **write**; **written by** geschrieben von
wrong [rɒŋ] falsch
wrote → write [rəʊt] *simple past* von **write**

X

XL (= extra large) [eks 'el] sehr groß, XL (Kleidung) *U1: 13*
X-ray ['eks reɪ] Röntgenaufnahme

Y

yard: back yard [bæk 'jɑːd] Hinterhof *U2: 27*
yeah *(ugs.)* [jeə] ja *U2: 27*
year [jɪə] Jahr, Jahrgang; **new year** Neujahr(stag) **U5:** 70
yellow ['jeləʊ] gelb
yes [jes] ja; **Yes, she does.** Ja (tut sie).
yesterday ['jestədeɪ] gestern
yoga ['jəʊgə] Yoga
yogurt ['jɒgət] Jogurt
you [juː] du/ihr/Sie; **you and your ...** du mit deinem/deiner ...; **you're (= you are)** du bist/ihr seid/Sie sind
young [jʌŋ] jung
your [jɔː] dein/euer/Ihr
Yours [jɔːz] dein(e)/Ihr(e) *(im Brief)*; **Yours sincerely** mit freundlichen Grüßen
yourself [jə'self] (du/Sie) selbst, selber
yourselves [jɔː'selvz] (ihr/euch) selbst, selber; **Help yourselves.** [help jɔː'selvz] Bedient euch! Nehmt euch!
youth: youth club ['juːθ klʌb] Jugendclub, -zentrum; **youth hostel** Jugendherberge
Yuk! [jʌk] Igitt! U3: 39

Z

zero/0 ['zɪərəʊ] null
zone [zəʊn]**: time zone** Zeitzone **U2:** 23
zoo [zuː] Zoo

[v] seven [w] **w**e [s] **s**ix [z] hi**s** [ʃ] **sh**e [tʃ] tea**ch**er [dʒ] **j**eans [j] **y**es [θ] **th**ing [ð] **th**e [iː]

WÖRTERVERZEICHNIS

Alphabetische Liste der Wörter aus Band 1–5 (Deutsch–Englisch)

A

abbiegen: links abbiegen take a left [teɪk ə 'left]; **nach links/rechts abbiegen** turn left/right [tɜ:n 'left, tɜ:n 'raɪt]

Abdruck mark [mɑ:k]

Abend: (später) Abend night [naɪt]; **heute Abend** tonight [tə'naɪt]

Abendessen dinner ['dɪnə]

abends in the evening [ɪn ði 'i:vnɪŋ]; p.m. [pi: 'em]

Abenteuer adventure [əd'ventʃə]

aber but [bʌt]; though [ðəʊ]

abfahren leave [li:v]

Abfall garbage *(AE)* ['gɑ:bɪdʒ]; rubbish ['rʌbɪʃ]

abgesehen von apart from [ə'pɑ:t frəm]; except for [ɪ'ksept fə]

abhängig von dependent on [dɪ'pendənt 'ɒn]

abholen pick up [pɪk 'ʌp]; **Ich hole dich vom Bahnhof ab.** I'll meet you at the station. [aɪl 'mi:t ju: ət ðə 'steɪʃn]

abkühlen: (sich) abkühlen cool off [ku:l 'ɒf]

abschreiben copy ['kɒpi]

abseilen abseil ['æbseɪl]

absetzen drop off [drɒp 'ɒf]

abstimmen vote [vəʊt]

abwaschen wash up [wɒʃ 'ʌp]

Abzeichen badge [bædʒ]

acht eight [eɪt]; **achte(r,s)** eighth [eɪtθ]

achtzehn eighteen [eɪ'ti:n]

achtzig eighty ['eɪti]

achzehn: achzehnte(r,s) eighteenth [eɪ'ti:nθ]

Action action ['ækʃn]

Adresse address [ə'dres]

afghanisches Kamel Afghan camel ['æfgæn 'kæml]

Afrikaans Afrikaans [æfrɪ'kɑ:ns]

Afrikaner/in African ['æfrɪkən]

afrikanisch African ['æfrɪkən]

Afrikanischer Nationalkongress African National Congress (= ANC) [æfrɪkən næʃnəl 'kɒngres, ei en 'si]

aggressiv aggressive [ə'gresɪv]

Ahnung idea [aɪ'dɪə]; **keine Ahnung haben** have no idea [hæv nəʊ aɪ'dɪə]

Ahornblatt maple leaf ['meɪpl li:f]

Aids AIDS [eɪdz]

Aktion action ['ækʃn]; campaign [kæm'peɪn]

Aktivität action ['ækʃn]; activity [æk'tɪvəti]

Aktualisierung update ['ʌpdeɪt]

Akzent accent ['æksent]; **aufgrund Ihres/deines Akzents** by your accent [baɪ yʊə 'æksent]

albern silly ['sɪli]

Album album ['ælbəm]

Alkohol alcohol ['ælkəhɒl]

alle all [ɔ:l]; everybody ['evribɒdi]; everyone ['evriwʌn]

Allee avenue ['ævənju:]

allein alone [ə'ləʊn]

alles everything ['evriθɪŋ]

allgemein general ['dʒenrəl]

Alligator alligator ['ælɪgeɪtə]

alphabetisch: alphabetische Reihenfolge alphabetical order [ælfə'betɪkl 'ɔ:də]

als as [æz]; when [wen]; **als (unsere) neue Heimat** for our new home [fə aʊə nju: 'həʊm]

also well [wel]

alt old [əʊld]; **Wie alt bist du?** How old are you? [haʊ 'əʊld ə ju:]

Alter age [eɪdʒ]

älteste oldest ['əʊldɪst]

Amerika America [ə'merɪkə]

Amerikaner/in American [ə'merɪkən]

amerikanisch American [ə'merɪkən]; **amerikanische/r Ureinwohner/in** Native American ['neɪtɪv ə'merɪkən]

Amt office ['ɒfɪs]

amüsieren: sich gut amüsieren have a good time [hæv ə gʊd 'taɪm]

an at [æt]; on [ɒn]; **an ... vorbei** past [pɑ:st]

anbauen grow [grəʊ]

Andenken souvenir [su:və'nɪə]

andere(r,s) different ['dɪfrənt]; other ['ʌðə]; **ein/e andere(r,s)** another [ə'nʌðə]; **einige andere** some others [sʌm 'ʌðəz]

anders: anders sein als stand out from [stænd 'aʊt frɒm]

Anfang beginning [bɪ'gɪnɪŋ]

anfangen: (sie) fingen an zu essen (they) started eating [i:tɪŋ]

Anfeuerer/in cheerleader ['tʃɪəli:də]

anfühlen: sich anfühlen feel [fi:l]

Angeln: (das) Angeln fishing ['fɪʃɪŋ]

Angriff attack [ə'tæk]

Angst: Angst haben be frightened [bi 'fraɪtnd]; **ich hatte Angst** I was scared [ai wəz 'skeəd]; **Sie hatten Angst.** They were frightened. [ðeɪ wə 'fraɪtnd]

anhaben wear *(Kleidung)* [weə]

anhalten stop [stɒp]

Anhang: Anhang an eine E-Mail email attachment ['i:meɪl ə'tætʃmənt]

anhören: sich anhören listen (to) ['lɪsn tə]

ankommen arrive [ə'raɪv]

anlächeln smile at ['smaɪl ət]

Anmeldung desk [desk]; **Herr/Dame an der Anmeldung** receptionist [rɪ'sepʃnɪst]

annehmen expect [ɪk'spekt]

Anruf: (Telefon-)Anruf (phone) call ['fəʊn kɔ:l]

anrufen call [kɔ:l]; phone [fəʊn]; **Ruf(t) mich einfach an.** Just phone me. [jəst 'fəʊn mi]

anschauen look at ['lʊk ət]

anschließen: sich anschließen join [dʒɔɪn]

Anschrift address [ə'dres]

ansehen check out *(ugs.)* [tʃek 'aʊt]; view [vju:]; **sich ansehen** watch [wɒtʃ]

Ansichtssache matter of opinion ['mætər əv ə'pɪnjən]

Ansprache speech [spi:tʃ]

Antenne antenna [æn'tenə]

Antrag: einen Antrag stellen apply [ə'plaɪ]

Antwort answer ['ɑ:nsə]; **Antwort = AW** *(E-Mail)* re [ri:]

antworten answer ['ɑ:nsə]

Anwaltskanzlei law firm ['lɔ: fɜ:m]

Anzeige advert ['ædvɜ:t]

anziehen: (Kleidung) anziehen put on [pʊt 'ɒn]; **schnell anziehen** slip on [slɪp 'ɒn]

Anziehungspunkt attraction [ə'trækʃn]

Apartheid apartheid [ə'pɑ:thaɪt]

Apfel apple ['æpl]

Apfelsine orange ['ɒrɪndʒ]

April April ['eɪprəl]
Arbeit job [dʒɒb]; work [wɜːk]; **(lästige) Arbeit** chore [tʃɔː]; **ihm Arbeit machen** keep him busy [kiːp hɪm 'bɪzi]; **schriftliche Arbeit** coursework ['kɔːswɜːk]
arbeiten work [wɜːk]
Arbeiter/in worker ['wɜːkə]
Arbeitsbedingungen working conditions ['wɜːkɪŋ kən'dɪʃnz]
Arbeitserfahrung work experience ['wɜːk ɪk'spɪəriəns]
Arbeitsplatz job [dʒɒb]
Ärger trouble ['trʌbl]
ärgerlich angrily ['æŋgrili]; annoying [ə'nɔɪɪŋ]
Arktis the Arctic ['ɑːktɪk]
arktisch Arctic ['ɑːktɪk]
arm poor [pʊə]
Arm arm [ɑːm]
Armee army ['ɑːmi]
arrogant arrogant ['ærəgənt]
Art way [weɪ]; **Arten** *(Tiere und Pflanzen)* kinds of ['kaɪndz əv]
Artikel article ['ɑːtɪkl]
Arzt/Ärztin doctor ['dɒktə]
Asiate/Asiatin Asian ['eɪʃn]
asiatisch Asian ['eɪʃn]
Ast branch [brɑːntʃ]
Astronaut/in astronaut ['æstrənɔːt]
Atem: er hielt den Atem an he held his breath [hi held hɪz 'breθ]
Attacke attack [ə'tæk]
Attraktion attraction [ə'trækʃn]
attraktiv good-looking [gʊd'lʊkɪŋ]
auch also ['ɔːlsəʊ]; too [tuː]
Audioguide audio guide ['ɔːdiəʊ gaɪd]
auf in [ɪn]; on [ɒn]; onto ['ɒntə]; **auf ... zu** towards [tə'wɔːdz]
Auf Wiedersehen. Goodbye. ['gʊdbaɪ]
aufbauen: ein Zelt aufbauen put up a tent ['pʊt ʌp ə 'tent]
aufbleiben stay up [steɪ 'ʌp]
Aufführung act [ækt]
auffüllen fill (in) [fɪl 'ɪn]
Aufgabe job [dʒɒb]; task [tɑːsk]
aufgeben give up [gɪv 'ʌp]
aufgeregt excited [ɪk'saɪtɪd]; nervous ['nɜːvəs]
aufgrund: aufgrund Ihres/deines Akzents by your accent [baɪ yʊə 'æksent]
aufhängen hang [hæŋ]
aufhören: Hör(t) auf! Stop it! ['stɒp ɪt]
Aufkleber sticker ['stɪkə]
aufmachen open ['əʊpən]
aufnehmen record [rɪ'kɔːd]; take [teɪk]
aufprallen: aufprallen (auf) crash (into) [kræʃ]
aufräumen clear [klɪə]; tidy ['taɪdi]
aufrecht stehen stand up [stænd 'ʌp]
aufregend exciting [ɪk'saɪtɪŋ]
aufschreiben write down [raɪt 'daʊn]
Aufseher/in ranger ['reɪndʒə]; warden ['wɔːdən]
Aufsicht warden ['wɔːdən]
aufstehen get up [get 'ʌp]; stand up [stænd 'ʌp]
aufsteigen get on [get 'ɒn]
aufstellen: aufstellen (Zelt) pitch [pɪtʃ]; **das Aufstellen** the planting ['plɑːntiŋ]
Auftritt act [ækt]
aufwecken wake up [weɪk 'ʌp]
aufzeichnen record [rɪ'kɔːd]
Aufzug lift [lɪft]
Auge eye [aɪ]
Augenblick: Einen Augenblick. Just a minute. [dʒʌst ə 'mɪnɪt]
August August ['ɔːgəst]
aus from [frɒm]; **aus unterschiedlichen Gründen** for different reasons [fə 'dɪfrənt riːznz]
Ausdruck phrase [freɪz]
Ausflug: (Schul-)Ausflug (school) trip [trɪp]; **(Tages-) Ausflug** day out [deɪ 'aʊt]
ausfüllen fill (in) [fɪl 'ɪn]
ausgeben: (Geld) ausgeben spend (money) [spend 'mʌni]
Auskunft tourist office ['tʊərɪst ɒfɪs]
Ausland: im Ausland abroad [ə'brɔːd]
Ausländer/in foreigner ['fɒrənə]
ausleihen hire ['haɪə]
ausprobieren try [traɪ]
ausräumen clear [klɪə]
Ausrüstung equipment *(no pl.)* [ɪ'kwɪpmənt]
aussehen look [lʊk]
Außen- outdoor ['aʊtdɔː]
außer apart from [ə'pɑːt frəm]; except [ɪ'ksept]
außerhalb: außerhalb (des Museums) outside (the museum) [aʊt'saɪd]
Außerirdischer alien ['eɪliən]
Aussicht view (of) [vjuː]
aussteigen: (Busverbindung) zum Zu- und Aussteigen hop-on hop-off (bus service) [hɒp ɒn hɒp 'ɒf]; **aussteigen (aus)** get out (of) [get 'aʊt]; **aussteigen lassen** drop off [drɒp 'ɒf]
Ausstellung exhibition [eksɪ'bɪʃn]
ausstrecken: eine Hand ausstrecken hold out a hand [həʊld aʊt ə 'hænd]
Australien Oz *(ugs.)* [ɒz]
Australier/in Australian [ɒ'streɪliən]
australisch Australian [ɒ'streɪliən]; **australische Ureinwohner/innen** Aboriginal people [æbə'rɪdʒənl piːpl]; **australischer Football** Australian rules football [ɒ'streɪliən ruːlz 'fʊtbɔːl]; **australisches Englisch** Strine *(ugs.)* [straɪn]; **Leben der australischen Ureinwohner/innen** Aboriginal life [æbə'rɪdʒənl laɪf]
Auswahl choice [tʃɔɪs]
auswählen choose [tʃuːz]; select [sɪ'lekt]
auswandern emigrate ['emɪgreɪt]
Auswirkung impact ['ɪmpækt]
Auto car [kɑː]; **(das) Autofahren** driving ['draɪvɪŋ]
Autobahn freeway *(US)* ['friːweɪ]; highway *(US + Kanada)* ['haɪweɪ]; motorway *(Großbritannien)* ['məʊtəweɪ]
Autogramm autograph ['ɔːtəgrɑːf]
AW: AW = Antwort *(E-Mail)* re [riː]
Ayers Rock Uluru [uːlʊ'ruː]

B

Baby baby ['beɪbi]
Babysitter babysitter ['beɪbɪsɪtə]
Badeanzug swimsuit ['swɪmsuːt]
Badehose swimsuit ['swɪmsuːt]
Badezimmer bathroom ['bɑːθruːm]
Bagel bagel *(AE)* ['beɪgl]
Bahnhof station ['steɪʃn]; **Ich hole dich vom Bahnhof ab.** I'll meet you at the station. [aɪl 'miːt juː ət ðə 'steɪʃn]
bald soon [suːn]
Ball ball [bɔːl]

Banane banana [bəˈnɑːnə]
Band band [bænd]
Bank bank [bæŋk]
Bankgeschäfte: Bankgeschäfte über das Internet abwickeln online banking [ˈɒnlaɪn bæŋkɪŋ]
Bär bear [beə]
Barista barista [bəˈriːstə]
Baseball baseball [ˈbeɪsbɔːl]
Basis: Basis(station) base [beɪs]; **Basiswissen: Lesen** basic reading [beɪsɪk ˈriːdɪŋ]
Basketball basketball [ˈbɑːskɪtbɔːl]
Batterie battery *(pl.: batteries)* [ˈbætərɪ]
Bauarbeiter/in construction worker [kənˈstrʌkʃn wɜːkə]
bauen build [bɪld]
Bauernhof farm [fɑːm]
Baum tree [triː]
Baumwolle cotton [ˈkɒtn]
Bayer/in Bavarian [bəˈveəriən]
bayerisch Bavarian [bəˈveəriən]
Bayern Bavaria [bəˈveəriə]
Beamter/Beamtin officer [ˈɒfɪsə]
beantworten answer [ˈɑːnsə]
bedauern feel sorry for [fiːl ˈsɒri fə]
bedeuten mean [miːn]
bedienen serve [sɜːv]; **Bedient euch!** Help yourselves. [help jɔːˈselvz]
beeilen: Beeilt euch!/Beeil dich! Hurry! [ˈhʌri]
beenden finish [ˈfɪnɪʃ]
befestigen: befestigen an attach to [əˈtætʃ tʊ]
Beförderung transport *(no pl.)* [ˈtrænspɔːt]
befragen interview [ˈɪntəvjuː]
befreien free [friː]
beginnen start [stɑːt]
Begrüßer/in greeter [ˈgriːtə]
behalten keep [kiːp]
behilflich helpful [ˈhelpfəl]
bei at [æt]; with [wɪð]; **bei … zu Hause** at … house [ət haʊs]
beide both [bəʊθ]
Beifall: Beifall klatschen applaud [əˈplɔːd]
Bein leg [leg]
beinahe almost [ˈɔːlməʊst]
Beispiel: zum Beispiel for example [fər ɪgˈzɑːmpl]
bekommen get [get]
belaubt leafy [ˈliːfi]
beliebt popular [ˈpɒpjələ]; **beliebt bei** popular with [ˈpɒpjələ]; **beliebteste(r,s)** most popular [məʊst ˈpɒpjələ]; **nicht so beliebt wie …** not so popular as … [nɒt səʊ ˈpopjʊlə æz]
bemerken notice [ˈnəʊtɪs]
benehmen: sich benehmen behave [bɪˈheɪv]
benutzen use [juːz]
bequem comfortable [ˈkʌmftəbl]
bereisen tour [tʊə]
bereits already [ɔːlˈredi]
Berg hill [hɪl]; mountain [ˈmaʊntən]
Bergarbeiter/in miner [ˈmaɪnə]
Bericht report [rɪˈpɔːt]
berichten tell [tel]; **berichten über** report on [rɪˈpɔːt ɒn]; tell about [tel əˈbaʊt]
Beruf career [kəˈrɪə]
berühmt famous [ˈfeɪməs]
beschäftigen: ihn beschäftigen keep him busy [kiːp hɪm ˈbɪzi]
beschäftigt busy [ˈbɪzi]
Bescheinigung certificate [səˈtɪfɪkət]
beschließen decide [dɪˈsaɪd]
beschreiben describe [dɪˈskraɪb]
beschützen protect [prəˈtekt]
beschweren: sich beschweren complain [kəmˈpleɪn]
Besichtigung sightseeing [ˈsaɪtsiːɪŋ]; tour [tʊə]; **Besichtigung von Sehenswürdigkeiten** sightseeing [ˈsaɪtsiːɪŋ]
Besitzer/in owner [ˈəʊnə]
besonders specially [ˈspeʃəli]; **besonderer Tag** special day [ˈspeʃl deɪ]
besser better [ˈbetə]
beste(r,s) best [best]
bestellen order [ˈɔːdə]
Bestseller bestseller [bestˈselə]
Besuch visit [ˈvɪzɪt]
besuchen go see *(ugs.)* [gəʊ ˈsiː]; visit [ˈvɪzɪt]
Besucher/in visitor [ˈvɪzɪtə]
betrachten view [vjuː]
Betreff *(E-Mail)* subject [ˈsʌbdʒɪkt]
betreuen look after [lʊk ˈɑːftə]
Bett bed [bed]
Beutel bag [bæg]
Bevölkerung population [pɒpjuˈleɪʃn]
bevor before [bɪˈfɔː]
bevorzugen prefer [prɪˈfɜː]
bevorzugt favorite *(AE)* [ˈfeɪvərɪt]
bewegen: sich bewegen move [muːv]
bewegungslos still [stɪl]
Bewerbung (auf eine Arbeitsstelle) application [æplɪˈkeɪʃn]
Bewerbungsformular application form [æplɪˈkeɪʃn fɔːm]
bewölkt cloudy [ˈklaʊdi]
bewundern admire [ədˈmaɪə]
bezahlen pay for [ˈpeɪ fə]
Bezahlung: Bezahlung stundenweise pay by the hour [peɪ baɪ ði ˈaʊə]
Bibliothek library [ˈlaɪbrəri]
Bild painting [ˈpeɪntɪŋ]; picture [ˈpɪktʃə]
bilden form [fɔːm]
Bildschirm screen [skriːn]
billig cheap [tʃiːp]; **am billigsten** the cheapest [ˈtʃiːpɪst]
bin: ich bin I'm (= I am) [aɪm]
Bindewort conjunction [kənˈdʒʌŋkʃn]
Bindfaden string [strɪŋ]
Biographie biography [baɪˈɒgrəfi]
bis until [ənˈtɪl]; **bis auf** except for [ɪˈksept fə]; **bis spät** till late [tɪl ˈleɪt]; **Bis später.** See you later. [siː ju ˈleɪtə]; **von … bis** from … till [frəm tɪl]; from … to [frɒm tʊ]
bisher so far [ˈsəʊ fɑː]
Bison bison [ˈbaɪsn]
bisschen: ein bisschen a bit [ə ˈbɪt]; a little [ə ˈlɪtl]
bitte please [pliːz]; **(hier) Bitte.** Here you are. [hɪə ju ˈɑː]; **Wie bitte?** Pardon? [ˈpɑːdən]
Blase bubble [ˈbʌbl]
Blatt leaf *(pl.: leaves)* [liːf, liːvz]
blau blue [bluː]
bleiben stay [steɪ]; **Bleib(t) cool!** Chill out! [tʃɪl ˈaʊt]
Bleistift pencil [ˈpensl]
Blick (auf/über) view (of) [vjuː]
blöd silly [ˈsɪli]; stupid [ˈstjuːpɪd]
blond fair [feə]
bloß only [ˈəʊnli]
Blume flower [ˈflaʊə]
Blumenbeet flower-bed [ˈflaʊəbed]
Blut blood [blʌd]
Blüte flower [ˈflaʊə]
Boden ground [graʊnd]; **Grund und Boden** land [lænd]
Bohne bean [biːn]; **gebackene Bohnen (in Tomatensoße)** baked beans [beɪkt ˈbiːnz]

[ʊə] **s**ure [b] **b**ike [p] **p**en [d] **d**ay [t] **t**en [k] boo**k** [g] **g**o [ŋ] morni**ng** [l] **l**ike [r] **r**uler

Bonbon candy *(AE)* ['kændi]; sweet [swi:t]
Boom boom [bu:m]
Boot boat [bəʊt]
Bordkarte boarding card ['bɔ:dɪŋ kɑ:d]
böse angry ['æŋgri]
Boulevard avenue ['ævənju:]
Brathähnchen roast chicken [rəʊst 'tʃɪkɪn]
brauchen need [ni:d]; take [teɪk]
braun brown [braʊn]
Braunschlange: Westliche Braunschlange Western Brown [westən 'braʊn]
Brause pop [pɒp]; soda (pop) ['səʊdə pɒp]
Breakdance breakdance ['breɪkdɑ:ns]
brechen: (zer)brechen break [breɪk]
Brett board [bɔ:d]
Brief letter ['letə]; **(kurzer) Brief** note [nəʊt]
Briefmarke stamp [stæmp]
Brille glasses *(pl.)* ['glɑ:sɪz]
bringen bring [brɪŋ]; take [teɪk]
Brite/Britin British ['brɪtɪʃ]
britisch British ['brɪtɪʃ]
Brokkoli broccoli ['brɒkəli]
Broschüre brochure ['brəʊʃə]
Brot bread [bred]
Brötchen roll [rəʊl]
Brücke bridge [brɪdʒ]
Bruder brother ['brʌðə]
brummig grumpy ['grʌmpi]
Buch book [bʊk]
buchen book [bʊk]
Bücherei library ['laɪbrəri]
Büchse can [kæn]; tin [tɪn]
Buchstabe letter ['letə]
buchstabieren: Kannst du ... buchstabieren? Can you spell ...? [kən ju 'spel]
Bucht bay [beɪ]
Buchung booking ['bʊkɪŋ]
Büffel buffalo *(pl.: buffalo)* ['bʌfələʊ]
Bühnenbild set [set]
Bumerang boomerang ['bu:məræŋ]
Bundesland state [steɪt]
Bundesstaat state [steɪt]
Burg castle ['kɑ:sl]
Bürgersteig sidewalk *(CanE/AE)* ['saɪdwɔ:k]
Büro office ['ɒfɪs]
bürsten brush [brʌʃ]
Bus bus [bʌs]; **Bus(rund)reise** bus tour ['bʌs tʊə]; **Busverbindung von Haus zu Haus** door-to-door bus service [dɔ: tə 'dɔ:]; **Busverbindung zum Zu- und Aussteigen** hop-on hop-off bus service [hɒp ɒn hɒp 'ɒf]; **im Bus** on the bus [ɒn ðə 'bʌs]
Busch: der Busch (Australiens) the outback ['aʊtbæk]
Buschlandschaft bush [bʊʃ]
Busfahrer/in bus driver ['bʌs draɪvə]
Bushaltestelle bus stop ['bʌs stɒp]
Butterbrotdose lunch box ['lʌntʃ bɒks]
Button badge [bædʒ]

C

Café café ['kæfeɪ]
Call-Center call centre ['kɔ:l sentə]
Camp camp [kæmp]
Campingplatz campsite ['kæmpsaɪt]
Camping-Urlaub camping holiday ['kæmpɪŋ hɒlədeɪ]
Caravan-Campingplatz caravan park ['kærəvæn pɑ:k]
CD CD [si:'di:]
CD-Player CD player ['si:'di: pleɪə]
Celsius: unter null Grad Celsius below 0° C = Celsius [bɪ'ləʊ 'zɪərəʊ dɪ'gri:z 'selsiəs]
Cent cent [sent]
Center center *(AE)* ['sentə]
Chance chance [tʃɑ:ns]
Checkliste checklist ['tʃeklɪst]
Cheeseburger cheeseburger ['tʃi:zbɜ:gə]
Chef-Barista head barista ['hed bə'ri:stə]
Chinese/Chinesin Chinese [tʃaɪ'ni:z]
chinesisch Chinese [tʃaɪ'ni:z]
Chinook Chinook [tʃɪ'nu:k]
Clique gang [gæŋ]
Cocktail cocktail ['kɒkteɪl]
Cola cola ['kəʊlə]
Comic(heft) comic ['kɒmɪk]
Computer computer [kəm'pju:tə]
cool cool [ku:l]; laid-back [leɪd 'bæk]; **Bleib(t) cool!** Chill out! [tʃil 'aʊt]
Cornflakes cornflakes ['kɔ:nfleɪks]
Couch couch [kaʊtʃ]
Cousin/Cousine cousin ['kʌzn]
Cousine/Kusine cousin ['kʌzn]
Cowboy cowboy ['kaʊbɔɪ]
Cowgirl cowgirl ['kaʊgɜ:l]
Creme cream [kri:m]

D

da there [ðeə]; **da drüben** over there [əʊvə 'ðeə]
daher so [səʊ]; that's why ['ðæts waɪ]
Dame madam ['mædəm]
dämlich stupid ['stju:pɪd]
danke: Danke (schön). Thank you. [θæŋk]; **Danke!** Cheers! *(ugs.)* [tʃɪəz]; **Danke.** Thanks. [θæŋk]
danken thank [θæŋk]
dann then [ðen]
darstellen act [ækt]
das that *(Relativpronomen)* [ðæt]; which *(Relativpronomen)* [wɪtʃ]; who *(Relativpronomen)* [hu:]; **das ist** that's (= that is) [ðæts]; **der, die, das** the [ðə]
dasselbe wie the same as [ðə 'seɪm əz]
Datenbank database ['deɪtəbeɪs]
Datum date [deɪt]
dauern last [lɑ:st]; take [teɪk]; **es würde dauern** it would take [ɪt wʊd 'teɪk]
Daumen: Ich drücke die Daumen. fingers crossed ['fɪŋgə krɒst]
defekt broken ['brəʊkən]
dein your [jɔ:]; **dein(e)** Yours [jɔ:z]
dein/e thy *(veraltet)* [ðai]
Delfin dolphin ['dɒlfɪn]
denken think [θɪŋk]; **daran denken** remember [rɪ'membə]; **ich denke** I guess [aɪ 'ges]
Denkmal memorial [mə'mɔ:riəl]
Deo deodorant [di'əʊdərənt]
Deodorant deodorant [di'əʊdərənt]
deprimiert sick [sɪk]
der that *(Relativpronomen)* [ðæt]; which *(Relativpronomen)* [wɪtʃ]; who *(Relativpronomen)* [hu:]; **der, die, das** the [ðə]
derartig such [sʌtʃ]
deshalb so [səʊ]; that's why ['ðæts waɪ]
Detail detail ['di:teɪl]

deutsch German ['dʒɜ:mən]; **auf Deutsch** in German [ɪn 'dʒɜ:mən]
Deutschland Germany ['dʒɜ:məni]
Dezember December [dɪ'sembə]
Dia slide [slaɪd]
Dialog dialogue ['daɪəlɒg]
dich thee *(veraltet)* [ði:]; you [ju:]
dicht close [kləʊs]
Dichter/in poet ['pəʊɪt]
Dichtung poetry ['pəʊətri]
Didgeridoo didgeridoo [dɪdʒəri'du:]
die that *(Relativpronomen)* [ðæt]; which *(Relativpronomen)* [wɪtʃ]; who *(Relativpronomen)* [hu:]; **der, die, das** the [ðə]; **die (da)** those *(pl.)* [ðəʊz]
Dienst service ['sɜ:vɪs]
Dienstag Tuesday ['tju:zdeɪ]
dies this [ðɪs]
diese these *(pl.)* [ði:z]
Digital- digital ['dɪdʒɪtl]
Ding thing [θɪŋ]
Dingo dingo ['dɪŋgəʊ]
Dinosaurier dinosaur ['daɪnəsɔ:]
dir thee [ði:]; you [ju:]
direkt: direkt (übertragen) live [laɪv]
Direktor/in principal ['prɪnsɪpl]
Distrikt province ['prɒvɪns]
Dock dock [dɒk]
Dollar buck *(AE) (ugs.)* [bʌk]; dollar ($) ['dɒlə]
dolmetschen interpret [ɪn'tɜ:prɪt]
Donnerstag Thursday ['θɜ:zdeɪ]
Doppel- double ['dʌbl]
doppelt double ['dʌbl]
Dorf village ['vɪlɪdʒ]
dort there [ðeə]; **dort drüben** over there [əʊvə 'ðeə]
Dose can [kæn]; tin [tɪn]; **Dose Bier** tinny *(AustE)* ['tɪni]
downloaden download ['daʊnləʊd]
Drachen kite [kaɪt]
draufklatschen slap on *(ugs.)* [slæp 'ɒn]
draußen outdoors [aʊt'dɔ:z]; outside [aut'saɪd]; **draußen vor dem Haus** out front [aʊt 'frʌnt]
drehen: (ab-, an-)drehen turn (on, off) [tɜ:n]
Drehort set [set]
drei three [θri:]
Dreieck triangle ['traɪæŋgl]
dreißig thirty ['θɜ:ti]; **dreißigste(r,s)** thirtieth ['θɜ:tiəθ]
dreizehn thirteen [θɜ:'ti:n]; **dreizehnte(r,s)** thirteenth [θɜ:'ti:nθ]
drinnen indoors [ɪn'dɔ:z]; **für drinnen** indoor ['ɪndɔ:]
dritte(r,s) third (= 3rd) [θɜ:d]
Drittel: ein Drittel a third [θɜ:d]
Drogen drugs [drʌgz]
drucken print [prɪnt]
drücken push [pʊʃ]; **Ich drücke die Daumen.** fingers crossed ['fɪŋgə krɒst]
du you [ju:]; **du bist** you're (= you are) [jʊə]; **du mit deinem/deiner ...** you and your ... ['ju ənd jɔ:]
dunkel dark [dɑ:k]
durch through [θru:]; **durch das Museum gehen** walk round the museum [wɔ:k 'raʊnd]
Durcheinander mess [mes]
durchsuchen search [sɜ:tʃ]
dürfen: du darfst/Sie dürfen nicht you mustn't ['mʌsnt]; **sie durften nicht** they weren't allowed to [ə'laʊd]
dürftig poor [pʊə]
Durst: Ich habe Durst. I'm thirsty. [aɪm 'θɜ:sti]
DVD DVD [di: vi: 'di:]; **DVD-Spieler** DVD player [di: vi: 'di: pleɪə]

E

eben flat [flæt]
Ebene level ['levl]
echt really ['rɪəli]
Ehrenmal memorial [mə'mɔ:riəl]
Ei egg [eg]
Eidechse lizard ['lɪzəd]
eigen own [əʊn]
eigentlich: eigentlich nicht not really [nɒt 'ri:əli]
ein/eine a [ə]; an [ən]
eincremen: sich mit reichlich Sonnencreme eincremen slop on sunscreen *(ugs.)* [slɒp ɒn 'sʌnskri:n]
einfach easy ['i:zi]; simple ['sɪmpl]; **Ruf(t) mich einfach an.** Just phone me. [jəst 'fəʊn mi]
einfache Strecke (Fahrkarte) one way [wʌn 'weɪ]
Einführung introduction [ɪntrə'dʌkʃn]
einige a few [ə 'fju:]; some [sʌm]; **einige andere** some others [sʌm 'ʌðəz]
einkaufen: einkaufen gehen go to the shops [gəʊ tə ðə 'ʃɒps]
Einkaufsbummel: einen Einkaufsbummel machen go to the shops [gəʊ tə ðə 'ʃɒps]
Einkaufszentrum mall [mɔ:l]; shopping centre ['ʃɒpɪŋ sentə]
Einladung invitation [ɪnvɪ'teɪʃn]
einleben: sich einleben settle in [setl 'ɪn]
Einleitung introduction [ɪntrə'dʌkʃn]
einmal once [wʌns]; **auf einmal** suddenly ['sʌdnli]; **noch einmal** again [ə'gen]; **schon einmal** before [bɪ'fɔ:]
Einmal- disposable [dɪ'spəʊzəbl]
einnehmen capture ['kæptʃə]
eins one [wʌn]
einsammeln collect [kə'lekt]
einschlafen fall asleep [fɔ:l ə'sli:p]
einschließlich included [ɪn'klu:dɪd]
einsteigen get on [get 'ɒn]
Einsteigen boarding ['bɔ:dɪŋ]
eintauschen gegen trade for ['treɪd fə]
eintreffen arrive [ə'raɪv]
Eintrittskarte ticket ['tɪkɪt]
Einwanderer/Einwanderin immigrant ['ɪmɪgrənt]
Einwanderung immigration [ɪmɪ'greɪʃn]; **Punkte für den Einwanderungsantrag** visa points ['vi:zə pɔɪnts]
Einwanderungsquote immigration rate [ɪmɪ'greɪʃn reɪt]
Einzelheit detail ['di:teɪl]
einzige(r/s) only ['əʊnli]
Eis ice [aɪs]; **(Speise-)Eis** ice cream [aɪs 'kri:m]; **Eis laufen** skate [skeɪt]
Eisbär polar bear ['pəʊlə beə]
Eisbrecher ice-breaker ['aɪs breɪkə]
Eisenbahn railroad *(AE)* ['reɪlrəʊd]; railway ['reɪlweɪ]
Eishockey ice hockey ['aɪs hɒki]
Eisläufer/in skater ['skeɪtə]
Eistee iced tea [aɪst 'ti:]
Elch elk [elk]
Elefant elephant ['elɪfənt]
Elektriker/in electrician [ɪlek'trɪʃn]
Elektroapparat electronic gadget [ɪlek'trɒnɪk 'gædʒɪt]
Elektrogerät electronic gadget [ɪlek'trɒnɪk 'gædʒɪt]
elektronisch: elektronische Postkarte ecard ['i:kɑ:d]

[i:] he [ɑ:] car [ɔ:] or [u:] too [ɜ:] girl [i] sorry [u] July [ɪ] big [e] yes [æ] cat [ʌ] bus

elf eleven [ɪ'levn]; **elfte(r,s)** eleventh [ɪ'levnθ]
Eltern parents *(pl.)* ['peərənts]
E-Mail email ['i:meɪl]; **als E-Mail verschicken** email ['i:meɪl]; **Anhang an eine E-Mail** email attachment ['i:meɪl ə'tætʃmənt]; **per E-Mail** by email [baɪ 'i:meɪl]
Empfang desk [desk]; reception [rɪ'sepʃn]
Emu emu ['i:mju:]
Ende end [end]; **am Ende** in the end [ɪn ði 'end]; **am oberen Ende** at the top [æt ðə 'tɒp]; **zu Ende machen** finish ['fɪnɪʃ]
endlich at last [æt 'lɑ:st]
England England ['ɪŋglənd]
Engländer/in pom *(AustE)* [pɒm]
englisch English ['ɪŋglɪʃ]; **auf Englisch** in English [ɪn 'ɪŋglɪʃ]
enorm: enorm viel (Land) a whole lot of (land) [ə 'həʊl lɒt əv lænd]
entdecken find out [faɪnd 'aʊt]
entfernt: weit entfernt von a long way from [ə 'lɒŋ weɪ frɒm]
Entfernung distance ['dɪstəns]
entfliehen escape [ɪ'skeɪp]
entgegen towards [tə'wɔ:dz]
entlang along [ə'lɒŋ]
entlanggehen go along [gəʊ ə'lɒŋ]
entscheiden: (sich) entscheiden decide [dɪ'saɪd]; **sich entscheiden** make a decision ['meɪk ə dɪ'sɪʒn]
Entscheidung decision [dɪ'sɪʒn]; **eine Entscheidung treffen** make a decision [meɪk ə dɪ'sɪʒn]
entschuldigen: Entschuldigen Sie. Excuse me. [ɪk'skju:z mi]
Entschuldigung. Excuse me. [ɪk'skju:z mi]
entspannen: sich entspannen chill out *(ugs.)* [tʃil 'aʊt]
entspannt relaxed [rɪ'lækst]
enttäuscht disappointed [dɪsə'pɔɪntɪd]
entwerfen design [dɪ'zaɪn]
Entwicklungsländer developing countries [dɪ'veləpɪŋ kʌntriz]
er: er ist he's (= he is) [hi:z]
Erdatmosphäre: Erwärmung der Erdatmosphäre global warming [gləʊbl 'wɔ:mɪŋ]
Erdbeben earthquake ['ɜ:θkweɪk]
Erde ground [graʊnd]; **(die) Erde** earth [ɜ:θ]
Erdgeschoss ground floor ['graʊnd flɔ:]
Erdkunde geography [dʒi'ɒgrəfi]
erfahren: etwas erfahren über learn about ['lɜ:n əbaʊt]
Erfahrung experience [ɪk'spɪəriəns]
Erfolg: Erfolg haben succeed [sək'si:d]
erfolgreich successful [sə'ksesfl]
erforschen explore [ɪk'splɔ:]
Ergebnis result [rɪ'zʌlt]
erinnern: es erinnert uns an ... it reminds us of ... [ɪt rɪ'maɪndz ʌs əf]; **sich erinnern** remember [rɪ'membə]
erkennen recognize ['rekəgnaɪz]
erklären explain [ɪk'spleɪn]
erkunden explore [ɪk'splɔ:]
erleichtert relieved [rɪ'li:vd]
ernst: es ernst nehmen take it seriously [teɪk ɪt 'sɪəriəsli]
ernst(haft) serious ['sɪəriəs]
Erntedankfest Thanksgiving Day *(CanE/AE)* [θæŋks'gɪvɪŋ]
erobern capture ['kæptʃə]
erraten guess [ges]
erreichen get [get]; reach [ri:tʃ]
erschaffen create [kri:'eɪt]
erschrecken scare [skeə]
Ersparnisse savings ['seivɪŋz]
erst only ['əʊnli]
erstaunt amazed [ə'meɪzd]
erste(r,s) first [fɜ:st]; **der erste Mai (1. Mai)** May the first (= 1st May) [meɪ ðə 'fɜ:st]; **zum ersten Mal** first [fɜ:st]
Erwachsene/r adult ['ædʌlt]
erwähnen mention ['menʃn]
Erwärmung: Erwärmung der Erdatmosphäre global warming [gləʊbl 'wɔ:mɪŋ]
erwarten expect [ɪk'spekt]
erwecken command [kə'mɑ:nd]
erwischen catch [kætʃ]
erzählen tell [tel]; tell about [tel ə'baʊt]
Erzählung story ['stɔ:ri]
es: es ist it's (= it is) [ɪts]
Espresso espresso [e'spresəʊ]
essen eat [i:t]; have [hæv]; **(sie) fingen an zu essen** (they) started eating [i:tɪŋ]; **essen gehen** go out for a meal [geʊ aʊt fər ə 'mi:l]
Essen food [fu:d]; pot-luck meal [pɒt lʌk 'mɪ:l]; **(zubereitetes) Essen** meal [mi:l]; **Essen, zu dem alle Gäste etwas mitbringen** pot-luck meal [pɒt lʌk 'mɪ:l]
ethnisch ethnic ['eθnɪk]
etwas anything ['eniθɪŋ]; something ['sʌmθɪŋ]
euer your [jɔ:]
Euro euro ['jʊərəʊ]
Europa Europe ['jʊərəp]
Europäer/in European [jʊərə'pi:ən]
Expedition expedition [ekspə'diʃn]
Experiment experiment [ɪk'sperɪmənt]
Experte/Expertin expert ['ekspɜ:t]

F

Fabrik factory ['fæktəri]
Fach: (Schul-)Fach subject ['sʌbdʒɪkt]
Fachmann/Fachfrau expert ['ekspɜ:t]
Fähigkeit skill [skɪl]
Fahne flag [flæg]
Fähre ferry ['feri]
fahren drive [draɪv]; go [gəʊ]; travel ['trævl]; **in die (Innen-) Stadt fahren** go to town [gəʊ tə 'taʊn]; **in Urlaub fahren** go on holiday [gəʊ ɒn 'hɒlədeɪ]; **mit dem/der ... fahren** go by ... ['gəʊ baɪ]; **schnell fahren** speed [spi:d]
Fahrkarte ticket ['tɪkɪt]
Fahrplan schedule ['ʃedju:l]
Fahrrad bike [baɪk]
Fahrstuhl lift [lɪft]
Fahrt journey ['dʒɜ:ni]; ride [raɪd]; **eine Fahrt machen** take a trip [teɪk ə 'trɪp]
fair fair [feə]
Fakt fact [fækt]
fallen fall [fɔ:l]
falsch false [fɔ:ls]; wrong [rɒŋ]; **Richtig oder falsch?** Right or wrong? ['raɪt ɔ: 'rɒŋ]
Familie family ['fæməli]; **meine Familie** my folks *(ugs.)* [maɪ 'fəʊks]
Fan fan [fæn]
Fanatiker/in freak [fri:k]
fangen catch [kætʃ]
fantastisch fantastic [fæn'tæstɪk]; terrific [tə'rɪfɪk]
Farbe color *(AE)* ['kʌlə]; colour ['kʌlə]
Farm farm [fɑ:m]
fast almost ['ɔ:lməʊst]
faul lazy ['leɪzi]
Februar February ['februəri]
Federmäppchen pencil case ['pensl keɪs]
fegen: (Schnee) fegen clear [klɪə]

[ɒ] dog [ʊ] put [ə] again [eɪ] name [aɪ] time [ɔɪ] boy [əʊ] no [aʊ] house [ɪə] here [eə] chair

fehlen: ein Wort fehlt one word is missing [wʌn wɜːd ɪz 'mɪsɪŋ]
Feier party ['pɑːti]
feiern celebrate ['selɪbreɪt]
Feiertag anniversary [ænɪ'vɜːsəri]; **gesetzlicher Feiertag** public holiday [pʌblɪk 'hɒlədeɪ]
Feld field [fiːld]
Fell pelt [pelt]
Fels rock [rɒk]
Fenster window ['wɪndəʊ]
Ferien holiday ['hɒlədeɪ]; vacation *(AE)* [və'keɪʃn]
Ferienhaus cottage ['kɒtɪdʒ]
Ferienort resort [rɪ'zɔːt]
Fernbedienung remote control [rɪ'məʊt kən'trəʊl]
Fernsehapparat TV [tiː'viː]
fernsehen watch TV [wɒtʃ tiː'viː]
Fernsehen television ['telɪvɪʒn]
Fernseher TV [tiː'viː]
Fernsehraum TV lounge [tiː'viː laʊndʒ]
Fernsehsender TV station [tiː'viː steɪʃn]
Fernsehsendung programme ['prəʊgræm]
fertig ready ['redi]
Festessen: Festessen mit anschließendem Tanz dinner dance ['dɪnə dɑːns]
festhalten hold [həʊld]
Festival festival ['festɪvl]
Festland mainland ['meɪnlænd]
Festung fortress ['fɔːtrəs]
feucht wet [wet]
Feuer: Feuer schlucken/speien eat fire [iːt 'faɪə]
Feuerwehrmann/Feuerwehrfrau firefighter ['faɪəfaɪtə]
Feuerwerkskörper firework ['faɪəwɜːk]
Film film [fɪlm]
Filmführer film guide ['fɪlm gaɪd]
Filmprogrammheft film guide ['fɪlm gaɪd]
Filmtheater movie theater *(AE)* ['muːvi 'θɪətə]
Filzstift felt-tip ['felttɪp]
finden find [faɪnd]; **(neue) Freunde/Freundinnen finden** make (new) friends [meɪk 'frendz]
Finger finger ['fɪŋgə]
Firma company ['kʌmpəni]; firm [fɜːm]
Firmenzeichen logo ['ləʊgəʊ]
Fisch: Fisch und Pommes frites fish and chips [fɪʃ ənd 'tʃɪps]
Fischstäbchen fish fingers [fɪʃ 'fɪŋgəz]
Fitness fitness ['fɪtnəs]
flach flat [flæt]
Flagge flag [flæg]
Flasche: eine Flasche ... a bottle of ... [ə 'bɒtl əv]
Fleisch meat [miːt]
flexibel flexible ['fleksəbl]
Fliege fly [flaɪ]
fliegen fly [flaɪ]
fliehen escape [ɪ'skeɪp]
fließen flow [fləʊ]
Floß raft [rɑːft]
Flöte: (Quer-)Flöte flute [fluːt]
Flug flight [flaɪt]
Flugblatt leaflet ['liːflet]
Flughafen airport ['eəpɔːt]
Flugplatz airfield ['eəfiːld]
Flugschalter airport desk ['eəpɔːt desk]
Flugsteig gate [geɪt]
Flugzeug plane [pleɪn]
Fluss river ['rɪvə]
Flyer flyer ['flaɪə]
folgen follow ['fɒləʊ]
Folie slide [slaɪd]
Football: australischer Football Australian rules football [ɒ'streɪliən ruːlz 'fʊtbɔːl]
Football-Pokalendspiel Super Bowl ['suːpə bəʊl]
Form form [fɔːm]
Formular form [fɔːm]
Foto photo ['fəʊtəʊ]; **Fotos von ... machen** take photos (of) [teɪk 'fəʊtəʊz]
Fotoapparat camera ['kæmərə]
fotokopieren photocopy ['fəʊtəkɒpi]
Frage question ['kwestʃən]; **häufig gestellte Fragen** FAQ (= frequently asked questions) [ef eɪ 'kju, 'friːkwəntli ɑːskt 'kwestʃnz]
fragen ask [ɑːsk]; **eine(n) Partner/in fragen über/nach** ask a partner about [ɑːsk ə 'pɑːtnə əbaʊt]; **sie fragt nach** she's asking about [ʃiːz 'ɑːskɪŋ ə'baʊt]
Frankreich France [frɑːns]
französisch French [frentʃ]
Französisch French [frentʃ]
Frau Mrs ['mɪsɪz]; sheila *(AustE)* ['ʃiːlə]; woman *(pl.: women)* ['wʊmən]
Freak freak [friːk]
frei free [friː]; **im Freien** outdoor ['aʊtdɔː]; outdoors [aʊt'dɔːz]
Freibad swimming pool ['swɪmɪŋ puːl]
Freiheit freedom ['friːdəm]
Freiheitsstatue Statue of Liberty ['stætʃuː əv 'lɪbəti]
Freilichtmuseum outdoor museum [aʊtdɔː mju'ziːəm]
Freitag Friday ['fraɪdeɪ]
Freizeit free time [friː'taɪm]
Freizeitort: Ferien- und Freizeitort resort [rɪ'zɔːt]
Freizeitpark theme park ['θiːm pɑːk]
Fremdenverkehrsamt tourist office ['tʊərɪst ɒfɪs]
Fremdsprache foreign language [fɒrən 'læŋgwɪdʒ]
fressen: zu fressen geben feed [fiːd]
freuen: sich auf etwas freuen look forward to sth. [lʊk 'fɔːwəd tʊ]
Freund mate *(ugs.)* [meɪt]
Freund/Freundin: (neue) Freunde/Freundinnen finden make (new) friends [meɪk 'frendz]
Freund/in friend [frend]
Freundin: (feste) Freundin girlfriend ['gɜːlfrend]
freundlich friendly ['frendli]; **mit freundlichen Grüßen** Yours sincerely [jɔːz sɪn'sɪəli]
Friede(n) peace [piːs]
Friedensnobelpreis Nobel Peace Prize [nəʊbel 'piːs praɪz]
friedlich peaceful ['piːsfl]
frisch fresh [freʃ]
Friseur/in hairdresser ['heədresə]
froh glad [glæd]; happy ['hæpi]
Fruchtsaft fruit juice ['fruːt dʒuːs]
früh early ['ɜːli]
Frühling spring [sprɪŋ]
Frühstück breakfast ['brekfəst]; **Zimmer mit Frühstück** Bed & Breakfast (B&B) [bed ənd 'brekfəst]
frühstücken have breakfast [hæv 'brekfəst]
Frühstückspension Bed & Breakfast (B&B) [bed ən 'brekfəst]
frühzeitig early ['ɜːli]
fühlen: (sich) fühlen feel [fiːl]
Führerschein auf Probe probationary driver's license *(CanE/AE)* [prə'beɪʃnri draɪvəz laɪsns]
Führung tour [tʊə]
füllen fill (in) [fɪl 'ɪn]
Füller pen [pen]

[ʊə] sure [b] bike [p] pen [d] day [t] ten [k] book [g] go [ŋ] morning [l] like [r] ruler

fünf five [faɪv]; **fünfte(r,s)** fifth [fɪfθ]
fünfzehn fifteen [fɪf'tiːn]; **fünfzehnte(r,s)** fifteenth [fɪf'tiːnθ]
fünfzig fifty ['fɪfti]
Funk: über Funk by radio [baɪ 'reɪdiəʊ]
Funkmeldung radio message ['reɪdiəʊ mesɪdʒ]
funktionieren: Rechner sind heruntergefahren/funktionieren nicht computers are down [daʊn]
für for [fɔː]
furchtbar terrible ['terəbl]
Fuß foot [fʊt]
Fußball football ['fʊtbɔːl]
Fußballplatz football field ['fʊtbɔːl fiːld]
Fußballtrikot shirt [ʃɜːt]
füttern feed [fiːd]

G

Gameboy gameboy ['geɪmbɔɪ]
Gangster/in gangster *(ugs.)* ['gæŋstə]
ganz whole [həʊl]; **der/die/das ganze** all (the) [ɔːl]
Garage garage ['gærɑːʒ]
Gardine curtain ['kɜːtn]
Garten garden ['gɑːdn]
Gas gas [gæs]
Gast guest [gest]
Gate gate [geɪt]
Gaukler/in juggler ['dʒʌglə]
gebacken: gebackene Bohnen (in Tomatensoße) baked beans [beɪkt 'biːnz]; **gebackene Kartoffel** baked potato *(pl.: potatoes)* [beɪkt pə'teɪtəʊ]
Gebäude building ['bɪldɪŋ]
geben give [gɪv]; **es gibt** there is/are [ðeər ɪz, ðeər ɑː]
Gebiet area ['eəriə]; territory ['terətri]
geboren: Ich bin ... geboren. I was born in ... [aɪ wəz 'bɔːn ɪn]; **Wann bist du geboren?** When were you born? ['wen wə ju 'bɔːn]
Gebrauchsanweisung handbook ['hændbʊk]
gebraucht second-hand [sekənd'hænd]
gebrochen broken ['brəʊkən]
Gebühren commission [kə'mɪʃən]
Geburtstag birthday ['bɜːθdeɪ]
Gedanke idea [aɪ'dɪə]
Gedicht lyrics *(pl.)* ['lɪrɪks]; poem ['pəʊɪm]
Gefahr danger ['deɪndʒə]
gefährlich dangerous ['deɪndʒərəs]
Gefängnis prison ['prɪzn]
gegen against [ə'geɪnst]; at about [æt ə'baʊt]
Gegend neighbourhood ['neɪbəhʊd]
Gegenteil opposite ['ɒpəzɪt]
Gegenwart present ['preznt]
gehen go [gəʊ]; **(spazieren) gehen** walk [wɔːk]; **durch das Museum gehen** walk round the museum [wɔːk 'raʊnd]; **es geht darum, stark zu sein** it's about being strong [ə'baʊt biːɪŋ 'strɒŋ]; **es geht/ging so** not bad [nɒt 'bæd]; **in Urlaub gehen** go on holiday [gəʊ ɒn 'hɒlədeɪ]; **Was geht hier vor?** What's happening? [wɒts 'hæpənɪŋ]; **Wie geht es dir/euch/Ihnen?** How are you? [haʊ ə 'juː]; **Wie geht's?** How are things? *(ugs.)* [haʊ ɑː 'θɪŋz]
gehören (zu) belong to [bɪ'lɒŋ tə]
Geist spirit ['spɪrɪt]
geizig mean [miːn]
gelangen get [get]; travel ['trævl]
gelangweilt bored [bɔːd]
gelassen laid-back [leɪd 'bæk]
gelb yellow ['jeləʊ]
Geld money ['mʌni]; **kein Geld** no money [nəʊ 'mʌni]
Geld ausgeben spend money [spend 'mʌni]
Geld verdienen make money [meɪk 'mʌni]
Geldautomat cash machine [kæʃ mə'ʃiːn]
Geldbeutel purse [pɜːs]
Geldgeber/in sponsor ['spɒnsə]
Gelegenheit chance [tʃɑːns]
Gemälde painting ['peɪntɪŋ]
gemeinsam together [tə'geðə]
Gemüse vegetables ['vedʒtəblz]
genau accurate ['ækjərət]; **wenn man mal genau hinschaut** when you get down to it [wen juː get 'daʊn tʊ ɪt]
genauso: genauso freundlich wie as friendly as [æz 'frendli æz]; **genauso wie** the same as [ðə 'seɪm əz]
Genehmigung permit ['pɜːmɪt]
genießen enjoy [ɪn'dʒɔɪ]
genug enough [ɪ'nʌf]
geöffnet open ['əʊpən]
Geographie geography [dʒi'ɒgrəfi]
Geologe/Geologin geologist [dʒi'ɒlədʒɪst]
gerade just [dʒʌst]; **gerade nach oben** straight up [steɪt 'ʌp]
geradeaus: geradeaus (weiter) gehen Go straight on. [gəʊ streɪt 'ɒn]
Gerät machine [mə'ʃiːn]
Geräusch noise [nɔɪz]; sound [saʊnd]
gerecht fair [feə]
Geruch smell [smel]
Gerümpel junk [dʒʌŋk]
Gesamtschule: (US) Gesamtschule für 13- bis 18-Jährige high school ['haɪ skuːl]
Geschäft shop [ʃɒp]; store *(AE)* [stɔː]
geschäftlich for business [fə 'bɪznəs]
Geschäftsleiter/in manager ['mænɪdʒə]
geschehen happen ['hæpən]
Geschenk present ['preznt]
Geschichte history ['hɪstri]; story ['stɔːri]; **die Geschichte handelt von** the story is about [ðə 'stɔːri ɪz ə'baʊt]
Geschirrspülmaschine dishwasher ['dɪʃwɒʃə]
geschlossen closed [kləʊzd]
geschrieben: geschrieben von written by ['rɪtn baɪ]
Gesellschaft corporation [kɔːpə'reɪʃn]
gesellschaftlich social ['səʊʃl]
Gesetz law [lɔː]
gesetzlich: gesetzlicher Feiertag public holiday [pʌblɪk 'hɒlədeɪ]
Gesicht face [feɪs]
gestern yesterday ['jestədeɪ]
gesund healthy ['helθi]
Getränk drink [drɪŋk]
getrennt separated ['sepəreɪtɪd]
Getto ghetto ['getəʊ]
Gewalt(tätigkeit) violence ['vaɪələns]
gewaltsam violent ['vaɪələnt]
gewalttätig violent ['vaɪələnt]
Gewinn prize [praɪz]
gewinnen win [wɪn]; **(das) Gewinnen** winning ['wɪnɪŋ]
gewöhnlich ordinary ['ɔːdnəri]
gießen: es gießt wie aus Kübeln it's raining cats and dogs [ɪts 'reɪnɪŋ kæts ən 'dɒgz]
glänzend shining ['ʃaɪnɪŋ]
Glas glass [glɑːs]

[v] seven [w] we [s] six [z] his [ʃ] she [tʃ] teacher [dʒ] jeans [j] yes [θ] thing [ð] the

glauben believe [bɪ'li:v]; think [θɪŋk]; **ich glaube** I guess [aɪ 'ges]; **Was glaubst du ...?** What do you think ...? [wɒt də ju 'θɪŋk]
Glocke bell [bel]
Glück: (viel) Glück good luck [gʊd 'lʌk]; **Du hast Glück!** You're lucky! ['lʌki]; **wir hatten Glück** we were lucky ['lʌki]
glücklich happy ['hæpi]; lucky ['lʌki]
glücklos unlucky [ʌn'lʌki]
Glücks- lucky ['lʌki]
Glückwunsch: Herzlichen Glückwunsch! Congratulations! [kɒngrætʃʊ'leɪʃnz]
glühende Herzen glowing hearts [gləʊɪŋ 'hɑ:ts]
Gold gold [gəʊld]
Goldrausch gold rush ['gəʊld rʌʃ]
Golf golf [gɒlf]
Gott God [gɒd]
Gouverneur/in governor ['gʌvənə]
Grad degrees *(pl.)* [dɪ'gri:z]; **unter null Grad Celsius** below 0° C = Celsius [bɪ'ləʊ 'zɪərəʊ dɪ'gri:z 'selsiəs]
Graffiti graffiti [grə'fi:ti]
Gramm gram [græm]
Gras grass [grɑ:s]
Grasland grassland ['grɑ:slænd]
grau grey [greɪ]
Grillfest barbie *(AustE)* ['bɑ:bi]; braai *(südafrikanisch)* [braɪ]
Grillparty barbecue ['bɑ:bɪkju:]
Grislibär grizzly bear ['grɪzli beə]
groß big [bɪg]; great [greɪt]; large [lɑ:dʒ]; tall *(bei Menschen)* [tɔ:l]; **sehr groß** XL (= extra large) *(Kleidung)* [eks 'el]; **ungeheuer groß** enormous [ɪ'nɔ:məs]
großartig great [greɪt]; **großartig in** great at ['greɪt ət]
Großbritannien Britain ['brɪtn]
Größe size [saɪz]
Großeltern grandparents ['grænpeərənts]
größer bigger ['bɪgə]; **größer als** bigger than ['bɪgə ðən]
Großmutter grandmother ['grænmʌðə]
Großstadt city ['sɪti]
Großvater grandfather ['grænfɑ:ðə]
Ground Zero Ground Zero [graʊnd 'zɪərəʊ]
grün green [gri:n]; leafy ['li:fi]
Grund reason ['ri:zn]; **aus unterschiedlichen Gründen** for different reasons [fə 'dɪfrənt ri:znz]; **Grund und Boden** land [lænd]
Gruppe group [gru:p]; **(Musik-) Gruppe** band [bænd]
Grüße: mit freundlichen Grüßen Yours sincerely [jɔ:z sɪn'sɪəli]; **Viele Grüße** Best wishes [best 'wɪʃɪz]
grüßen: Grüße mir ... Give my greetings to ... [gɪv maɪ 'gri:tɪŋz tə]
gucken look [lʊk]
günstig: günstig (gelegen) convenient [kən'vi:niənt]
gut fine [faɪn]; **gut (in)** good (at) ['gʊd æt]; **gut aussehend** good-looking [gʊd'lʊkɪŋ]; **gut besuchter Laden** busy shop [bɪzi 'ʃɒp]; **Gut gemacht!** Well done! [wel 'dʌn]; **Guten Abend.** Good evening. [gʊd 'i:vnɪŋ]; **Guten Morgen.** Good morning. [gʊd 'mɔ:nɪŋ]; **Guten Tag!** G'day! *(AustE)* [gə'deɪ]; **Guten Tag.** *(nachmittags)* Good afternoon. [gʊd ɑ:ftə'nu:n]
Güter goods [gʊdz]

H

Haar(e) hair [heə]
haben have [hæv]; **er hat keinen/keine/kein** he doesn't have [hi 'dʌznt hæv]; **ich habe keinen/keine/kein** I don't have [aɪ 'dəʊnt hæv]; **ich hätte gern** I'd like (= I would like) [aɪd 'laɪk]; **Kann ich eine(n)/ein ... haben?** Can I have a ...? [kən aɪ 'hæv ə]; **wir haben viel** we gotta lot of = we've got a lot of ['gɒtə 'lɒt əv]
Hafen dock [dɒk]; harbor *(AE)* ['hɑ:bə]; port [pɔ:t]
Hai shark [ʃɑ:k]; **Hai-Tauchen mit Käfigen** shark cage diving [ʃɑ:k keɪdʒ 'daɪvɪŋ]
halb half past [hɑ:f 'pɑ:st]
Halbbruder half-brother ['hɑ:fbrʌðə]
halbtags: halbtags arbeiten work part-time [wɜ:k 'pɑ:ttaɪm]
Halbzeit half-time [hɑ:f'taɪm]
Hälfte half *(pl.: halves)* [hɑ:f, hɑ:vz]
Hallo. Hi. [haɪ]
Halloween Halloween [hæləʊ'i:n]
halten hold [həʊld]; keep [ki:p]; **einen Vortrag halten** give a talk [gɪv ə 'tɔ:k]; **er hielt den Atem an** he held his breath [hi held hɪz 'breθ]; **Versprechen werden manchmal nicht gehalten** promises can be broken ['prɒmɪsəz kæn bi 'brəʊkən]
Hamburger burger ['bɜ:gə]; hamburger ['hæmbɜ:gə]
Hamster hamster ['hæmstə]
Hand hand [hænd]; **eine Hand ausstrecken** hold out a hand [həʊld aʊt ə 'hænd]
Handel trade [treɪd]
handeln: die Geschichte handelt von the story is about [ðə 'stɔ:ri ɪz ə'baʊt]
Handlung action ['ækʃn]
Handtasche purse *(AE)* [pɜ:s]
Handy cellphone *(AE)* ['selfəʊn]; mobile ['məʊbaɪl]
Handzettel flyer ['flaɪə]; leaflet ['li:flet]
hängen hang [hæŋ]
Hardware hardware ['hɑ:dweə]
hart hard [hɑ:d]; **Das ist hart.** That's tough. [ðæts 'tʌf]
hassen hate [heɪt]
häufig: häufig gestellte Fragen FAQ (= frequently asked questions) [ef eɪ 'kju, 'fri:kwəntli ɑ:skt 'kwestʃnz]
hauptsächlich mainly ['meɪnli]; mostly ['məʊstli]
Hauptstadt capital ['kæpɪtl]
Haus house [haʊs]; **(Busverbindung) von Haus zu Haus** door-to-door (bus service) [dɔ: tə 'dɔ:]; **bei ... zu Hause** at ... house [ət haʊs]; **das Haus verlassen** leave the house ['li:v ðə haʊs]; **draußen vor dem Haus** out front [aʊt 'frʌnt]; **im Haus** indoors [ɪn'dɔ:z]; **nach Hause** home [həʊm]; **zu Hause** at home [ət 'həʊm]
Hausaufgabe(n) homework ['həʊmwɜ:k]
Häuschen cottage ['kɒtɪdʒ]
Haut skin [skɪn]
Hautkrebs skin cancer ['skɪn kɑ:nsə]
heilig sacred ['seɪkrɪd]
Heim home [həʊm]
Heimat home [həʊm]; **als (unsere) neue Heimat** for our new home [fə aʊə nju: 'həʊm]

[i:] he [ɑ:] car [ɔ:] or [u:] too [ɜ:] girl [i] sorry [u] July [ɪ] big [e] yes [æ] cat [ʌ] bus

Heimatland native land ['neɪtɪv 'lænd]
Heimatstadt hometown ['həʊmtaʊn]
Heimweh: Heimweh haben/ bekommen be/get homesick [bɪ, get 'həʊmsɪk]
heiraten marry ['mæri]
heiß hot [hɒt]; **heiße Schokolade** hot chocolate [hɒt 'tʃɒklət]
heißen: Wie heißt du? What's your name? [wɒts jɔː 'neɪm]
Held/in hero ['hɪərəʊ]
helfen help [help]; **(aus)helfen bei** help out with [help 'aʊt wɪð]
hell bright [braɪt]; light [laɪt]
Helm helmet ['helmɪt]
Hemd shirt [ʃɜːt]
herauf up [ʌp]
herausbekommen work out [wɜːk 'aʊt]
herausfinden find out [faɪnd 'aʊt]; **mehr herausfinden über** check out [tʃek 'aʊt]
Herbst autumn ['ɔːtəm]; fall *(AE)* [fɔːl]
Herkunft background ['bækgraʊnd]
Herr Mr ['mɪstə]; sir [sɜː]
herum around [ə'raʊnd]; **herumhängen** hang out [hæŋ 'aʊt]; **herumkommen** get around [get ə'raʊnd]; **um ... herum** round [raʊnd]
herunter down [daʊn]; **(Daten) herunterladen** download ['daʊnləʊd]; **herunterhüpfen von** jump off [dʒʌmp 'ɒf]; **herunterspringen von** jump off [dʒʌmp 'ɒf]
herunterfahren: Rechner sind heruntergefahren/ funktionieren nicht computers are down [daʊn]
hervorragend terrific [tə'rɪfɪk]
hervorstechen: hervorstechen aus stand out from [stænd]
Herz: glühende Herzen glowing hearts [gləʊɪŋ 'hɑːts]
herzlich: Herzlichen Glückwunsch! Congratulations! [kɒngrætʃʊ'leɪʃnz]
heute today [tə'deɪ]; **heute Abend** tonight [tə'naɪt]; **heute Nacht** tonight [tə'naɪt]
Hey! Hey! [heɪ]
hier here [hɪə]; **hier ist** here's (= here is) [hɪəz]; **hier sind** here are ['hɪə ɑː]
Hightech- hi-tech ['haɪ tek]
hilfreich helpful ['helpfəl]
Himmel: am Himmel in the sky [in ðə 'skaɪ]
hinauf up [ʌp]
hindurch through [θruː]
hinein: in ... hinein into ['ɪntə]
hineintun, -stecken put in [pʊt 'ɪn]
hinfahren take [teɪk]
hinfallen fall over [fɔːl 'əʊvə]
hinkommen get [get]; travel ['trævl]
hinschauen: wenn man mal genau hinschaut when you get down to it [wen juː get 'daʊn tʊ ɪt]
hinsetzen: sich hinsetzen sit down [sɪt]
hinstellen (auf) put (on) [pʊt]
hinter behind [bɪ'haɪnd]
Hintergrund background ['bækgraʊnd]
Hinterhof back yard [bæk 'jɑːd]
Hinterland backcountry ['bækkʌntri]; **das Hinterland (Australiens)** the outback ['aʊtbæk]
hinunter down [daʊn]; **hinunterhüpfen von** jump off [dʒʌmp 'ɒf]; **hinunterspringen von** jump off [dʒʌmp 'ɒf]
Hinweis tip [tɪp]
Hispano-Amerikaner/in Hispanic [hɪ'spænɪk]
historisch historical [hɪ'stɒrɪkl]
Hit hit ['hɪt]
Hobby hobby ['hɒbi]; interest ['ɪntrəst]; **Welches Hobby hast du?** What's your hobby? ['wɒts jə hɒbi]
hoch high [haɪ]; tall [tɔːl]
hochheben pick up [pɪk 'ʌp]
hochschauen look up [lʊk 'ʌp]
hochziehen pull up [pʊl 'ʌp]
Hockey hockey ['hɒki]
hoffen hope [həʊp]
Höhe level ['levl]
holen get [get]
Holz wood [wʊd]
Homepage home page ['həʊm peɪdʒ]
Hoodoo hoodoo ['huːduː]
hören hear [hɪə]; listen (to) ['lɪsn tə]
Hose: kurze Hose(n) shorts *(pl.)* [ʃɔːts]
Hotdog hot dog ['hɒt dɒg]
Hotel hotel [həʊ'tel]
Hubschrauber helicopter ['helɪkɒptə]
huckelig: irgendwie huckelig kinda bumpy = kind of bumpy [kaində 'bʌmpi]
Hügel hill [hɪl]
Huhn chicken ['tʃɪkɪn]
Humor humour ['hjuːmə]; **Sinn für Humor** sense of humour [sens əv 'hjuːmə]
Hund dog [dɒg]; **mit dem Hund spazieren gehen** take the dog for a walk ['teɪk ðə dɒg fə ə 'wɔːk]
Hundejunges puppy ['pʌpi]
hundert hundred ['hʌndrəd]
Hundeschlitten dog sled ['dɒg sled]
Hunger: Ich habe Hunger. I'm hungry. [aɪm 'hʌŋgri]
Hut hat [hæt]

I

ich I [aɪ]; **ich bin's** it's me [ɪts 'miː]
ideal ideal [aɪ'dɪəl]
Idee idea [aɪ'dɪə]
Idol idol ['aɪdl]
Igitt! Yuk! [jʌk]
ihm him [hɪm]
ihn him [hɪm]
ihnen them [ðem]
ihr you [juː]; **ihr seid** you're (= you are) [jʊə]
Ihr your [jɔː]; **Ihr(e)** Yours [jɔːz]
ihr/ihre her [hɜː]; its [ɪts]; their (pl.) [ðeə]
Imbiss: (Feinkost-)Imbiss deli *(AE)* ['deli]
Imbiss-Bude chip shop ['tʃɪp ʃɒp]
immer always ['ɔːlweɪz]; **immer und immer wieder** over and over again ['əʊvə ənd əʊvə ə'gen]; **schrumpft immer weiter** keeps on shrinking [kiːps ɒn 'ʃrɪŋkɪŋ]
in at [æt]; in [ɪn]; **in ... (hinein)** into ['ɪntə]
Inder/in Indian ['ɪndiən]
indianisch: indianische Völker in Kanada First Nations [fɜːst 'neɪʃn]
indisch Indian ['ɪndiən]

Industrie industry ['ɪndəstri]
industrielle Revolution Industrial Revolution [ɪndʌstriəl revə'lu:ʃn]
Information(en) information [ɪnfə'meɪʃn]
Informationstechnologie information technology (IT) [ɪnfəmeɪʃn tek'nɒlədʒi]
Inlineskates skates [skeɪts]
Inlineskating inline skating ['ɪnlaɪn skeɪtɪŋ]
Innen- indoor ['ɪndɔ:]
Innenstadt downtown *(AE)* ['daʊntaʊn]
Insekt insect ['ɪnsekt]
Insektenspray insect spray ['ɪnsekt spreɪ]
Insel island ['aɪlənd]
Installateur/in plumber ['plʌmə]
Instrument: ein Instrument spielen play an instrument [pleɪ ən 'ɪnstrəmənt]
interessant interesting ['ɪntrəstɪŋ]; **interessanter als** more interesting than [mɔ: 'ɪntrəstɪŋ]
Interesse interest ['ɪntrəst]
interessiert an interested in ['ɪntrəstɪd ɪn]
international international [ɪntə'næʃənl]
Internet Internet ['ɪntənet]
Internet-Gebühren Internet rates ['ɪntənet reɪts]
Internet-Tagebuch blog [blɒg]
Internetzugang Internet access ['ɪntənet ækses]
Interview interview ['ɪntəvju:]
interviewen interview ['ɪntəvju:]
Intonation intonation [ɪntə'neɪʃn]
Inuit Inuit people ['ɪnjuɪt]
irgendein/e any ['eni]
irgendetwas anything ['eniθɪŋ]
irgendjemand anybody ['enibɒdi]
irgendwelche any ['eni]
irgendwie: irgendwie uneben/huckelig kinda bumpy = kind of bumpy *(ugs.)* [kaində 'bʌmpi]
irgendwo somewhere ['sʌmweə]
irgendwo(hin) anywhere ['eniweə]
Irrgarten: Verloren im Irrgarten. Lost in the maze. [lɒst ɪn ðə 'meɪz]
ist is [ɪz]; **Ist das ...?** Is that ...? ['ɪz ðæt]; **Ist es ...?** Is it ...? ['ɪz ɪt]; **ist nicht** isn't (= is not) [ɪznt]

J

ja yeah *(ugs.)* [jeə]; yes [jes]; **Ja (tut sie).** Yes, she does. [jes ʃi 'dʌz]
jagen hunt [hʌnt]; **in die Luft jagen** blow up [bləʊ 'ʌp]
Jäger/in hunter ['hʌntə]
Jahr year [jɪə]
Jahrestag anniversary [ænɪ'vɜ:səri]
Jahreszeit season ['si:zn]
Jahrgang year [jɪə]
Jahrhundert century ['sentʃəri]
Jahrmarkt fair [feə]
Januar January ['dʒænjuəri]
Jazz jazz [dʒæz]
je ever ['evə]
Jeans jeans *(pl.)* [dʒi:nz]
jede(r) everybody ['evribɒdi]; everyone ['evriwʌn]; **jede(r) (beliebige)** anybody ['enibɒdi]
jede(r,s) any ['eni]; each [i:tʃ]; every ['evri]; **jeden Tag** every day [evri 'deɪ]
jedoch though [ðəʊ]
jemals ever ['evə]; **Bist du jemals ... gewesen?** Have you ever been ...? [hæv ju: 'evə bɪn]
jemand anybody ['enibɒdi]; somebody ['sʌmbədi]
jene: jene (dort) those *(pl.)* [ðəʊz]
Jetlag jet lag ['dʒet læg]
jetzt at the moment [æt ðə 'məʊmənt]; now [naʊ]
Joggen: (das) Joggen jogging ['dʒɒgɪŋ]
Jogurt yogurt ['jɒgət]
Jongleur/in juggler ['dʒʌglə]
jonglieren juggle ['dʒʌgl]
Journalist/in journalist ['dʒɜ:nəlɪst]
jubeln cheer [tʃɪə]
Jugendclub youth club ['ju:θ klʌb]
Jugendherberge youth hostel ['ju:θ hɒstl]
Jugendliche(r) kid [kɪd]
Jugendzentrum youth club ['ju:θ klʌb]
Juli July [dʒu'laɪ]
jung young [jʌŋ]
Junge boy [bɔɪ]
Juni June [dʒu:n]
Junior Junior (Jr.) ['dʒu:niə]
Jura law [lɔ:]
Jury jury ['dʒʊəri]

K

Kaffee coffee ['kɒfi]
Kaffer kaffir ['kæfə]
Käfig cage [keɪdʒ]; **Hai-Tauchen mit Käfigen** shark cage diving [ʃa:k keɪdʒ 'daɪvɪŋ]
Kalender calendar ['kælɪndə]
Kalifornier/in Californian [kælɪ'fɔ:niən]
kalifornisch Californian [kælɪ'fɔ:niən]
kalt cold [kəʊld]
Kamel: afghanisches Kamel Afghan camel ['æfgæn 'kæml]
Kamera camera ['kæmərə]
Kampagne campaign [kæm'peɪn]
kämpfen: kämpfen (gegen) fight [faɪt]
Kämpfer/in fighter ['faɪtə]
Kanadier/in Canadian [kə'neɪdiən]
kanadisch Canadian [kə'neɪdiən]
Känguru kangaroo [kæŋgə'ru:]
Kanu: Kanu fahren canoe [kə'nu:]
Kapitän/in captain ['kæptɪn]
kaputt broken ['brəʊkən]
kaputtmachen break [breɪk]
Karneval carnival ['kɑ:nɪvəl]
Karotte carrot ['kærət]
Karriere career [kə'rɪə]
Karte: (Spiel-, Gruß-)Karte card [kɑ:d]
Kartoffel potato *(pl.: potatoes)* [pə'teɪtəʊ]; **gebackene Kartoffel** baked potato *(pl.: potatoes)* [beɪkt pə'teɪtəʊ]
Kartoffelchips crisps *(pl.)* [krɪsps]
Karton: ein Karton ... a carton of ... [ə 'kɑ:tn əv]
Käse cheese [tʃi:z]
Kasse checkout ['tʃekaʊt]
Kater cat [kæt]
Katze cat [kæt]
kaufen buy [baɪ]
Kaufhaus department store [dɪ'pɑ:tmənt stɔ:]
Kaugummi chewing gum ['tʃu:ɪŋ gʌm]
kaum barely ['beəli]
kein/e no [nəʊ]; not any [nɒt 'eni]; **kein Geld** no money [nəʊ 'mʌni]; **nicht mehr, keine/n ... mehr** not ... any more [nɒt eni 'mɔ:]
keine/r: keine Ahnung haben have no idea [hæv nəʊ aɪ'dɪə]
keiner nobody ['nəʊbədi]
Keks biscuit ['bɪskɪt]

Keller basement *(AE)* ['beɪsmənt]
kennen know [nəʊ]; **den Weg kennen** know the way [nəʊ ðə 'weɪ]
Ketschup ketchup ['ketʃəp]
Kette chain [tʃeɪn]
Kettensäge chainsaw ['tʃeɪnsɔ:]
kicken kick [kɪk]
Kilometer kilometre [kɪ'lɒmɪtə]
Kind kid [kɪd]
Kinder children ['tʃɪldrən]
Kino cinema ['sɪnəmə]; movie theater *(AE)* ['mu:vi 'θɪətə]
Kinofilm movie *(AE)* ['mu:vi]
Kiosk kiosk ['ki:ɒsk]
Kirche church [tʃɜ:tʃ]
Kissen cushion ['kʊʃn]
Klang sound [saʊnd]
Klasse: (Schul-)Klasse class [klɑ:s]
Klasse(nstufe) grade *(AE)* [greɪd]
Klassenarbeit test [test]
Klassenzimmer classroom ['klɑ:sru:m]
klatschen: Beifall klatschen applaud [ə'plɔ:d]
Kleid dress [dres]
Kleider clothes [kləʊðz]
Kleidung clothes [kləʊðz]; **(Kleidung) anziehen** put on [pʊt 'ɒn]
klein short [ʃɔ:t]; small [smɔ:l]; **der/die/das kleine, die kleinen** the small one/s [ðə 'smɔ:l wʌn]
kleinlich mean [mi:n]
Kletterer climber ['klaɪmə]
Kletterin climber ['klaɪmə]
klettern climb [klaɪm]
klicken: (an-, hin-)klicken click [klɪk]
Klima climate ['klaɪmət]
Klimaanlage air-conditioning ['eə kəndɪʃnɪŋ]
Klimatisierung air-conditioning ['eə kəndɪʃnɪŋ]
Klimaveränderung(en) climate change ['klaɪmət tʃeɪndʒ]
klingeln ring [rɪŋ]
klingen sound [saʊnd]
Klippe cliff [klɪf]
Klub club [klʌb]
klug clever ['klevə]
Kneipe pub [pʌb]
Knochen bone [bəʊn]
Knopf button ['bʌtn]
Koala(bär) koala (bear) [kəʊ'ɑ:lə]
kochen cook ['kʊk]; **(das) Kochen** cooking ['kʊkɪŋ]
Koffer suitcase ['su:tkeɪs]
Kofferraum boot [bu:t]
Kohle coal [kəʊl]
Kolonie colony ['kɒləni]
komisch funny ['fʌni]
Kommandobrücke bridge [brɪdʒ]
kommen come [kʌm]; **komm(t) mit uns** come with us [kʌm wɪð 'ʌs]; **Komm(t) nach ...** Come to ... ['kʌm tə]; **Wo kommst du her?** Where are you from? [weə ə ju: 'frɒm]
König king ['kɪŋ]
Königin queen [kwi:n]
königlich royal ['rɔɪəl]
Königreich: Vereinigtes Königreich United Kingdom (UK) [junaɪtɪd 'kɪŋdəm, ju: 'keɪ]
Konjunktion conjunction [kən'dʒʌŋkʃn]
können can [kæn]; **du kannst ... sehen** you get to see ... [get tə 'si:]; **Kann ich eine(n)/ein ... haben?** Can I have a ...? [kən aɪ 'hæv ə]; **nicht können** can't [kɑ:nt]
Konsole: (Spiel-)Konsole (games) console ['geɪmz kən'səʊl]
konstruieren design [dɪ'zaɪn]
Kontinent continent ['kɒntɪnənt]
kontrollieren check [tʃek]
Konzert concert ['kɒnsət]
Kopf head [hed]
Kopfhörer headphones ['hedfəʊnz]
kopieren copy ['kɒpi]
Korb basket ['bɑ:skɪt]
korrekt right [raɪt]
Kosmetiker/in beautician [bju:'tɪʃn]
kosten cost [kɒst]; **Was kostet das?** How much is it? [haʊ 'mʌtʃ ɪz ɪt]
kostenlos free [fri:]
Kraft power ['paʊə]
kräftig: so kräftig sie konnten as hard as they could [æz 'hɑ:d əz ðeɪ kʊd]
krank ill [ɪl]; sick [sɪk]
Krankenhaus hospital ['hɒspɪtl]
Krankheit illness ['ɪlnəs]
Krass! Wow! [waʊ]
kratzen scratch [skrætʃ]
Kreditkarte credit card ['kredɪt kɑ:d]
kreuzen cross [krɒs]
Kriebelmücken midges ['mɪdʒɪz]
Krieg war [wɔ:]
Kriminalität crime [kraɪm]
kritisch: kritisch gegenüber critical of ['krɪtɪkl əv]
Krokodil crocodile ['krɒkədaɪl]
Kübel: Es gießt wie aus Kübeln! It's raining cats and dogs! [ɪts 'reɪnɪŋ kæts ən 'dɒgz]
Küche kitchen ['kɪtʃɪn]
Kuchen cake [keɪk]
Kugelschreiber biro ['baɪrəʊ]
Kuh cow [kaʊ]
kühl cool [ku:l]
Kühlschrank fridge [frɪdʒ]
Kultur culture ['kʌltʃə]
kümmern: sich kümmern um look after [lʊk 'ɑ:ftə]
Kumpel mate *(ugs.)* [meɪt]
Kunde/Kundin customer ['kʌstəmə]
Kunst art [ɑ:t]
Kunstgalerie art gallery [ɑ:t 'gæləri]
Künstler/in artist ['ɑ:tɪst]
Kunststück trick [trɪk]
Kurs class [klɑ:s]
Kurve bend [bend]; **eine Kurve machen** bend [bend]
kurz short [ʃɔ:t]; **kurze Hose(n)** shorts *(pl.)* [ʃɔ:ts]; **zu kurz** too short [tu: 'ʃɔ:t]
Küste coast [kəʊst]; **an der Küste** on the coast [ɒn ðə 'kəʊst]

L

lächeln smile [smaɪl]
Lächeln smile [smaɪl]
lachen laugh [lɑ:f]
Laden shop [ʃɒp]; **gut besuchter Laden** busy shop [bɪzi 'ʃɒp]
Ladendieb/in shoplifter ['shɔplɪftə]
Lager warehouse ['weəhaʊs]
Lampe light [laɪt]
Land country ['kʌntri]; land [lænd]; **(Bundes-)Land** state [steɪt]; **auf dem Land** in the country [ɪn ðə 'kʌntri]; **unser Land** this land of ours [ðɪs 'lænd əv 'aʊəz]
Landebahn landing strip ['lændɪŋ strɪp]
landen land [lænd]
Landes- national ['næʃənl]
Landkarte map [mæp]
Landrover Land Rover ['lænd rəʊvə]
Landschaft countryside ['kʌntrisaɪd]; scenery ['si:nəri]

[v] seven [w] we [s] six [z] his [ʃ] she [tʃ] teacher [dʒ] jeans [j] yes [θ] thing [ð] the

Landung landing ['lændɪŋ]
lang long [lɒŋ]
langsam slow [sləʊ]; slowly (Adverb) ['sləʊli]
langweilen: du langweilst dich you're bored [bɔːd]; **Ich langweile mich.** I'm bored. [bɔːd]
langweilig boring ['bɔːrɪŋ]; **dir ist langweilig** you're bored [bɔːd]
Laptop laptop ['læptɒp]
Lärm noise [nɔɪz]
lärmend noisy ['nɔɪzi]
lassen leave [liːv]; **(stehen) lassen** leave [liːv]; **Lass(t) uns ...** Let's ... [lets]
lästig annoying [ə'nɔɪɪŋ]
Lastwagen truck *(AE)* [trʌk]
laufen run [rʌn]; **um die Wette laufen** have a race [hæv ə 'reɪs]; race against ['reɪs əgeɪnst]; **Wie läuft's?** How are things? *(ugs.)* [həʊ ɑː 'θɪŋz]
lausig lousy ['laʊzi]
laut loud [laʊd]; noisy ['nɔɪzi]
Lautsprecher loudspeaker ['laʊdspiːkə]
Leadsänger/in lead singer [liːd 'sɪŋə]
leben be alive [ə'laɪv]; live [lɪv]
Leben life [laɪf]; **am Leben sein** be alive [ə'laɪv]; **Leben der australischen Ureinwohner/innen** Aboriginal life [æbə'rɪdʒənl laɪf]; **Renn/t um dein/euer Leben!** Run for your life! [rʌn fə jɔː 'laɪf]
lebendig lively ['laɪvli]
Lebensbeschreibung biography [baɪ'ɒgrəfi]
lebenslänglich for life [fə 'laɪf]
Lebenslauf curriculum vitae = CV *(BE)* [kərɪkjəltʃəm 'viːtaɪ]; CV = curriculum vitae *(BE)* [siː 'viː]; résumé ['rezjumeɪ]
Lebensmittel food [fuːd]
Lebensstil lifestyle ['laɪfstaɪl]
Lebensweise way of life [weɪ əv 'laɪf]
lebhaft lively ['laɪvli]
leer empty ['empti]
legen (auf) put (on) [pʊt]
Legende legend ['ledʒənd]
Lehrer/in teacher ['tiːtʃə]
leicht easy ['iːzi]
leid tun: Es tut mir leid. I'm sorry. [aɪm 'sɒri]
leiden: leiden an/unter suffer from ['sʌfə frɒm]
leihen hire ['haɪə]; lend [lend]; rent [rent]
leise quiet ['kwaɪət]
leiten: leitende Position senior job ['siːniə 'dʒɒb]; **leitende/r Pilot/in** chief pilot [tʃiːf 'paɪlət]
lernen learn [lɜːn]; study ['stʌdi]
lesen read [riːd]; **(das) Lesen** reading ['riːdɪŋ]
Lesen: Basiswissen: Lesen basic reading [beɪsɪk 'riːdɪŋ]
Leser/in reader ['riːdə]
letzte(r,s) last [lɑːst]
Leute people ['piːpl]; **hallo Leute!** hi there, guys! *(ugs.)* [gaɪz]; **meine Leute** my folks *(ugs.)* [maɪ 'fəʊks]
Licht light [laɪt]
Liebe love [lʌv]
Liebe(r,s) ..., Dear ..., [dɪə]
lieben love [lʌv]
lieber: lieber haben/mögen prefer [prɪ'fɜː]; **Lieber spät als gar nicht.** Better late than never. [betə 'leɪt ðən 'nevə]
Liebhaber/in lover ['lʌvə]
Lieblings- favorite *(AE)* ['feɪvərɪt]; favourite ['feɪvərɪt]
Lied song [sɒŋ]
Liedtext lyrics *(pl.)* ['lɪrɪks]
liefern deliver [dɪ'lɪvə]
liegen: liegen (auf) lie (on) [laɪ]
Limonade lemonade [lemə'neɪd]; pop [pɒp]; soda (pop) *(AE)* ['səʊdə pɒp]
Lineal ruler ['ruːlə]
Linie line [laɪn]
Link link [lɪŋk]
links to the left [tə ðə 'left]; **links abbiegen** take a left [teɪk ə 'left]; **nach links abbiegen** turn left [tɜːn 'left]
Liste list [lɪst]; **eine Liste schreiben** make a list [meɪk ə 'lɪst]
Literatur literature ['lɪtrətʃə]
live live [laɪv]
Loch hole [həʊl]
Logo logo ['ləʊgəʊ]
Lokal pub [pʌb]
Londoner/in Londoner ['lʌndənə]
Löwe lion ['laɪən]
Luft air [eə]; **in die Luft jagen** blow up [bləʊ 'ʌp]
lustig funny ['fʌni]

M

machen do [duː]; make [meɪk]; **Das macht doch nichts.** it doesn't matter ['mætə]; **Fotos von ... machen** take photos (of) [teɪk 'fəʊtəʊz]; **Gut gemacht!** Well done! [wel 'dʌn]; **Mach(t) es so.** Do it this way. [duː ɪt 'ðɪs weɪ]; **macht nichts** never mind [nevə 'maɪnd]; **wir machen (gerade)** we're making [wɪə 'meɪkɪŋ]
Macht power ['paʊə]
Mädchen girl [gɜːl]
Mahlzeit meal [miːl]
Mai May [meɪ]; **der erste Mai (1. Mai)** May the first (= 1st May) [meɪ ðə 'fɜːst]
mailen email ['iːmeɪl]
Mais maize [meɪz]
mal times [taɪmz]
Mal: zum ersten Mal first [fɜːst]
malen paint [peɪnt]
Mama mom *(AE)* [mɒm]; mum *(BE)* [mʌm]
manchmal sometimes ['sʌmtaɪmz]
Mann man *(pl.: men)* [mæn, men]
Mannschaft team [tiːm]
Marke brand [brænd]; **Marken- (Spielwaren)** branded (toys) [brændɪd tɔɪz]
Markenname brand name ['brænd neɪm]
Markenzeichen brand name ['brænd neɪm]
Markt market ['mɑːkɪt]
Markthalle market hall ['mɑːkɪt hɔːl]
März March [mɑːtʃ]
Maschine machine [mə'ʃiːn]
Maske mask [mɑːsk]
Masse mass [mæs]
Mathe(matik) maths [mæθs]
Matsch mud [mʌd]
Mauer wall [wɔːl]
Maus mouse *(pl.: mice)* [maʊs, maɪs]
Mechaniker/in: (Auto-)Mechaniker/in (car) mechanic [mə'kænɪk]
Medikamente drugs [drʌgz]
medizinisch medical ['medɪkl]
Meer sea [siː]; **am Meer** at the seaside [ət ðə 'siːsaɪd]
mehr more [mɔː]; **mehr als** over ['əʊvə]
mehrere several ['sevrəl]
Meile mile [maɪl]

[iː] he [ɑː] car [ɔː] or [uː] too [ɜː] girl [i] sorry [u] July [ɪ] big [e] yes [æ] cat [ʌ] bus

mein/meine my [maɪ]
meinen mean [mi:n]; **Was meinst du ...?** What do you think ...? [wɒt də ju 'θɪŋk]
Meinung idea [aɪ'dɪə]; opinion [ə'pɪniən]
meisten: die meisten most [məʊst]
Meisterschaft championship ['tʃæmpiənʃɪp]
Menge: (Menschen-)Menge crowd [kraʊd]; **eine Menge** a lot of [ə 'lɒt əv]; lots of ['lɒts əv]
Menschen people ['pi:pl]
Menschen- human ['hju:mən]
menschlich human ['hju:mən]
merkwürdig funny ['fʌni]
Meter metre ['mi:tə]
mich me [mi:]
mies lousy ['laʊzi]
mieten hire ['haɪə]; rent [rent]
Milch milk [mɪlk]
Milchmann milkman ['mɪlkmən]
Million million ['mɪljən]
Minderheit minority [maɪ'nɒrəti]
Mindest- minimum ['mɪnɪməm]
Mineralwasser mineral water ['mɪnərəl wɔ:tə]
Minigolf minigolf ['mɪnigɒlf]
minus minus ['maɪnəs]
Minute minute ['mɪnɪt]
mir me [mi:]
Mischung mix [mɪks]; mixture ['mɪkstʃə]
mit with [wɪð]
mitbringen bring [brɪŋ]; **Essen, zu dem alle Gäste etwas mitbringen** pot-luck meal [pɒt lʌk 'mi:l]
mitgerechnet included [ɪn'klu:dɪd]
Mitglied member ['membə]
Mitleid: Mitleid haben mit feel sorry for [fi:l 'sɒri fə]
mitmachen (bei) join [dʒɔɪn]
Mitnehmen: ... zum Mitnehmen take-away ... ['teɪkəweɪ]
Mittag(essen) lunch [lʌntʃ]
Mittagszeit lunchtime ['lʌntʃtaɪm]
Mitte middle ['mɪdl]
Mittelpunkt centre ['sentə]
Mittwoch Wednesday ['wenzdeɪ]
Mixer mixer ['mɪksə]
Möbel furniture ['fɜ:nɪtʃə]
Mobiltelefon mobile ['məʊbaɪl]
Mode fashion ['fæʃn]
Modelleisenbahn model train [mɒdl 'treɪn]
modern modern ['mɒdn]
mögen like [laɪk]; **gar nicht mögen** hate [heɪt]; **Ich mag ... nicht.** I don't like ... [aɪ dəʊnt laɪk]; **ich möchte** I'd like (= I would like) [aɪd 'laɪk]; **nicht mögen** dislike [dɪs'laɪk]; **sehr mögen** love [lʌv]
Möglichkeit opportunity [ɒpə'ju:nəti]; way [weɪ]
Möhre carrot ['kærət]
Moment: in diesem Moment at the moment [æt ðə 'məʊmənt]
Monat month [mʌnθ]
Monster monster ['mɒnstə]
Montag Monday ['mʌndeɪ]
montieren fit [fɪt]
morgen tomorrow [tə'mɒrəʊ]
morgens a.m. [eɪ'em]; in the morning [ɪn ðə 'mɔ:nɪŋ]
Motel motel [məʊ'tel]
Motor motor ['məʊtə]
Mountainbike mountain bike ['maʊntən baɪk]; **Mountainbike fahren** mountain bike ['maʊntən baɪk]
MP3-Spieler MP3 player [empi:'θri: 'pleɪə]
müde tired ['taɪəd]
Mühe: sich die Mühe machen, zu gehen/fahren bother to go ['bɒðə tə gəʊ]
Müll junk [dʒʌŋk]; rubbish ['rʌbɪʃ]
Müllmann dustman ['dʌstmən]
multinational multinational [mʌlti'næʃnəl]
mürrisch grumpy ['grʌmpi]
Museum museum [mju'zi:əm]
Musik music ['mju:zɪk]; **(Musik-)Gruppe** band [bænd]
Musiker/in musician [mju'zɪʃn]
müssen have to ['hæv tə]; must [mʌst]
mutig brave [breɪv]
Mutter mother ['mʌðə]
Mutti mom *(AE)* [mɒm]; mum *(BE)* [mʌm]
Mütze hat [hæt]

N

nach after ['ɑ:ftə]; to [tu]; **nach draußen** outside [aut'saɪd]; **nach Hause** home [həʊm]; **nach links/rechts abbiegen** turn left/right [tɜ:n 'left, tɜ:n 'raɪt]; **nach oben** up [ʌp]; **nach oben steigen** rise [raiz]; **Viertel nach ...** quarter past ... ['kwɔ:tə pɑ:st]
Nachbar/in neighbour ['neɪbə]
Nachmittag: heute Nachmittag this arvo *(AustE)* [ðɪs 'ɑ:vəʊ]
nachmittags p.m. [pi: 'em]
Nachricht message ['mesɪdʒ]
nachschauen look [lʊk]; look up [lʊk 'ʌp]
nächste(r,s) next [nekst]; **als Nächstes** next [nekst]; **Wo ist der/die/das nächst(e) ...?** Where's the nearest ...? ['nɪərɪst]
Nacht night [naɪt]; **heute Nacht** tonight [tə'naɪt]; **über Nacht** overnight [əʊvə'naɪt]
nah close [kləʊs]
nahe near [nɪə]
Nähe: in der Nähe von near [nɪə]
Nahverkehrssystem: öffentliches Nahverkehrssystem public transportation system [pʌblɪk trænspɔ:'teɪʃn sɪstəm]
Name name [neɪm]
NASA NASA ['næsə]
Nase nose [nəʊz]; **Asif hatte die Nase voll.** Asif was fed up. ['æsi:f wəz fed 'ʌp]; **die Nase voll haben** be fed up [bi fed 'ʌp]
nass wet [wet]
Nation nation ['neɪʃn]; **Vereinte Nationen (UNO)** United Nations (UN) [ju:'naɪtɪd 'neɪʃnz, ju: 'en]
national national ['næʃənl]
National- national ['næʃənl]
Nationalhymne national anthem [næʃənl 'ænθəm]
Nationalität nationality [næʃə'næləti]
natürlich of course [əf 'kɔ:s]
neben next to ['nekst tə]
neblig foggy ['fɒgi]
nehmen take [teɪk]; **Nehmt euch!** Help yourselves. [help jɔ:'selvz]
nein no [nəʊ]; **Nein (tut sie nicht).** No, she doesn't. [nəʊ ʃi 'dʌzənt]
nennen call [kɔ:l]
nervös nervous ['nɜ:vəs]
nett friendly ['frendli]; nice [naɪs]
Netz net [net]; Web (= World Wide Web) *(= Internet)* [web]
neu new [nju:]; **neueste(r,s)** latest ['leɪtəst]
Neujahr(stag) new year [nju: 'jɪə]
neun nine [naɪn]; **neunte(r,s)** ninth [naɪnθ]
neunzehn nineteen [naɪn'ti:n]; **neunzehnte(r,s)** nineteenth [naɪn'ti:nθ]

[ɒ] dog [ʊ] put [ə] again [eɪ] name [aɪ] time [ɔɪ] boy [əʊ] no [aʊ] house [ɪə] here [eə] chair

neunzig ninety ['naɪnti]
nicht not [nɒt]; **nicht mehr, keine/n ... mehr** not ... any more [nɒt eni 'mɔː]
nichts nothing ['nʌθɪŋ]; **macht nichts** never mind [nevə 'maɪnd]
nie never ['nevə]
niedlich cute [kjuːt]; sweet [swiːt]
niedrig low [ləʊ]
niemals never ['nevə]
niemand nobody ['nəʊbədi]
nirgendwo nowhere ['nəʊweə]
nirgendwohin nowhere ['nəʊweə]
noch still [stɪl]; **noch einmal** again [ə'gen]; **Sonst noch etwas?** Anything else? [eniθɪŋ 'els]
Norden north [nɔːθ]
Nordirland Northern Ireland [nɔːðən 'aɪələnd]
nördlich north [nɔːθ]
normal normal ['nɔːml]; ordinary ['ɔːdnəri]
normalerweise usually ['juːʒuəli]
Notiz note [nəʊt]
Notizen machen take notes [teɪk 'nəʊts]
November November [nəʊ'vembə]
null zero/0 ['zɪərəʊ]
Nummer number ['nʌmbə]
nun well [wel]
nur just [dʒʌst]; only ['əʊnli]
nützlich useful ['juːsfl]

O

O.K. OK ['əʊkeɪ]
oben at the top [æt ðə 'tɒp]; **gerade nach oben** straight up [steɪt 'ʌp]; **nach oben** up [ʌp]; **nach oben steigen** rise [raiz]
Obst fruit [fruːt]
obwohl though [ðəʊ]
oder or [ɔː]
öffentlich public ['pʌblɪk]; **öffentliches Nahverkehrs-system** public transportation system [pʌblɪk trænspɔː'teɪʃn sɪstəm]
offiziell official [ə'fɪʃl]
öffnen open ['əʊpən]
Offroad-Motorrad dirt bike ['dɜːt baɪk]
Offroad-Motorradfahren dirt biking ['dɜːt baɪkɪŋ]
Offroad-Strecke dirt track ['dɜːt træk]
oft often ['ɒfn]
ohne without [wɪ'ðaʊt]
Ökosystem ecosystem ['iːkəʊsɪstəm]
Oktober October [ɒk'təʊbə]
Öl oil [ɔɪl]
Oma grandma ['grænmɑː]
Onkel uncle ['ʌŋkl]
online online ['ɒnlaɪn]
Onlinebanking online banking ['ɒnlaɪn bæŋkɪŋ]
Opa grandad *(ugs.)* ['grændæd]
Opernhaus opera house ['ɒprə haʊs]
Orange orange ['ɒrɪndʒ]
Ordnung: in Ordnung all right [ɔːl 'raɪt]; OK ['əʊkeɪ]
Organisation organisation [ɔːgənaɪ'zeɪʃn]
organisieren organise ['ɔːgənaɪz]
Ort place [pleɪs]; scene [siːn]; **am/vom Ort** local ['ləʊkl]
örtlich local ['ləʊkl]
Ost east [iːst]
Österreich Austria ['ɒstriə]

P

paar: ein paar a few [ə 'fjuː]; some [sʌm]
Paar couple ['kʌpl]; pair [peə]
Päckchen packet ['pækɪt]
packen pack [pæk]
paddeln paddle ['pædl]
Paket packet ['pækɪt]
Pakistan Pakistan [pækɪ'stɑːn]
Panik: Panik bekommen panic ['pænɪk]
Panther panther ['pænθə]
Panzer tank [tæŋk]
Papa dad [dæd]
Papiere papers ['peɪpəz]
Paprika(schote) pepper ['pepə]
Park park [pɑːk]
Parkaufseher/in park ranger [pɑːk 'reɪndʒə]
Parkhaus car park ['kɑː pɑːk]
Parkplatz car park ['kɑː pɑːk]; parking lot *(AE)* ['pɑːkɪŋ lɒt]
Parkzeit: das Überziehen der Parkzeit late parking [leɪt 'pɑːkɪŋ]
Parlament parliament ['pɑːləmənt]
Partner/in partner ['pɑːtnə]; **eine(n) Partner/in fragen über/nach** ask a partner about [ɑːsk ə 'pɑːtnə əbaʊt]
Party party ['pɑːti]
Pass passport ['pɑːspɔːt]
Passagier/in passenger ['pæsɪndʒə]
passieren happen ['hæpən]
Patient/in patient ['peɪʃnt]
Pause break [breɪk]
Pelz pelt [pelt]
Pence pence *(pl.)* [pens]
per: per E-Mail by email [baɪ 'iːmeɪl]
Person person ['pɜːsn]
Pfad path [pɑːθ]; trail [treɪl]
Pfannkuchen pancake ['pænkeɪk]
Pferd horse [hɔːs]
Pflanze plant [plɑːnt]
Pflegeheim care home ['keə həʊm]
Pfleger/in care worker ['keə wɜːkə]; nurse [nɜːs]
Pflicht chore [tʃɔː]
Pforte gate [geɪt]
Pfund pound *(britisches Geld)* [paʊnd]
Picknick picnic ['pɪknɪk]
Pilot/in pilot ['paɪlət]; **leitende/r Pilot/in** chief pilot [tʃiːf 'paɪlət]
Pinsel brush [brʌʃ]
Pirat/in pirate ['paɪrət]
Pizza pizza ['piːtsə]
Plan plan [plæn]
planen plan [plæn]
Planet planet ['plænɪt]
Plasmafernseher plasma TV ['plæzmə tiː viː]
Platz space [speɪs]
plaudern chat [tʃæt]
plötzlich suddenly ['sʌdnli]
Podcast: (Video-)Podcast video podcast ['vɪdiəʊ 'pɒdkɑːst]
Politiker/in politician [pɒlə'tɪʃn]
politisch political [pə'lɪtɪkl]
Polizei police [pə'liːs]
Polizeibeamter/Polizeibeam-tin officer ['ɒfɪsə]; police officer [pə'liːs ɒfɪsə]
Polizeirevier police station [pə'liːs steɪʃn]
Polizeiwache police station [pə'liːs steɪʃn]
Pommes frites: Fisch und Pommes frites fish and chips [fɪʃ ənd 'tʃɪps]
Pommes-frites-Bude chip shop ['tʃɪp ʃɒp]
Pool pool [puːl]
Pop-Art pop art ['pɒp ɑːt]
Popgruppe pop group ['pop gruːp]
Popmusik pop music [pɒp 'mjuːzɪk]

Portion portion ['pɔːʃn]
Position: leitende Position senior job ['siːniə 'dʒɒb]
Postamt post office ['pəʊst ɒfɪs]
Poster poster ['pəʊstə]
Postkarte postcard ['pəʊstkɑːd]; **elektronische Postkarte** ecard ['iːkɑːd]
Postleitzahl postcode ['pəʊstkəʊd]
Postskript(um) PS [piː 'ɛs]
Praktikum work experience ['wɜːk ɪk'spɪəriəns]
praktisch convenient [kən'viːniənt]
Präposition preposition [prepə'zɪʃn]
Prärie prairie ['preəri]
Präsentation presentation [prezn'teɪʃn]
Präsident/in president ['prezɪdənt]
präzise accurate ['ækjərət]
Preis prize [praɪz]; **(Kauf-)Preis** price [praɪs]
preisgünstig good value [gʊd 'væljuː]
pro: pro (Tag) a (day) [ə 'deɪ]
probieren try [traɪ]
Problem problem ['prɒbləm]; **kein Problem!** no worries *(AustE)* [nəɪ 'wʌriz]
Programm program *(AE)* ['prəʊgræm]; programme ['prəʊgræm]
Projekt project ['prɒdʒekt]
Prospekt brochure ['brəʊʃə]
Protest protest ['prəʊtest]
Provider provider [prə'vaɪdə]
Provinz province ['prɒvɪns]
Prozent per cent (%) [pə 'sent]
prüfen test [test]; **(über)prüfen** check [tʃek]
Prüfung test [test]
PS PS [piː 'ɛs]
Pullover jumper ['dʒʌmpə]
Punkt point [pɔɪnt]
Punkte: Punkte für den Einwanderungsantrag visa points ['viːzə pɔɪnts]
Puppe doll [dɒl]
putzen brush [brʌʃ]; clean [kliːn]

Q

Quadrat square [skweə]
Qualität quality ['kwɒləti]
Quelle spring [sprɪŋ]
Quiz quiz [kwɪz]

R

Rad wheel [wiːl]; **Rad fahren** ride a bike [raɪd ə 'baɪk]
Radiergummi rubber ['rʌbə]
Radio radio ['reɪdiəʊ]
Rand: Rand *(südafrikanische Währung)* rand = R [rænd]
Rap rap [ræp]
rappen rap [ræp]
Rapper/in rapper ['ræpə]
rasen speed [spiːd]
raten guess [ges]; **(einmal) Raten** (a) guess [ges]
Ratte rat [ræt]
rauchend smoky ['sməʊki]
Raum room [ruːm]; space [speɪs]
rausgehen: mit dem Hund rausgehen take the dog for a walk ['teɪk ðə dɒg fə ə 'wɔːk]
Recht law [lɔː]; right [raɪt]; **Du hast Recht.** You're right. [jʊə 'raɪt]
rechts to the right [tə ðə 'raɪt]; **nach rechts abbiegen** turn right [tɜːn 'raɪt]
Rechtsanspruch right [raɪt]
Rechtschreibung: (Recht-)Schreibung spelling ['spelɪŋ]
Rechtswissenschaft law [lɔː]
Rede speech [spiːtʃ]
reden: reden mit talk to ['tɔːk tʊ]
Redewendung phrase [freɪz]
Referat presentation [prezn'teɪʃn]
Regal shelf *(pl.: shelves)* [ʃelf, ʃelvz]
Regel rule [ruːl]
Regierung government ['gʌvnmənt]
Regisseur director [də'rektə]
regnen rain [reɪn]
regnerisch rainy ['reɪni]
reich rich [rɪtʃ]
Reihenfolge: (alphabetische) Reihenfolge (alphabetical) order [ælfə'betɪkl 'ɔːdə]
Reise travel ['trævl]; **(lange) Reise** journey ['dʒɜːni]; **eine Reise machen** take a trip [teɪk ə 'trɪp]
Reiseführer guide book ['gaɪd bʊk]
Reiseführer/in tour guide ['tʊə gaɪd]
reisen travel ['trævl]; **durch etw. reisen** tour [tʊə]
Reisende/r traveller ['trævələ]
reiten ride [raɪd]
relaxen chill out *(ugs.)* [tʃil 'aʊt]
Religions- religious [rɪ'lɪdʒəs]
religiös religious [rɪ'lɪdʒəs]
rennen run [rʌn]; **Renn/t um dein/euer Leben!** Run for your life! [rʌn fə jɔː 'laɪf]
Rennen race [reɪs]
reparieren repair [rɪ'peə]
Reservat(ion) reserve [rɪ'zɜːv]
reservieren book [bʊk]
Reservierung booking ['bʊkɪŋ]
Respekt respect [rɪ'spekt]
Rest rest [rest]
Restaurant diner *(AE)* ['daɪnə]; restaurant ['restrɒnt]
Reste scraps [skræps]
Revolution: industrielle Revolution Industrial Revolution [ɪndʌstriəl revə'luːʃn]
rhythmisch rhythmic ['rɪðmɪk]
Rhythmus rhythm ['rɪðəm]; **der Rhythmus der Straße** the beat of the street [biːt əv ðə 'striːt]
richten auf: eine Waffe richten auf point a gun at [pɔɪnt ə 'gʌn æt]
richtig right [raɪt]; **Richtig oder falsch?** Right or wrong? ['raɪt ɔː 'rɒŋ]
Richtung direction [də'rekʃn]; **in Richtung auf** towards [tə'wɔːdz]
riechen smell [smel]
Rieseneisvogel kookaburra ['kʊkəbʌrə]
Riesenhaufen: ein Riesenhaufen (Arbeit) a whole lotta (work) *(ugs.)* [ə 'həʊl lɒtə wɜːk]
riesig huge [hjuːdʒ]
Rock(musik) rock [rɒk]
Rockband rock band ['rɒk bænd]
Rodeo rodeo ['rəʊdiəʊ]
roh raw [rɔː]
Rollenspiel role-play ['rəʊlpleɪ]
Rollschuhe skates [skeɪts]
Rollschuhlaufen skating ['skeɪtɪŋ]
Rollstuhl wheelchair ['wiːltʃeə]
Röntgenaufnahme X-ray ['eks reɪ]
rosa pink [pɪŋk]
rot red [red]
Route route [ruːt]
Rubellos lottery scratchcard ['lɒtəri 'skrætʃkɑːd]; scratchie *(AustE)* ['skrætʃi]
Rückfahrkarte: ohne Rückfahrkarte one way [wʌn 'weɪ]

Rucksack backpack ['bækpæk]
Rucksackreisen backpacking ['bækpækɪŋ]
Rucksacktourist/in backpacker ['bækpækə]
rückwärts backwards ['bækwədz]
Ruf: (An-)Ruf (phone) call ['fəʊn kɔ:l]
rufen shout [ʃaʊt]
Rugby rugby ['rʌgbi]
ruhig calm [kɑ:m]; quiet ['kwaɪət]
ruhmreich glorious ['glɔ:riəs]
Rundfunk radio ['reɪdiəʊ]
Russland Russia ['rʌʃə]

S

Sache thing [θɪŋ]
Sack bag [bæg]
Safari safari [sə'fɑ:ri]
Saft fruit juice ['fru:t dʒu:s]
Sage legend ['ledʒənd]
sagen say [seɪ]
Salat salad ['sæləd]; **(Kopf-)Salat** lettuce ['letɪs]
Salsa salsa ['sælsə]
sammeln collect [kə'lekt]
Samstag Saturday ['sætədeɪ]; **am Samstag** on Saturday [ɒn 'sætədeɪ]
Sand sand [sænd]; **Schrift im Sand** writing in the sand ['raɪtɪŋ ɪn ðə 'sænd]
Sand- sandy ['sændi]
sandig sandy ['sændi]
Sandstein sandstone ['sændstəʊn]
Sandwich sandwich ['sænwɪtʃ]
Sänger/in singer ['sɪŋə]
Satellitentechnik satellite technology ['sætəlaɪt teknɒlədʒi]
Satz sentence ['sentəns]
sauber clean [kli:n]
Saubermachen: (das) Saubermachen cleaning ['kli:nɪŋ]
Sauna sauna ['sɔ:nə]
Saxophon saxophone ['sæksəfəʊn]
Schachtel packet ['pækɪt]
schade: Das ist schade. That's a pity. [ðæts ə 'pɪti]; That's too bad. *(ugs.)* [ðæts 'tu: bæd]
schaden harm [hɑ:m]
Schaden: Schaden zufügen harm [hɑ:m]
Schaf sheep *(pl.: sheep)* [ʃi:p]
schaffen create [kri:'eɪt]
scharf cool [ku:l]
Schatten shadow ['ʃædəʊ]
schauen look [lʊk]; look [lʊk]

scheiden: sich scheiden lassen divorce [dɪ'vɔ:s]
scheinen seem [si:m]; **die Sonne scheint** the sun is shining [ðə sʌn iz 'ʃaɪnɪŋ]
Schere scissors *(pl.)* ['sɪzəz]
Scherz joke [dʒəʊk]
schicken send [send]
Schicksal destiny ['destəni]
schieben push [pʊʃ]
schießen shoot [ʃu:t]
Schiff boat [bəʊt]; ship [ʃɪp]
Schild sign [saɪn]
Schildkröte turtle ['tɜ:tl]
Schlacht battle ['bætl]
Schlafanzug pyjamas *(pl.)* [pə'dʒɑ:məz]
schlafen be asleep [bi ə'sli:p]; sleep [sli:p]; **(das) Schlafen** sleeping ['sli:pɪŋ]; **nicht schlafen gehen** stay up [steɪ 'ʌp]
Schlafsack sleeping bag ['sli:pɪŋ bæg]
Schlafzimmer bedroom ['bedru:m]
schlagen hit ['hɪt]
Schlager hit ['hɪt]
Schlagzeile headline ['hedlaɪn]
Schlagzeug drums *(pl.)* [drʌmz]
Schlagzeuger/in drummer ['drʌmə]
Schlamm mud [mʌd]
Schlange snake [sneɪk]; **Westliche Braunschlange** Western Brown [westən 'braʊn]
schlau clever ['klevə]
schlecht bad [bæd]; **der/die/das schlechteste** the worst [ðə 'wɜ:st]; **nicht schlecht** not bad [nɒt 'bæd]; **schlecht in** bad at ['bæd ət]; **schlechter** worse [wɜ:s]
schließen close [kləʊz]
schließlich in the end [ɪn ði 'end]
schlimm bad [bæd]; serious ['sɪəriəs]; **der/die/das schlimmste** the worst [ðə 'wɜ:st]; **schlimmer** worse [wɜ:s]
Schlitten: (Hunde-)Schlitten dog sled ['dɒg sled]
Schlittschuh: Schlittschuh laufen skate [skeɪt]; **Schlittschuhlaufen** skating ['skeɪtɪŋ]
Schlittschuhe skates [skeɪts]
Schloss castle ['kɑ:sl]
schlucken: Feuer schlucken eat fire [i:t 'faɪə]
Schlüssel key [ki:]

schmal narrow ['nærəʊ]
schmerzen hurt [hɜ:t]
Schnee snow [snəʊ]; **(Schnee) fegen** clear [klɪə]; **Snowshoeing** *(mit speziellen Schuhen über Schnee und Eis wandern)* snowshoeing ['snəʊʃu:ɪŋ]; **wenn viel Schnee gefallen ist** after bad snow [ɑ:ftə bæd 'snəʊ]
Schneefall: starker Schneefall a big dump of snow *(ugs.)* [ə bɪg dʌmp əv 'snəʊ]
Schneemobil snowmobile ['snəʊməbi:l]
Schneeschuhe snowshoes ['snəʊʃu:z]
Schneesturm snowstorm ['snəʊstɔ:m]
schneiden: in Stücke schneiden cut ... in pieces [kʌt ɪn 'pi:sɪz]
schneien snow [snəʊ]
schnell fast [fɑ:st]; quick [kwɪk]; quickly (Adverb) ['kwɪkli]; **schnell fahren** speed [spi:d]
Schnitt! Cut! [kʌt]
Schnur string [strɪŋ]
Schokolade chocolate ['tʃɒklət]; **heiße Schokolade** hot chocolate [hɒt 'tʃɒklət]
schon already [ɔ:l'redi]; **schon einmal** before [bɪ'fɔ:]
schön beautiful ['bju:tɪfəl]
schottisch Scottish ['skɒtɪʃ]
Schottland Scotland ['skɒtlənd]
Schrank cupboard ['kʌbəd]
schrecklich terrible ['terəbl]
schreiben write [raɪt]; **eine Liste schreiben** make a list [meɪk ə 'lɪst]
Schreiben writing ['raɪtɪŋ]
Schreibtisch desk [desk]
Schreibweise spelling ['spelɪŋ]
schreien scream [skri:m]; shout [ʃaʊt]
Schrift: Schrift im Sand writing in the sand ['raɪtɪŋ ɪn ðə 'sænd]
schriftlich: schriftliche Arbeit coursework ['kɔ:swɜ:k]
schrumpfen: schrumpft immer weiter keeps on shrinking [ki:ps ɒn 'ʃrɪŋkɪŋ]
Schuh shoe [ʃu:]
Schulabschlussfeier grad *(CanE/AE) (ugs.)* [græd]; graduation *(CanE/AE)* [grædʒu'eɪʃn]
Schulausflug (school) trip [trɪp]

he [ɑ:] car [ɔ:] or [u:] too [ɜ:] girl [i] sorry [u] July [ɪ] big [e] yes [æ] cat [ʌ] bus

Schule school [sku:l]; **in der Schule** at school [æt 'sku:l]; **Schule für 11- bis 14-Jährige** middle school ['mɪdl sku:l]
Schüler/in pupil ['pju:pl]; student ['stju:dnt]
Schulfach subject ['sʌbdʒɪkt]
Schulklasse class [klɑ:s]
Schulleiter/in principal *(AE)* ['prɪnsɪpl]
Schultasche bag [bæg]
Schulter shoulder ['ʃəʊldə]
Schuss gunshot ['gʌnʃɒt]
schützen protect [prə'tekt]
Schützer pad [pæd]
schwach poor [pʊə]
schwarz black [blæk]
Schwarze/r black [blæk]
Schwein pig [pɪg]
Schweiz Switzerland ['swɪtsələnd]
schwer difficult ['dɪfɪkəlt]
Schwester sister ['sɪstə]
schwierig difficult ['dɪfɪkəlt]; hard [hɑ:d]
Schwierigkeiten trouble ['trʌbl]
Schwimmbad pool [pu:l]; swimming pool ['swɪmɪŋ pu:l]
Schwimmbecken swimming pool ['swɪmɪŋ pu:l]
schwimmen swim [swɪm]; **(das) Schwimmen** swimming ['swɪmɪŋ]
Schwirrholz bullroarer ['bʊlrɔ:rə]
Science-Fiction science fiction [saɪəns 'fɪkʃn]
sechs six [sɪks]; **sechste(r,s)** sixth [sɪksθ]
sechzehn sixteen [sɪk'sti:n]; **sechzehnte(r,s)** sixteenth [sɪks'ti:nθ]
sechzig sixty ['sɪksti]
See: (Binnen-)See lake [leɪk]; **die See** sea [si:]
Seehund seal [si:l]
Seekuh manatee [mænə'ti:]
segeln sail [seɪl]
sehen see [si:]
Sehenswürdigkeit sight [saɪt]
Sehenswürdigkeiten: Besichtigung von Sehenswürdigkeiten sightseeing ['saɪtsi:ɪŋ]
sehr really ['rɪəli]; very ['veri]
Seife soap [səʊp]
Seifenoper: TV-Seifenoper soap [səʊp]
Seil line [laɪn]
sein be [bi]
sein/seine his [hɪz]; its [ɪts]
seit since [sɪns]; **seit Jahren** for years [fə 'yɪəz]
Seite page [peɪdʒ]; side [saɪd]
Sekunde second ['sekənd]
selber herself [hɜ:'self]; himself [hɪm'self]; itself [ɪt'self]; myself [maɪ'self]; ourselves [aʊə'selvz]; themselves [ðəm'selvz]; yourself [jə'self]; yourselves [jɔ:'selvz]
selbst herself [hɜ:'self]; himself [hɪm'self]; itself [ɪt'self]; myself [maɪ'self]; ourselves [aʊə'selvz]; themselves [ðəm'selvz]; yourself [jə'self]; yourselves [jɔ:'selvz]
selbstverständlich of course [əf 'kɔ:s]
selten rare [reə]; seldom ['seldəm]
seltsam strange [streɪndʒ]
senden send [send]
Sendung: (Fernseh-)Sendung programme ['prəʊgræm]; **(Fernseh-, Radio-)Sendung** show [ʃəʊ]
Senf mustard ['mʌstəd]
September September [sep'tembə]
Service service ['sɜ:vɪs]
servieren serve [sɜ:v]
setzen: Setz dich hierhin. Sit here. [sɪt 'hɪə]; **sich setzen** sit [sɪt]
Shake milkshake ['mɪlkʃeɪk]
Sheriff Sheriff ['ʃerɪf]
Shorts shorts *(pl.)* [ʃɔ:ts]
sicher safe [seɪf]; **sicher sein** be sure [bi 'ʃʊə]
Sicherheit security [sɪ'kjʊərəti]
sie she [ʃi:]; them [ðem]; they [ðeɪ]; **sie ist** she's (= she is) [ʃi:z]; **sie sind** they're (= they are) [ðeə]
Sie you [ju:]; **Sie sind** you're (= you are) [jʊə]
sieben seven ['sevn]; **siebte(r,s)** seventh ['sevnθ]
siebzehn seventeen [sevn'ti:n]; **siebzehnte(r,s)** seventeenth [sevn'ti:nθ]
siebzig seventy ['sevnti]
Siedler/in settler ['setlə]
Siedlung settlement ['setlmənt]
siegen win [wɪn]
Sieger/in winner ['wɪnə]
Signal signal ['sɪgnəl]
Silikon silicon ['sɪlɪkən]
Silizium silicon ['sɪlɪkən]
sind: sind nicht aren't (= are not) [ɑ:nt]; **Sind sie ...?** Are they ...? [ɑ: ðeɪ]
singen sing [sɪŋ]
Sinn für Humor sense of humour [sens əv 'hju:mə]
Situation situation [sɪtʃu'eɪʃn]
Sitz: mit Sitz (nahe Ottawa) based (near Ottawa) [beɪst]
sitzen sit [sɪt]
Sitzplatz seat [si:t]
Skateboard board [bɔ:d]; skateboard ['skeɪtbɔ:d]; **Skateboard fahren** skate [skeɪt]; **zum Skateboarden gehen** go skateboarding [gəʊ 'skeɪtbɔ:dɪŋ]
Skateboarder/in skateboarder ['skeɪtbɔ:də]
Skateboardfahrer/in boarder ['bɔ:də]; skateboarder ['skeɪtbɔ:də]
skaten skate [skeɪt]
Ski: Ski fahren skiing ['ski:ɪŋ]
Skilaufen: (das) Skilaufen skiing ['ski:ɪŋ]
Skisport skiing ['ski:ɪŋ]
Sklave/Sklavin slave [sleɪv]
Slang slang [slæng]
Slogan slogan ['sləʊgən]
SMS-Nachricht text message ['tekst mesɪdʒ]
Snack snack [snæk]
Snowboard: Snowboard fahren snowboarding ['snəʊbɔ:dɪŋ]
snowboarden snowboarding ['snəʊbɔ:dɪŋ]
Snowshoeing: Snowshoeing *(mit speziellen Schuhen über Schnee und Eis wandern)* snowshoeing ['snəuʃu:ɪŋ]
so so [səʊ]; such [sʌtʃ]; **Mach(t) es so.** Do it this way. [du: ɪt 'ðɪs weɪ]; **nicht so beliebt wie ...** not so popular as ... [nɒt səʊ 'popjʊlə æz]; **so kräftig sie konnten** as hard as they could [æz 'hɑ:d əz ðeɪ kʊd]
Socke sock [sɒk]
Sofa couch [kaʊtʃ]
Software software ['sɒftweə]
sogar even ['i:vn]
Sohn son [sʌn]
solange as long as [æz 'lɒŋ æz]
sollte: sollte/solltest/sollten/solltet should [ʃʊd]
Solo solo ['səʊləʊ]
Sommer summer ['sʌmə]
Sonderangebot special offer [speʃl 'ɒfə]
sonderbar strange [streɪndʒ]

[ɒ] dog [ʊ] put [ə] again [eɪ] name [aɪ] time [ɔɪ] boy [əʊ] no [aʊ] house [ɪə] here [eə] chair

Sonnabend Saturday ['sætədeɪ]; **am Sonnabend** on Saturday [ɒn 'sætədeɪ]
Sonne sun [sʌn]; **die Sonne scheint** the sun is shining [ðə sʌn iz 'ʃaɪnɪŋ]
Sonnenbrille sunglasses *(pl.)* ['sʌnglɑːsɪz]; sunnies *(AustE)* ['sʌniːz]
Sonnencreme sun cream ['sʌn kriːm]; sunscreen ['sʌnskriːn]; **sich mit reichlich Sonnencreme eincremen** slop on sunscreen *(ugs.)* [slɒp ɒn 'sʌnskriːn]
Sonnenschein sunshine ['sʌnʃaɪn]
sonnig sunny ['sʌni]
Sonntag Sunday ['sʌndeɪ]; **am Sonntag** on Sundays [ɒn 'sʌndeɪz]
sonntags on Sundays [ɒn 'sʌndeɪz]
sonst: Sonst noch etwas? Anything else? [eniθɪŋ 'els]
Sorgen: Mach dir keine Sorgen. Don't worry. ['dəʊnt wʌri]
sorgfältig careful ['keəfl]
Sorte brand [brænd]
Soße sauce [sɔːs]
Souvenir souvenir [suːvə'nɪə]
sozial social ['səʊʃl]
Spaghetti spaghetti [spə'geti]
Spanien Spain [speɪn]
Spanisch Spanish ['spænɪʃ]
spannend exciting [ɪk'saɪtɪŋ]
Sparkasse bank [bæŋk]
Spaß fun [fʌn]; **sie haben Spaß** they enjoy themselves [ɪn'dʒɔɪ]; **Spaß machen** be fun [bi 'fʌn]; **viel Spaß beim Zuhören!** happy listening! [hæpi 'lɪsnɪŋ]; **zum Spaß** for fun [fə 'fʌn]
spät late [leɪt]; **bis spät** till late [tɪl 'leɪt]; **er kommt zu spät** he is late [leɪt]; **Lieber spät als gar nicht.** Better late than never. [betə 'leɪt ðən 'nevə]; **Wie spät ist es?** What time is it? [wɑt 'taɪm ɪz ɪt]
später: Bis später. See you later. [siː ju 'leɪtə]
spazieren gehen walk [wɔːk]; **mit dem Hund spazieren gehen** take the dog for a walk ['teɪk ðə dɒg fə ə 'wɔːk]
Spazierfahrt: eine Spazierfahrt machen go out in the car [gəʊ aʊt ɪn ðə 'kɑː]
Spaziergang walk [wɔːk]
speien: Feuer speien eat fire [iːt 'faɪə]
Spiel game [geɪm]; match [mætʃ]
spielen play [pleɪ]; **ein Instrument spielen** play an instrument [pleɪ ən 'ɪnstrəmənt]; **einen Streich spielen** play a trick [pleɪ ə 'trɪk]; **Hast du mit ... gespielt?** Did you play with ...? [dɪd ju 'pleɪ wɪð]
Spieler/in player ['pleɪə]
Spielkonsole games console ['geɪmz kən'səʊl]
Spielstand score [skɔː]
Spielzeug toy [tɔɪ]
Spinne spider ['spaɪdə]
spitz pointy ['pɔɪnti]
Spitze: an der Spitze at the top [æt ðə 'tɒp]
Spitzname nickname ['nɪkneɪm]
Sponsor/in sponsor ['spɒnsə]
Sport sport [spɔːt]; **Sport treiben** play sport [pleɪ 'spɔːt]; **verrückt nach Sport** crazy about sport ['kreɪzi əbaʊt 'spɔːt]
Sporthalle gym [dʒɪm]
Sportzentrum sports centre ['spɔːts sentə]
Sprache language ['læŋgwɪdʒ]
Spray spray [spreɪ]
sprechen speak [spiːk]; **sprechen mit** talk to ['tɔːk tʊ]; **sprechen über** talk about [tɔːk ə'baʊt]
spülen wash up [wɒʃ 'ʌp]
Spur mark [mɑːk]
Staat: (Bundes-)Staat state [steɪt]
Stadion stadium ['steɪdiəm]
Stadt city ['sɪti]; town [taʊn]
Stadtplan map [mæp]
Stadtzentrum downtown *(AE)* ['daʊntaʊn]
Stand: (Verkaufs-)Stand stall [stɔːl]
Standbesitzer/in stallholder ['stɔːlhəʊldə]
Star idol ['aɪdl]; star [stɑː]
stark cool [kuːl]; strong [strɒŋ]; **es geht darum, stark zu sein** it's about being strong [ə'baʊt biːɪŋ 'strɒŋ]; **stark werden** rise [raɪz]
Start start [stɑːt]
starten start [stɑːt]
Startseite home page ['həʊm peɪdʒ]
Staubsauger vacuum cleaner ['vækjuəm kliːnə]
Steak steak [steɪk]
stehen stand [stænd]; **aufrecht stehen** stand up [stænd 'ʌp]
stehlen steal [stiːl]
steigen: nach oben steigen rise [raiz]
Steigerung(sform) comparison [kəm'pærɪsən]
Stein rock [rɒk]; stone [stəʊn]
Stelle job [dʒɒb]; place [pleɪs]
stellen (auf) put (on) [pʊt]
Stellenanzeige job advert ['dʒɒb 'ædvɜːt]; job advertisement ['dʒɒb əd'vɜːtɪsmənt]
sterben die [daɪ]
Sticker sticker ['stɪkə]
Stiefel boot [buːt]
Stiefmutter stepmother ['stepmʌðə]
Stiefvater stepfather ['stepfɑːðə]
Stil style [staɪl]
still quiet ['kwaɪət]; still [stɪl]
Stimme voice [vɔɪs]
stimmen: Stimmt. You're right. [jʊə 'raɪt]
Stinktier skunk [skʌŋk]
Stock stick [stɪk]
Stockcar stock car ['stɒk kɑː]
stolz proud [praʊd]
Storch stork [stɔːk]
stoßen hit ['hɪt]
Strafe punishment ['pʌnɪʃmənt]
Strand beach [biːtʃ]
Straße road [rəʊd]; street [striːt]
Straßenbahn tram [træm]
Strauß ostrich ['ɒstrɪtʃ]
Strecke line [laɪn]; route [ruːt]; **einfache Strecke (Fahrkarte)** one way [wʌn 'weɪ]
Streich: einen Streich spielen play a trick [pleɪ ə 'trɪk]
Strom electricity [ɪlek'trɪsəti]
Stromschnellen rapids ['ræpɪdz]
Strömung current ['kʌrənt]
Struktur structure ['strʌktʃə]
Strumpf sock [sɒk]
Stück piece [piːs]; **in Stücke schneiden** cut ... in pieces [kʌt ɪn 'piːsɪz]
Student/in student ['stjuːdnt]
studieren study ['stʌdi]
Studio studio ['stjuːdiəʊ]
Studium: (sein) Studium (his) studies ['stʌdiz]
Stufen: (Treppen-)Stufen stairs [steəz]
Stuhl chair [tʃeə]
Stunde hour ['aʊə]; **(Unterrichts-)Stunde** lesson ['lesn]
Stundenplan schedule *(AE)* ['ʃedjuːl]; timetable ['taɪmteɪbl]

[ʊə] sure [b] **b**ike [p] **p**en [d] **d**ay [t] **t**en [k] boo**k** [g] **g**o [ŋ] morni**ng** [l] **l**ike [r] **r**uler

stundenweise: Bezahlung stundenweise pay by the hour [peɪ baɪ ði 'aʊə]
stürzen fall [fɔ:l]
suchen look for ['lʊk fə]; search [sɜ:tʃ]
Südafrikaner/in South African [saʊθ 'æfrɪkən]
südafrikanisch South African [saʊθ 'æfrɪkən]
Süden south [saʊθ]
südlich: südlich (von) south (of) [saʊθ]
super super ['su:pə]; **super in** great at ['greɪt ət]
Supermarkt supermarket ['su:pəmɑ:kɪt]
Suppe soup [su:p]
surfen surf [sɜ:f]; **im Internet surfen** surf the Internet [sɜ:f ði 'ɪntənet]
süß cute [kju:t]; sweet [swi:t]
Süßigkeit sweet [swi:t]
Süßigkeiten candy *(AE)* ['kændi]
Sweatshirt sweatshirt ['swetʃɜ:t]
Symbol symbol ['sɪmbl]
System system ['sɪstəm]
Szene scene [si:n]

T

Tabak tobacco [tə'bækəʊ]
Taekwondo tae kwon do [tai kwɒn 'dəʊ]
Tafel board [bɔ:d]
Tag day [deɪ]; **besonderer Tag** special day ['speʃl deɪ]; **jeden Tag** every day [evri 'deɪ]
Tagebuch diary ['daɪəri]
Tagesablauf timetable ['taɪmteɪbl]
Tagesausflug day out [deɪ 'aʊt]; **einen Tagesausflug machen** have a day out [hæv ə deɪ 'aʊt]
Tal valley ['væli]
Tankstelle garage ['gærɑ:ʒ]
Tante aunt [ɑ:nt]
Tanz: Festessen mit anschließendem Tanz dinner dance ['dɪnə dɑ:ns]
tanzen dance [dɑ:ns]; **(das) Tanzen** dancing ['dɑ:nsɪŋ]
Tänzer/in dancer ['dɑ:nsə]
Tapete wallpaper ['wɔ:lpeɪpə]
tapfer brave [breɪv]
Tasche pocket ['pɒkɪt]; **(Schul-) Tasche** bag [bæg]
Taschengeld pocket money ['pɒkɪt mʌni]
Taschenlampe flashlight *(AE)* ['flæʃlaɪt]; torch [tɔ:tʃ]
Taschenrechner calculator ['kælkjuleɪtə]
Tasse cup [kʌp]
Tatsache fact [fækt]
tauchen dive [daɪv]; **Hai-Tauchen mit Käfigen** shark cage diving [ʃa:k keɪdʒ 'daɪvɪŋ]
tauschen gegen trade for ['treɪd fə]
tausend thousand ['θaʊznd]
Taxi taxi ['tæksi]
Team team [ti:m]
Teddybär teddy bear ['tedi beə]
Tee tea [ti:]
Teenager teenager ['ti:neɪdʒə]; **für/von Teenager, Teenager-** teenage ['ti:neɪdʒ]
Teil part [pɑ:t]
Teilzeit: (in) Teilzeit arbeiten work part-time [wɜ:k 'pɑ:ttaɪm]; **Teilzeitstelle** part-time job ['pɑ:ttaɪm dʒɒb]
Telefon telephone ['telɪfəʊn]
Telefonanruf (phone) call ['fəʊn kɔ:l]
Telefonbuch phone book ['fəʊn bʊk]
Teller plate [pleɪt]
Temperatur temperature ['temprətʃə]
Tennis tennis ['tenɪs]
Territorium territory ['terətri]
Test test [test]
testen test [test]
teuer: zu teuer too expensive [tu: ɪk'spensɪv]
Text text [tekst]
Theater theater *(AE)* ['θɪətə]; theatre ['θɪətə]
Thema topic ['tɒpɪk]
Themenbereich topic ['tɒpɪk]
tief deep [di:p]; low [ləʊ]
Tier animal ['ænɪml]
Tierhandlung pet shop ['pet ʃɒp]
Tierheim animal home ['ænɪml həʊm]
Tipp tip [tɪp]
Tisch table ['teɪbl]
Tischtennis table tennis ['teɪbl tenɪs]
Titel title ['taɪtl]
Toast toast [təʊst]
Tochter daughter ['dɔ:tə]
Tod death [deθ]
Toilette toilet ['tɔɪlət]
toll fantastic [fæn'tæstɪk]; great [greɪt]; super ['su:pə]; terrific [tə'rɪfɪk]
Tomate tomato *(pl.: tomatoes)* [tə'mɑ:təʊ]
Tonfall intonation [ɪntə'neɪʃn]
Tor gate [geɪt]; goal [gəʊl]
Tortillachips tortilla chip [tɔ:'ti:ə tʃɪp]
tot dead [ded]
töten kill [kɪl]
Tourismus tourism ['tʊərɪzəm]
Tourist/in tourist ['tʊərɪst]
Township township ['taʊnʃɪp]
Tradition tradition [trə'dɪʃn]
traditionell traditional [trə'dɪʃənl]
tragen carry ['kæri]; wear *(Kleidung)* [weə]
trainieren work out [wɜ:k 'aʊt]
Training working out ['wɜ:kɪŋ aʊt]
Tram tram [træm]
Transport transport *(no pl.)* ['trænspɔ:t]; transportation [trænspɔ:'teɪʃn]
Transportmittel transportation [trænspɔ:'teɪʃn]
Traum dream [dri:m]
träumen dream [dri:m]
Traumzeit Dreamtime ['dri:mtaɪm]
traurig sad [sæd]
treffen hit ['hɪt]; meet [mi:t]; **sich treffen** meet up [mi:t 'ʌp]; **sich treffen (mit)** meet [mi:t]
Treppenstufen stairs [steəz]
treten kick [kɪk]
Trick trick [trɪk]
trinken drink [drɪŋk]; have [hæv]
trocken dry [draɪ]
Trockenbootrennen dry boat race [draɪ 'bəʊt reɪs]
Trödelmarkt: (eine Art) Trödelmarkt car-boot sale [kɑ: 'bu:t seɪl]
Trommel drum [drʌm]
Truppe gang [gæng]
Tschüs! Bye(-bye)! [baɪ, bə 'baɪ]; Cheers! [tʃɪəz]
T-Shirt T-shirt ['ti:ʃɜ:t]
tun do [du:]
Tunnel tunnel ['tʌnl]
Tür door [dɔ:]
Türkei Turkey ['tɜ:ki]
Turnhalle gym [dʒɪm]
Turnschuhe trainers *(pl.)* ['treɪnəz]
Tüte bag [bæg]
typisch typical ['tɪpɪkl]

U

U-Bahn subway *(AE)* ['sʌbweɪ]; underground ['ʌndəgraʊnd]
übel sick [sɪk]
üben practise ['præktɪs]
über about [ə'baʊt]; above [ə'bʌv]; over ['əʊvə]; **(quer) über** across [ə'krɒs]
über Nacht overnight [əʊvə'naɪt]
überall all over [ɔ:l 'əʊvə]; everywhere ['evriweə]
übereinstimmen agree [ə'gri:]
übernachten: übernachten in (einem Hotel) stay at (a hotel) ['steɪ æt]
überprüfen check [tʃek]
überqueren cross [krɒs]
überrascht surprised [sə'praɪzd]
Überraschung surprise [sə'praɪz]
Überraschungs- surprise [sə'praɪz]
Überschrift headline ['hedlaɪn]; title ['taɪtl]
übersetzen interpret [ɪn'tɜ:prɪt]
überziehen slip on [slɪp 'ɒn]; **das Überziehen der Parkzeit** late parking [leɪt 'pɑ:kɪŋ]
übrigens by the way [baɪ ðə 'weɪ]
Übung exercise ['eksəsaɪz]; practice ['præktɪs]
Uhr clock [klɒk]; **zwei Uhr** two o'clock [tu: ə'klɒk]
Uhrzeit time [taɪm]
um: um ... herum round [raʊnd]; **um ... Uhr** at ... o'clock [ət ə'klɒk]; **um zu** to [tu]
umbringen kill [kɪl]
umdrehen: (sich) umdrehen turn [tɜ:n]; **sich umdrehen** turn around [tɜ:n ə'raʊnd]
Umfrage report [rɪ'pɔ:t]
Umgangssprache slang [slæŋ]
umher around [ə'raʊnd]; **im Museum umhergehen** walk round the museum [wɔ:k 'raʊnd]
Umwelt environment [ɪn'vaɪrənmənt]
Umweltverschmutzung pollution [pə'lu:ʃn]
umziehen move [mu:v]; **ihre Familie ist umgezogen** their family has moved [ðeə 'fæmɪli həz 'mu:vd]
unabhängig independent [ɪndɪ'pendənt]
Unabhängigkeit independence [ɪndɪ'pendəns]; **Unabhängigkeitstag der USA** Independence Day [ɪndɪ'pendəns deɪ]
unangenehm unpleasant [ʌn'pleznt]
unbezahlbar priceless ['praɪsles]
und and [ænd]
uneben: irgendwie uneben kinda bumpy = kind of bumpy [kaində 'bʌmpi]
unfair unfair [ʌn'feə]
Unfall accident ['æksɪdənt]
unfreundlich unfriendly [ʌn'frendli]
ungefähr about [ə'baʊt]
Ungeheuer monster ['mɒnstə]
ungeheuer groß enormous [ɪ'nɔ:məs]
unglücklich unhappy [ʌn'hæpi]; unlucky [ʌn'lʌki]
Uniform uniform ['ju:nɪfɔ:m]
Universität university [ju:nɪ'vɜ:səti]
uns us [ʌs]
unscharf fuzzy ['fʌzi]
unser/e our ['aʊə]; **unser Land** this land of ours [ðɪs 'lænd əv 'aʊəz]
unsere(r,s): (Häuser wie) unseres (houses like) ours [aʊəz]
unten below [bɪ'ləʊ]
unter below [bɪ'ləʊ]; under ['ʌndə]; **unter null Grad Celsius** below 0° C = Celsius [bɪ'ləʊ 'zɪərəʊ dɪ'gri:z 'selsiəs]
unterhalb (von) below [bɪ'ləʊ]
unterhalten: sich unterhalten chat [tʃæt]; **sich unterhalten wollen** want a word [wɒnt ə 'wɜ:d]
Unterlagen papers ['peɪpəz]
Unternehmen company ['kʌmpəni]
Unterschied: (Zeit-)Unterschied (time) difference ['taɪm dɪfrəns]
unterschiedlich: aus unterschiedlichen Gründen for different reasons [fə 'dɪfrənt ri:znz]
Untersuchung: (ärztliche) Untersuchung medical ['medɪkl]
unterwegs en route *(Französisch)* [ã 'ʀut]; on the way [ɒn ðə 'weɪ]
Uran uranium [ju'reɪniəm]
Ureinwohner/in: amerikanische/r Ureinwohner/in Native American ['neɪtɪv ə'merɪkən]; **australische Ureinwohner/innen** Aboriginal people [æbə'rɪdʒənl pi:pl]; **Leben der australischen Ureinwohner/innen** Aboriginal life [æbə'rɪdʒənl laɪf]
Ureinwohner/innen aboriginal people [æbə'rɪdʒənl 'pi:pl]
Urkunde certificate [sə'tɪfɪkət]
Urlaub holiday ['hɒlədeɪ]; vacation *(AE)* [və'keɪʃn]; **im Urlaub** on holiday ['hɒlədeɪ]; **in Urlaub gehen/fahren** go on holiday [gəʊ ɒn 'hɒlədeɪ]
Urlaubs- holiday ['hɒlədeɪ]
Urlaubsort resort [rɪ'zɔ:t]
USA USA [ju: es 'eɪ]
USA-Festland continental USA [kɒntɪ'nentl ju: es 'eɪ]

V

Valentinskarte valentine card ['væləntaɪnz kɑ:d]
Vater father ['fɑ:ðə]
Vaterlandsliebe patriot love ['peɪtrɪət lʌv]
Vati dad [dæd]
Verabredung date [deɪt]
verändern change [tʃeɪndʒ]
Veränderung change [tʃeɪndʒ]
verängstigt: verängstigt sein be frightened [bi 'fraɪtnd]
veranstalten organise ['ɔ:gənaɪz]
Verb verb [vɜ:b]
Verbindung link [lɪŋk]; **sich in Verbindung setzen mit** contact ['kɒntækt]
Verbrechen crime [kraɪm]
Verbrecher/in criminal ['krɪmɪnl]; gangster ['gæŋstə]
verbringen: (Zeit) verbringen spend (time) [spend 'taɪm]
verdienen earn [ɜ:n]; **Geld verdienen** make money [meɪk 'mʌni]
verehren admire [əd'maɪə]
Verein club [klʌb]
vereinigt: die Vereinigten Staaten USA [ju: es 'eɪ]; **Vereinigtes Königreich** United Kingdom (UK) [junaɪtɪd 'kɪŋdəm, ju: 'keɪ]
vereint: Vereinte Nationen (UNO) United Nations (UN) [ju:'naɪtɪd 'neɪʃnz, ju: 'en]

Vergangenheit history ['hɪstri]; past [pɑːst]
vergessen forget [fə'get]; **Vergesst/Vergiss nicht!** Don't forget! [dəʊnt fə'get]
Vergleich comparison [kəm'pærɪsən]
vergleiche! make comparisons! ['meɪk kəm'pærɪsənz]
verhaften arrest [ə'rest]
verkaufen sell [sel]
Verkäufer/in shop assistant ['ʃɒp ə'sɪstənt]
Verkehr traffic ['træfɪk]; transport *(no pl.)* ['trænspɔːt]
verknüpfen join [dʒɔɪn]
verlassen leave [liːv]; **das Haus verlassen** leave the house ['liːv ðə haʊs]
verletzen injure ['ɪndʒə]
verletzt hurt [hɜːt]; injured ['ɪndʒəd]
verlieren lose [luːz]
verloren: Verloren im Irrgarten. Lost in the maze. [lɒst ɪn ðə 'meɪz]
vermischen: alles miteinander vermischen mix everything [mɪks]
vermissen miss [mɪs]
vermuten expect [ɪk'spekt]
vernünftig: Sei(d) mal vernünftig! Grow up! [grəʊ 'ʌp]
verpassen miss [mɪs]
verreisen go away [gəʊ ə'weɪ]
verreist away [ə'weɪ]
verrückt: verrückt nach mad about ['mæd əbaʊt]; **verrückt nach Sport** crazy about sport ['kreɪzi əbaʊt 'spɔːt]
verschicken: als E-Mail verschicken email ['iːmeɪl]
verschieden different ['dɪfrənt]
Verschmutzung: (Umwelt-) Verschmutzung pollution [pə'luːʃn]
verschneit snowy ['snəʊi]
verschwinden disappear [dɪsə'pɪə]
verschwommen fuzzy ['fʌzi]
verschwunden gone [gɒn]
verspäten: er verspätet sich he is late [leɪt]; **sich verspäten** run late [rʌn 'leɪt]
Verspätung: Verspätung haben run late [rʌn 'leɪt]
Versprechen promise ['prɒmɪs]; **Versprechen werden manchmal nicht gehalten** promises can be broken ['prɒmɪsəz kæn bi 'brəʊkən]
verstehen understand [ʌndə'stænd]; **sich gut verstehen mit** get on well with [get ɒn 'wel wɪð]
Versuch experiment [ɪk'sperɪmənt]
versuchen try [traɪ]
Vertrag treaty ['triːti]
verursachen cause [kɔːz]
Verwandte/r relative ['relətɪv]
verwenden use [juːz]
verwöhnen spoil [spɔɪl]
Video video ['vɪdiəʊ]
Videoclip video clip ['vɪdiəʊ klɪp]
Video-Podcast video podcast ['vɪdiəʊ 'pɒdkɑːst]
Videorekorder video recorder ['vɪdiəʊ rɪ'kɔːdə]
Videospiel video game ['vɪdiəʊ geɪm]
viel a lot of [ə 'lɒt əv]; lots of ['lɒts əv]; much [mʌtʃ]; **viel Glück** good luck [gʊd 'lʌk]; **wie viel?** how much? [haʊ 'mʌtʃ]; **wie viele?** how many? [haʊ 'meni]; **wir haben viel** we gotta lot of = we've got a lot of *(ugs.)* ['gɒtə 'lɒt əv]
viele a lot of [ə 'lɒt əv]; lots of ['lɒts əv]; many ['meni]
vielleicht maybe ['meɪbi]; perhaps [pə'hæps]
vier four [fɔː]; **vierte(r,s)** fourth (= 4th) [fɔːθ]
Viertel quarter ['kwɔːtə]; **Viertel vor/nach ...** quarter to/past ... ['kwɔːtə tʊ, 'kwɔːtə pɑːst]
vierzehn fourteen [fɔː'tiːn]; **vierzehnte(r,s)** fourteenth [fɔː'tiːnθ]
vierzig forty ['fɔːti]
Visum visa ['viːzə]
Vogel bird [bɜːd]
Voicemail voicemail ['vɔɪsmeɪl]
Volkswirtschaft economy [ɪ'kɒnəmi]
voll: die Nase voll haben be fed up [bi fed 'ʌp]; **voll (mit, von)** full of ['fʊl əv]
Volleyball volleyball ['vɒlibɔːl]
von from [frɒm]; **eine/r von vier(en)** one in four [wʌn ɪn 'fɔː]; **geschrieben von** written by ['rɪtn baɪ]; **von ... bis** from ... till [frəm tɪl]; from ... to [frɒm tʊ]
vor ago [ə'gəʊ]; before [bɪ'fɔː]; in front of [ɪn 'frʌnt əv]; **draußen vor dem Haus** out front [aʊt 'frʌnt]; **Viertel vor ...** quarter to ... ['kwɔːtə tʊ]
vor- pre- [priː]
Voraus: im Voraus in advance [ɪn əd'vɑːns]
vorbei: an ... vorbei past [pɑːst]
vorbeifahren an pass [pɑːs]
Vorhaben plan [plæn]
Vorhang curtain ['kɜːtn]
vormittags a.m. [eɪ'em]
Vorort suburb ['sʌbɜːb]
Vorschrift rule [ruːl]
vorsichtig careful ['keəfl]
vorspielen act [ækt]
vorstellen: ich werde mich vorstellen I'll introduce myself [ɪntrə'djuːs]; **stell dir vor!** guess what! [ges 'wɒt]
Vorstellung idea [aɪ'dɪə]
Vortrag: einen Vortrag halten give a talk [gɪv ə 'tɔːk]
Vorwahl dialling code ['daɪəlɪŋ kəʊd]

W

wach awake [ə'weɪk]
wachsen grow [grəʊ]; rise [raiz]
Wachstum boom [buːm]
Waffe gun [gʌn]; **eine Waffe richten auf** point a gun at [pɔɪnt ə 'gʌn æt]
Wahl choice [tʃɔɪs]
wählen choose [tʃuːz]; select [sɪ'lekt]; vote [vəʊt]
Wahnsinn! Wow! [waʊ]
wahr true [truː]
während during ['djʊərɪŋ]; while [waɪl]
Wahrheit truth [truːθ]
Wal whale [weɪl]
Wald forest ['fɒrəst]; **(kleinerer) Wald** wood [wʊd]
Waliser: (die) Waliser Welsh [welʃ]
walisisch Welsh [welʃ]
Walkman Walkman ['wɔːkmən]
Wanderer/Wanderin hiker ['haɪkə]
wandern hike [haɪk]; **(das) Wandern** backpacking ['bækpækɪŋ]
Wanderschuh boot [buːt]
Wanderweg trail [treɪl]
wann when [wen]; **Wann bist du geboren?** When were you born? ['wen wə ju 'bɔːn]
war was [wɒz]
waren were [wɜː]
Waren goods [gʊdz]
warm warm [wɔːm]
Warnung warning ['wɔːnɪŋ]

[ɒ] dog [ʊ] put [ə] again [eɪ] name [aɪ] time [ɔɪ] boy [əʊ] no [aʊ] house [ɪə] here [eə] chair

warten wait [weɪt]
warum why [waɪ]; **Warum nicht?** Why not? [waɪ]
was: Was für ein/eine ... What a ... ['wɒt ə]; **Was ist ...?** What's ...? [wɒts]; **Was ist denn (los)?** What's the matter? [wɒts ðə 'mætə]; **Was ist los?/ Was geht hier vor?** What's happening? [wɒts 'hæpənɪŋ]; **Was kannst du ...?** What can you ...? [wɒt kən ju]; **Was kostet das?** How much is it? [haʊ 'mʌtʃ ɪz ɪt]; **Was würdest du gern ...?** What would you like ...? ['wɒt wʊd ju laɪk]
waschen wash [wɒʃ]; **sich waschen** have a wash [həv ə 'wɒʃ]
Wasser water ['wɔ:tə]
Wassersport water sports ['wɔ:tə spɔ:ts]
Wasserstelle watering hole ['wɔ:tərɪŋ həʊl]
Webcam webcam ['webkæm]
Webcamera webcam ['webkæm]
Webdesigner/in web designer ['web dɪzaɪnə]
Website website ['websaɪt]
Wechsel change [tʃeɪndʒ]
wechseln change [tʃeɪndʒ]; **ein Wort wechseln wollen** want a word [wɒnt ə 'wɜ:d]
wecken wake [weɪk]; wake up [weɪk 'ʌp]
Wecker alarm clock [ə'lɑ:m klɒk]
weg away [ə'weɪ]; gone [gɒn]
Weg path [pɑ:θ]; **auf dem Weg** en route *(Französisch)* [ã 'ʀut]; on the way [ɒn ðə 'weɪ]; **den Weg kennen** know the way [nəʊ ðə 'weɪ]
wegen because of [bɪ'kɒz əv]
wegschicken send off [send 'ɒf]
Wegwerf- disposable [dɪ'spəʊzəbl]
Weihnachten Christmas ['krɪsməs]
Weihnachtstag: der 1. Weihnachtstag Christmas Day ['krɪsməs deɪ]
weil because [bɪ'kɒz]; 'cause *(ugs.)* [kɔ:z]
Weile while [waɪl]
Wein wine [waɪn]
weinen cry [kraɪ]
Weise way [weɪ]
weiß white [waɪt]
weit far [fɑ:]; **weit entfernt von** a long way from [ə 'lɒŋ weɪ frɒm]
weiter: schrumpft immer weiter keeps on shrinking [ki:ps ɒn 'ʃrɪŋkɪŋ]
weitere other ['ʌðə]; **ein/e weitere(r,s)** another [ə'nʌðə]
welche(r,s) that *(Relativpronomen)* [ðæt]; what [wɒt]; which *(Relativpronomen)* [wɪtʃ]; who *(Relativpronomen)* [hu:]; **welche(r,s) ...?** which ...? [wɪtʃ]
Welpe puppy ['pʌpi]
Welt world [wɜ:ld]
Weltraum space [speɪs]
wenden: (sich) wenden turn [tɜ:n]
wenig: ein wenig a little [ə 'lɪtl]
wenige few [fju:]
weniger less [les]
wenn if [ɪf]; when [wen]
wer who [hu:]; **wer ist** who's (= who is) [hu:z]; **Wer ist es?** Who is it? [hu: 'ɪz ɪt]
Werbeprospekt leaflet ['li:flet]
Werbespruch slogan ['sləʊgən]
werden become [bɪ'kʌm]; will [wɪl]; **werden/wird nicht** won't (= will not) [wəʊnt]; **Wir werden keine Zeit haben.** We won't (= will not) have time. [wi wəʊnt hæv 'taɪm]; **wird sehr schön sein** will be very nice [wɪl bi: verɪ 'naɪs]
werfen throw [θrəʊ]
Werkstatt garage ['gærɑ:ʒ]
Werkzeug tool [tu:l]
wert: sie sind nicht viel wert they don't amount [ə'maunt]
Westen west [west]
westlich western ['westən]
Westliche Braunschlange Western Brown [westən 'braʊn]
Wettbewerb competition [kɒmpə'tɪʃn]
Wette: um die Wette laufen have a race [hæv ə 'reɪs]; race against ['reɪs əgeɪnst]
Wetter weather ['weðə]
Wettkampf match [mætʃ]
Wettlauf race [reɪs]
Whisky whisky ['wɪski]
wichtig important [ɪm'pɔ:tnt]
wie how [haʊ]; like [laɪk]; **(genau)so freundlich wie** as friendly as [æz 'frendli æz]; **(sein/aussehen) wie** be like ['bi: laɪk]; **nicht so beliebt wie ...** not so popular as ... [nɒt səʊ 'popjʊlə æz]; **Wie alt bist du?** How old are you? [haʊ 'əʊld ə ju:]; **Wie geht es dir/ euch/Ihnen?** How are you? [haʊ ə 'ju:]; **Wie geht's?** How are things? *(ugs.)* [həʊ ɑ: 'θɪŋz]; **Wie heißt du?** What's your name? [wɒts jɔ: 'neɪm]; **Wie ist/ war/waren ...?** What is/was/ were ... like? [wɒt ɪz, wəz, wɜ: 'laɪk]; **Wie läuft's?** How are things? *(ugs.)* [həʊ ɑ: 'θɪŋz]; **Wie spät ist es?** What time is it? [wɑt 'taɪm ɪz ɪt]; **wie viel?** how much? [haʊ 'mʌtʃ]; **wie viele?** how many? [haʊ 'meni]; **Wie wäre es mit ...?** What about ...? [wɒt ə'baʊt]; **wie wär's mit ...?** how about ...? [haʊ ə'baʊt]
Wie bitte? Pardon? ['pɑ:dən]
wieder again [ə'gen]; **immer und immer wieder** over and over again ['əʊvə ənd əʊvə ə'gen]
Wiese field [fi:ld]
wild wild [waɪld]
Wildhund: australischer Wildhund dingo ['dɪŋgəʊ]
Wildnis backcountry ['bækkʌntri]; wilderness ['wɪldənəs]
willkommen: willkommen heißen welcome ['welkəm]; **Willkommen!** Welcome! ['welkəm]
Wind wind [wɪnd]
windig windy ['wɪndi]
Winter winter ['wɪntə]
wir we [wi:]; **wir sind** we're (= we are) [wɪə]
wirklich real [rɪəl]; really ['rɪəli]
Wirkung impact ['ɪmpækt]
Wirtschaft: (Volks-)Wirtschaft economy [ɪ'kɒnəmi]
wissen know [nəʊ]
Wissenschaft: (Natur-)Wissenschaft science ['saɪəns]
Wissenschaftler/in scientist ['saɪəntɪst]
Witz joke [dʒəʊk]
witzig funny ['fʌni]
wo where [weə]; **Wo kommst du her?** Where are you from? [weə ə ju: 'frɒm]

[ʊə] **sure** [b] **bike** [p] **pen** [d] **day** [t] **ten** [k] **book** [g] **go** [ŋ] **morning** [l] **like** [r] **ruler**

Woche week [wi:k]
Wochenende weekend [wi:k'end]
Wochentag weekday ['wi:kdeɪ]
wohlhabend wealthy ['welθi]
wohltätig: wohltätige Zwecke charity ['tʃærəti]
Wohltätigkeit: Wohltätigkeit(sorganisation) charity ['tʃærəti]
wohnen live [lɪv]; **Wohnt dein Cousin/deine Kusine ...?** Does your cousin live...? [dʌz jʊə kʌzn 'lɪv]
Wohnung apartment *(AE)* [ə'pɑ:tmənt]; flat [flæt]
Wohnwagen-Campingplatz caravan park ['kærəvæn pɑ:k]
Wohnzimmer living room ['lɪvɪŋru:m]
Wolkenkratzer skyscraper ['skaɪskreɪpə]
wolkig cloudy ['klaʊdi]
wollen want [wɒnt]
Wort word [wɜ:d]; **ein Wort fehlt** one word is missing [wʌn wɜ:d ɪz 'mɪsɪŋ]; **ein Wort wechseln wollen** want a word [wɒnt ə 'wɜ:d]
Wörterbuch dictionary ['dɪkʃənri]
wunderbar terrific [tə'rɪfɪk]
wunderschön beautiful ['bju:tɪfəl]; lovely ['lʌvli]
wünschen: Ich wünschte, du wärst hier. Wish you were here. ['wɪʃ ju wə hɪə]
würde: es würde dauern it would take [ɪt wʊd 'teɪk]; **Was würdest du gern ...?** What would you like ...? ['wɒt wʊd ju laɪk]
Wurst sausage ['sɒsɪdʒ]
Würstchen sausage ['sɒsɪdʒ]
wütend angry ['æŋgri]

X

XL XL (= extra large) *(Kleidung)* [eks 'el]

Y

Yoga yoga ['jəʊgə]

Z

Zahl number ['nʌmbə]
zählen count [kaʊnt]
zahlen für pay for ['peɪ fə]
Zähne teeth [ti:θ]
Zaubershow magic show ['mædʒɪk ʃəʊ]
Zaun fence [fens]
zehn ten [ten]; **zehnte(r,s)** tenth ['tenθ]
Zeichen signal ['sɪgnəl]
zeigen show [ʃəʊ]; **Zeig(t) es mir bitte.** Show me, please. ['ʃəʊ mi pli:z]
Zeit time [taɪm]; **schöne Zeit des Zusammenseins** quality time ['kwɒləti taɪm]; **Wir werden keine Zeit haben.** We won't (= will not) have time. [wi wəʊnt hæv 'taɪm]; **Zeit haben** have time [həv 'taɪm]
Zeit verbringen spend time [spend 'taɪm]
Zeitplan schedule ['ʃedju:l]
Zeitraum period ['pɪəriəd]
Zeitschrift mag *(ugs.)* [mæg]; magazine [mægə'zi:n]
Zeitung newspaper ['nju:zpeɪpə]
Zeitungsartikel article ['ɑ:tɪkl]
Zeitzone time zone ['taɪm zəʊn]
Zelt tent [tent]; **aufstellen (Zelt)** pitch [pɪtʃ]; **ein Zelt aufbauen** put up a tent ['pʊt ʌp ə 'tent]
zelten camp [kæmp]
Zeltlager camp [kæmp]
zentral central ['sentrəl]
Zentral- central ['sentrəl]
Zentrum center *(AE)* ['sentə]; centre ['sentə]
zerbrechen break [breɪk]
zerbrochen broken ['brəʊkən]
Zeremonie ceremony ['serəməni]
Zeug junk [dʒʌŋk]
ziehen: (um)ziehen move [mu:v]
ziemlich pretty ['prɪti]; quite [kwaɪt]
Zimmer room [ru:m]; **Zimmer mit Frühstück** Bed & Breakfast (B&B) [bed ənd 'brekfəst]
zirka: (um) zirka at about [æt ə'baʊt]
Zoo zoo [zu:]
zu closed [kləʊzd]; to [tu]; too [tu:]; **(um) zu** to [tu]; **bei ... zu Hause** at ... house [ət haʊs]; **zu Hause** at home [ət 'həʊm]; **zu kurz** too short [tu: 'ʃɔ:t]; **zu teuer** too expensive [tu: ɪk'spensɪv]
Zu- und Aussteigen: (Busverbindung) zum Zu- und Aussteigen hop-on hop-off (bus service) [hɒp ɒn hɒp 'ɒf]
Zucker sugar ['ʃʊgə]
zuerst at first [ət 'fɜ:st]; first [fɜ:st]
zufügen: Schaden zufügen harm [hɑ:m]
Zug train [treɪn]; **im Zug** on the train [ɒn ðə 'treɪn]
Zuhause home [həʊm]
zuhören listen (to) ['lɪsn tə]; **viel Spaß beim Zuhören!** happy listening! [hæpi 'lɪsnɪŋ]
Zukunft future ['fju:tʃə]
zulächeln smile at ['smaɪl ət]
zumachen close [kləʊz]
zurück back [bæk]
zurückfinden get back [get 'bæk]
zurückkommen get back [get 'bæk]
zusammen together [tə'geðə]
Zusammensein: schöne Zeit des Zusammenseins quality time ['kwɒləti taɪm]
zusammensetzen put together [pʊt tə'geðə]
zusätzlich: zusätzliches (Taschengeld) extra (pocket money) ['ekstrə]
zuschauen watch [wɒtʃ]
zustimmen agree [ə'gri:]
zuwinken: ihm zuwinken wave at him ['weɪv ət hɪm]
zwanzig twenty ['twenti]; **zwanzigste(r,s)** twentieth ['twentiəθ]
zwei two [tu:]; **zweite(r,s) (= 2nd)** second ['sekənd]
zweimal twice [twaɪs]
Zwiebel onion ['ʌnjən]
zwischen between [bɪ'twi:n]
zwölf twelve [twelv]; **zwölfte(r,s)** twelfth [twelθ]

[v] seven [w] we [s] six [z] his [ʃ] she [tʃ] teacher [dʒ] jeans [j] yes [θ] thing [ð] the [i:]

LIST OF NAMES

GIRLS/WOMEN

Amber	['æmbə]
Amy	['eɪmi]
Angela	['ændʒələ]
Anna	['ænə]
Annie	['æni]
Beth	[beθ]
Carla	['kɑ:lə]
Carmen	['kɑ:men]
Carol	['kærəl]
Cathy	['kæθi]
Chris	[krɪs]
Chubi	['tʃu:bi]
Corrie	['kɒri]
Donna	['dɒnə]
Ella	['elə]
Ellie	['eli]
Emma	['emə]
Fi	[fi:]
Fiona	[fɪ'əʊnə]
Funani	[fʊ'nɑ:ni]
Gemma	['dʒemə]
Holly	['hɒli]
Jane	[dʒeɪn]
Jenny	['dʒeni]
Jessica	['dʒesɪkə]
Jill	[dʒɪl]
Kate	[keɪt]
Kelly	['keli]
Kylie	['kaɪli]
Laurie	['lɒri]
Linda	['lɪndə]
Lisa	['li:sə]
Liv	[lɪv]
Lucy	['lu:si]
Mallory	['mæləri]
Marie	[mə'ri:]
Meg	[meg]
Megan	['megən]
Molly	['mɒli]
Pat	[pæt]
Rina	['ri:nə]
Sally	['sæli]
Sarah	['seərə]
Sue	[su:]
Sunaina	[sʊ'naɪnə]
Tina	['ti:nə]
Trish	[trɪʃ]

BOYS/MEN

Adam	['ædəm]
Alan	['ælən]
Alex	['ælɪks]
Ben	[ben]
Bob	[bɒb]
Brad	[bræd]
Bruce	[bru:s]
Brucie	['bru:si]
Carl	[kɑ:l]
Dan	[dæn]
Daniel	['dænjəl]
Dave	[deɪv]
David	['deɪvɪd]
Dean	[di:n]
Del	[del]
Delani	[də'lɑ:ni]
Derek	['derik]
Dilip	['dɪlɪp]
Donald	['dɒnld]
Duncan	['dʌŋkən]
Ernest	['ɜ:nəst]
Gareth	['gærəθ]
Gary	['gæri]
Gavin	['gævɪn]
Geoff	[dʒef]
Greg	[greg]
Homer	['həʊmə]
Jack	[dʒæk]
Jake	[djeɪk]
Jason	['dʒeɪsn]
Jassim	['dʒʌsɪm]
Jerry	['dʒeri]
Jim	[dʒɪm]
Jo	[dʒəʊ]
John	[dʒɒn]
Kevin	['kevɪn]
Lachlan	['lɒklən, 'læklən]
Liam	['li:əm]
Matt	[mæt]
Mike	[maɪk]
Paul	[pɔ:l]
Peter	['pi:tə]
Pierre	[pɪ'eə]
Raoul	[raʊ'u:l, rɑ:'u:l]
Robyn	['rɒbɪn]
Ryan	['raɪən]
Sam	[sæm]
Simon	['saɪmən]
Steve	[sti:v]
Tom	[tɒm]

FAMILIES

Ali	['æli, 'ɑ:li]
Androssof	['ændrɒsɒf]
Bulkeley	['bʌlkəli]
Davis	['deɪvɪs]
Dunbar	[dʌn'bɑ:]
Goodway	['gʊdweɪ]
Green	[gri:n]
Grove	[grəʊv]
Haas	[hɑ:s, hæs]
Hale	[heɪl]
Handke	['hændkə]
Hill	[hɪl]
Holmes	[həʊmz]
Johnston	['dʒɒnstən]
Lee	[li:]
Marsden	['mɑ:zdn]
Maxwell	['mækswel]
McCarthy	[mə'kɑ:θi]
Mills	[mɪlz]
Pemmann	['pemæn]
Peters	['pi:təz]
Popescu	[pə'pesku]
Sampson	['sæmpsən]
Steel	[sti:l]
Wei	[weɪ]
Wilson	['wɪlsn]

PLACES AND SIGHTS

Adelaide	['ædəleɪd]
Alaska	[ə'læskə]
Alberta	[æl'bɜ:tə]
Alice Springs	[ælɪs 'spɪŋz]
Asia	['eɪʃə, 'eɪʒə]
Australia	[ɒ'streɪlɪə]
Bedford	['bedfəd]
Berlin	[bɜ:'lɪn]
Brisbane	['brɪzbən]
Broome	[bru:m]
Cairns	[keənz]
Calgary	['kælgəri]
Canada	['kænədə]
Canberra	['kænbərə]
Cape Town	['keɪp taʊn]
China	['tʃaɪnə]
Churchill	['tʃɜ:tʃɪl]
Darwin	['dɑ:wɪn]
Dawson City	['dɔ:sn sɪti]
Drumheller	[drʌm'helə]
Edmonton	['edməntən]
Florida	['flɒrədə]
Fraser Island	['freɪzə 'aɪlənd]
Glasgow	['glɑzgəʊ]
Grove Street	['grəʊv stri:t]
Hell	[hel]
Hobart	['həʊbɑ:t]
Holland	['hɒlənd]
Hudson Bay	['hʌdsn beɪ]
India	['ɪndɪə]
Iqaluit	[ɪ'kælʊɪt]
Iraq	[ɪ'rɑ:k]
Israel	['ɪzreɪəl]
Italy	['ɪtəli]
Jakarta	[dʒə'kɑ:tə]

Johannesburg, Joburg	[dʒəʊ'hænəzbɜ:g , 'dʒəʊbɜ:g]
Kalgoorlie	[kæl'gʊəli]
Kedron	['kedrən]
Kingsford Smith Airport	[kɪŋzfəd 'smɪθ eəpɔ:t]
Korea	[kə'rɪə]
Kruger Park	['kru:gə pɑ:k]
Lachine	[lə'ʃi:n]
Lake Erie	[leɪk 'ɪəri]
Lake Superior	[leɪk su:'pɪərɪə]
Launceston	['lɔ:nstən, 'lɑ:nstən]
Laverton	['lævətən]
London	['lʌndən]
Los Angeles	[lɒs 'ændʒəli:z]
Malaysia	[məleɪzɪə, mə'leɪʃə]
Manly	['mænli]
Melbourne	['melbən, 'melbɔ:n]
Mexico	['meksəkəʊ]
Montreal	[mɒntrɪ'ɔ:l]
Mullaloo	[mʌlə'lu:]
Munich	['mju:nɪk]
New York	[nju: 'jɔ:k]
Newfoundland	[nju:'faʊndlənd, 'nju:fndlənd]
Nunavut	['nʊnəvʊt]
Ontario	[ɒn'teərɪəʊ]
Ottawa	['ɒtəwə]
Perth	[pɜ:θ]
the Prairies	[ðə 'preəriz]
Quebec	[kwə'bek]
Queensland	['kwi:nzlənd]
Robben Island	[rɒbən 'aɪlənd]
the Rocky Mountains, the Rockies	[ðə rɒkɪ 'maʊntənz, ðə 'rɒkɪz]
Romania	[ru:'meɪnɪə]
Saskatoon	[sæskə'tu:n]
Singapore	[sɪŋgə'pɔ:]
Somalia	[sə'mɑ:lɪə]
South Africa	[saʊθ 'æfrəkə]
Soweto	[sə'wetəʊ]
Squamish	['skwɑ:mɪʃ]
St. Lawrence River	[sənt 'lɒrəns rɪvə]
Sunshine Coast	['sʌnʃaɪn kəʊst]
Sydney	['sɪdni]
Tailor's (= Tailor's Stitch)	['teɪləz, teɪləz 'stɪtʃ]
Tasmania	[tæz'meɪnɪə]
Toronto	[tə'rɒntəʊ]
Townsville	['taʊnzvɪl]
Vancouver	[væn'ku:və]
Victoria	[vɪk'tɔ:rɪə]
Uluru	[u:lʊ'ru:]
Warburton	['wɔ:bətən]
Wellington	['welɪŋtən]
Whistler	['wɪslə]
Whitsunday	[wɪt'sʌndeɪ]
Wirrawee	['wɪrəwi]
Yukon	['ju:kɒn]

FAMOUS PEOPLE

Arthur Mafokate	['ɑ:θə mafəʊ'kɑ:te]
Bryan Adams	[braɪən 'ædəmz]
Celine Dion	[sə'li:n di:ɔ̃]
David Beckham	[deɪvɪd 'bekəm]
Étienne Brûlé	[etɪ'en bru:'leɪ]
Frederik Willem de Klerk	['fredərɪk wɪləm də 'kleək]
Hillary Clinton	[hɪləri 'klɪntən]
James Cook	[dʒeɪmz 'kʊk]
John Marsden	[dʒɒn 'mɑ:zdən]
Keanu Reeves	[ki'ɑ:nu 'ri:vz]
Naomi Klein	[neɪ'əʊmi 'klaɪn]
Nelly Furtado	[neli fɜ'tɑ:dəʊ]
Nelson Mandela	[nelsn mæn'delə]
Orlando Bloom	[ɔ:'lændəʊ 'blu:m]
Paul Hogan	[pɔ:l 'həʊgən]
Samuel de Champlain	['sæmjɪəl də ʃæm'pleɪn]
Steve Irwin	[sti:v 'ɜ:wɪn]

OTHER NAMES

The Arrogant Worms	[ði 'ærəgənt 'wɜ:mz]
Barenaked Ladies	[beəneɪkəd 'leɪdɪz]
Baz Bus	['bæz bʌs]
Brownlove	['braʊnlʌv]
Canucks	[kə'nʌks]
Cool Clothes	[ku:l 'kləʊðz]
Crocodile Dundee	['krɒkədaɪl dʌn'di:]
Dash	[dæʃ]
Eskimo	['eskəməʊ]
Flash Cars	['flæʃ 'kɑ:z]
Fruity	['fru:ti]
Ghan	[gɑ:n]
Highway 99	['haɪweɪ naɪnti 'naɪn]
the Huron people	[ðə 'hjʊərɒn pi:pl]
the Iroquois people	[ðə 'ɪrəkwɔɪ pi:pl]
John Sears Coffee	[dʒɒn 'sɪəz 'kɒfi]
Kwaito	['kweɪtəʊ]
the Mounties (= Royal Canadian Mounted Police)	[ðə 'maʊntɪz]
Oscar	['ɒskə]
Radio YFM	[reɪdɪəʊ waɪ ef 'em]
Rocky Hotel	['rɒkɪ həʊ'tel]
skidoo	[skɪ'du:]
Stars beauticians	['stɑ:z bju:'tɪʃnz]
Teen magazine	['ti:n mægə'zi:n]
Three Dead Trolls in a Baggie	['θri: ded trɒlz ɪn ə 'bægi]
Yothu Yindi	['jɒtʊ 'jɪndi]
Zulu	['zu:lu:]

Wichtige Wörter zur Grammatik

Grammatical terms	Grammatische Begriffe	Beispiele
noun	Nomen (Substantiv)	*car, town, school, sister, dog*
singular	Singular (Einzahl)	*a car, a school, a sister, a dog*
plural	Plural (Mehrzahl)	*some cars, a lot of schools*
verb	Verb (Tätigkeitswort)	*have, eat, goes, went*
infinitive	Infinitiv (Grundform)	*have, eat, go*
regular verb	regelmäßiges Verb	*repair → repaired*
irregular verb	unregelmäßiges Verb	*make → made*
modal verb	modales Hilfsverb	*must, have to, should*
article	Artikel (Begleiter)	*the, a/an*
adjective	Adjektiv (Eigenschaftswort)	*easy, small, big, quiet, good*
adverb	Adverb (Umstandswort)	*often, never, today, there*
preposition	Präposition (Verhältniswort)	*after, before, at, next to*
personal pronoun	Personalpronomen	*I, you, he, she, it, we, they*
reflexive pronoun	Reflexivpronomen	*myself, yourself, ourselves*
conjunction	Konjunktion (Bindewort)	*and, but, so, because, when*

sentence	Satz	*I have a big car.*
question	Frage	*Do you have a car?* *Where did you buy your car?*
answer	Antwort	*Yes, I have. I bought it in Spain.*
phrase	Satzteil	*last year, at school*
word order	Wortstellung	
relative clause	Relativsatz	*This is the boy who I met.* *The jeans which you bought are great.* *I like the poster that you painted.*
comparison	Steigerung	*younger – youngest* *more careful – most careful*

tense	Zeitform	
simple past	Präteritum (einfache Vergangenheit)	*He did his homework.*
simple present	Präsens (einfache Gegenwart)	*He does his homework every day.*
present perfect	Perfekt (vollendete Vergangenheit)	*He has just done his homework.*
present progressive	Verlaufsform der Gegenwart	*He's doing his homework now.*
will-future	Futur	*He'll do his homework after school.*

IN ENGLISH

SOUNDS

[i:]	meet, team, he
[ɑ:]	answer, class, car
[ɔ:]	or, ball, door
[u:]	ruler, blue, too
[ɜ:]	girl, word, her
[i]	radio, video, sorry
[u]	July, February
[ɪ]	in, milk, big
[e]	empty, yes, bed
[æ]	cat, black
[ʌ]	bus, come
[ɒ]	on, dog, what
[ʊ]	put, good, woman
[ə]	again, today, sister
[eɪ]	eight, name, play
[aɪ]	I, time, my
[ɔɪ]	boy, toilet
[əʊ]	old, no, road
[aʊ]	house, now
[ɪə]	near, here, we're
[eə]	there, chair
[ʊə]	you're, sure
[b]	bike, hobby, job
[p]	pen, pupil, shop
[d]	day, window, good
[t]	ten, football, at
[k]	car, lucky, book
[g]	go, again, bag
[ŋ]	wrong, morning
[l]	like, old, small
[r]	ruler, friend, biro
[v]	very, seven, have
[w]	we, swim
[s]	six, poster, yes
[z]	zoo, visit, his
[ʃ]	she, action, English
[tʃ]	child, teacher, match
[dʒ]	jeans, German, badge
[j]	yes, you, young
[θ]	thing, maths, month
[ð]	the, father, with

ORDINAL NUMBERS

1st	**first**	[fɜ:st]
2nd	**second**	['sekənd]
3rd	**third**	[θɜ:d]
4th	**fourth**	[fɔ:θ]
5th	**fifth**	[fɪfθ]
6th	**sixth**	[sɪksθ]
7th	**seventh**	['sevnθ]
8th	**eighth**	[eɪtθ]
9th	**ninth**	[naɪnθ]
10th	**tenth**	[tenθ]
11th	**eleventh**	[ɪ'levnθ]
12th	**twelfth**	[twelfθ]
13th	**thirteenth**	[θɜ:'ti:nθ]
14th	**fourteenth**	[fɔ:'ti:nθ]
15th	**fifteenth**	[fɪf'ti:nθ]
16th	**sixteenth**	[sɪks'ti:nθ]
17th	**seventeenth**	[sevn'ti:nθ]
18th	**eighteenth**	[eɪ'ti:nθ]
19th	**nineteenth**	[naɪn'ti:nθ]
20th	**twentieth**	['twentiəθ]
21st	**twenty-first**	[twenti'fɜ:st]
22nd	**twenty-second**	[twenti'sekənd]
23rd	**twenty-third**	[twenti'θɜ:d]
24th	**twenty-fourth**	[twenti'fɔ:θ]
25th	**twenty-fifth**	[twenti'fɪfθ]
26th	**twenty-sixth**	[twenti'sɪksθ]
27th	**twenty-seventh**	[twenti'sevnθ]
28th	**twenty-eighth**	[twenti'eɪtθ]
29th	**twenty-ninth**	[twenti'naɪnθ]
30th	**thirtieth**	['θɜ:tiəθ]

DECIMAL NUMBERS

Immer ein Punkt – kein Komma:

3.5 = three **point** five
15.75 = fifteen **point** seven five

THE YEAR

1999 = nineteen ninety-nine
2000 = two thousand
2001 = two thousand **and** one
2002 = two thousand **and** two

ALPHABET

a	[eɪ]
b	[bi:]
c	[si:]
d	[di:]
e	[i:]
f	[ef]
g	[dʒi:]
h	[eɪtʃ]
i	[aɪ]
j	[dʒeɪ]
k	[keɪ]
l	[el]
m	[em]
n	[en]
o	[əʊ]
p	[pi:]
q	[kju:]
r	[ɑ:]
s	[es]
t	[ti:]
u	[ju:]
v	[vi:]
w	['dʌblju:]
x	[eks]
y	[waɪ]
z	[zed]

PARTS OF THINGS

half

a third
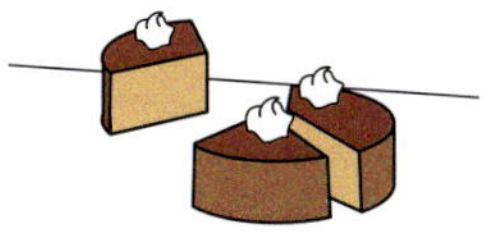

a quarter
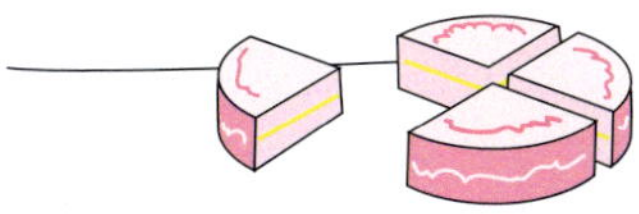

a fifth

You and your teacher

Sorry, I'm late.	Entschuldigung, dass ich zu spät komme.
Sorry, I've forgotten my book.	Entschuldigung, ich habe mein Buch vergessen.
I haven't done my homework.	Ich habe meine Hausaufgaben nicht gemacht.
Can I go to the toilet, please?	Darf ich bitte zur Toilette gehen?
Can I open/close the window, please?	Kann ich bitte das Fenster öffnen/schließen?

You need help

Can you help me, please?	Können Sie mir bitte helfen?
Can you write it on the board, please?	Können Sie es bitte an die Tafel schreiben?
Can you explain it to me, please?	Können Sie es mir bitte erkären?
Can you spell "...", please?	Können Sie bitte „..." buchstabieren?
Sorry, I can't find it. What page?	Entschuldigung, ich kann es nicht finden. Auf welcher Seite?
Which line/paragraph, please?	Welche Zeile / Welcher Absatz, bitte?
Can you say that again, please?	Können Sie das bitte wiederholen?
Can you speak louder, please?	Können Sie bitte lauter sprechen?
Can we listen to it again, please?	Könnten wir es noch einmal hören?
What's "..." in English / in German?	Was heißt „..." auf Englisch / auf Deutsch?
Is "..." the right word for ...?	Ist „..." das richtige Wort für ...?
Can I say it in German?	Kann ich es auf Deutsch sagen?

Homework and exercises

Can we work together, please?	Können wir bitte zusammen arbeiten?
Can we make notes?	Können wir uns Notizen machen?
Can I read the next sentence?	Kann ich den nächsten Satz lesen?
Can we act the dialogue?	Können wir den Dialog spielen?
Can I borrow your ruler/pencil/..., please?	Kann ich mir bitte dein Lineal / deinen Bleistift / ... ausleihen?
I can't do number 3.	Ich kann Nummer 3 nicht lösen.
I don't understand this exercise.	Ich verstehe diese Übung nicht.
I don't know. / I'm not sure.	Ich weiß es nicht. / Ich bin nicht sicher.
Pardon?	Wie bitte?
Is this right?	Ist das richtig?
Sorry, I haven't finished.	Entschuldigung, ich bin noch nicht fertig.
What's the homework?	Was haben wir (als Hausaufgabe) auf?
It's my turn.	Ich bin an der Reihe.
Can I take ...'s part, please?	Kann ich bitte ...s Teil/Rolle übernehmen?

Unregelmäßige Verben / Irregular verbs

Infinitive	Simple past	Present perfect	
be [bi:]	I **was**, you **were** [wɒz/wɜ:]	I've **been** [aɪv bi:n]	sein
become [bɪ'kʌm]	I **became** [bɪ'keɪm]	I've **become** [bɪ'kʌm]	werden
begin [bɪ'gɪn]	I **began** [bɪ'gæn]	I've **begun** [bɪ'gʌn]	beginnen
break [breɪk]	I **broke** [brəʊk]	I've **broken** ['brəʊkn]	(zer)brechen, kaputtmachen
bring [brɪŋ]	I **brought** [brɔ:t]	I've **brought** [brɔ:t]	bringen, mitbringen
buy [baɪ]	I **bought** [bɔ:t]	I've **bought** [bɔ:t]	kaufen
catch [kætʃ]	I **caught** [kɔ:t]	I've **caught** [kɔ:t]	fangen, erwischen
choose [tʃu:z]	I **chose** [tʃəʊz]	I've **chosen** ['tʃəʊzn]	(aus)wählen
come [kʌm]	I **came** [keɪm]	I've **come** [kʌm]	kommen
cost [kɒst]	I **cost** [kɒst]	I've **cost** [kɒst]	kosten
cut [kʌt]	I **cut** [kʌt]	I've **cut** [kʌt]	schneiden
do [du:]	I **did** [dɪd]	I've **done** [dʌn]	tun, machen
draw [drɔ:]	I **drew** [dru:]	I've **drawn** [drɔ:n]	zeichnen
drink [drɪŋk]	I **drank** [dræŋk]	I've **drunk** [drʌŋk]	trinken
drive [draɪv]	I **drove** [drəʊv]	I've **driven** ['drɪvn]	fahren
eat [i:t]	I **ate** [eɪt]	I've **eaten** ['i:tn]	essen
fall [fɔ:l]	I **fell** [fel]	I've **fallen** ['fɔ:lən]	fallen, stürzen
feed [fi:d]	I **fed** [fed]	I've **fed** [fed]	füttern, zu fressen geben
feel [fi:l]	I **felt** [felt]	I've **felt** [felt]	(sich) fühlen, sich anfühlen
find [faɪnd]	I **found** [faʊnd]	I've **found** [faʊnd]	finden
fly [flaɪ]	I **flew** [flu:]	I've **flown** [fləʊn]	fliegen
forget [fə'get]	I **forgot** [fə'gɒt]	I've **forgotten** [fə'gɒtn]	vergessen
get [get]	I **got** [gɒt]	I've **got** [gɒt]	holen, bekommen, erreichen
give [gɪv]	I **gave** [geɪv]	I've **given** ['gɪvn]	geben
go [gəʊ]	I **went** [went]	I've **gone** [gɒn]	gehen, fahren
grow [grəʊ]	I **grew** [gru:]	I've **grown** [grəʊn]	anbauen, wachsen
hang [hæŋ]	I **hung** [hʌŋ]	I've **hung** [hʌŋ]	hängen, aufhängen
have [hæv]	I **had** [hæd]	I've **had** [hæd]	haben, essen, trinken
hear [hɪə]	I **heard** [hɜ:d]	I've **heard** [hɜ:d]	hören
hit [hɪt]	I **hit** [hɪt]	I've **hit** [hɪt]	treffen, schlagen, stoßen
hold [həʊld]	I **held** [held]	I've **held** [held]	(fest)halten
hurt [hɜ:t]	I **hurt** [hɜ:t]	I've **hurt** [hɜ:t]	schmerzen
know [nəʊ]	I **knew** [nju:]	I've **known** [nəʊn]	kennen, wissen
leave [li:v]	I **left** [left]	I've **left** [left]	(stehen) lassen, verlassen, abfahren
lend [lend]	I **lent** [lent]	I've **lent** [lent]	leihen
let [let]	I **let** [let]	I've **let** [let]	lassen
lie [laɪ]	I **lay** [leɪ]	I've **lain** [leɪn]	liegen
lose [lu:z]	I **lost** [lɒst]	I've **lost** [lɒst]	verlieren

Infinitive	Simple past	Present perfect	
make [meɪk]	I **made** [meɪd]	I've **made** [meɪd]	machen
mean [mi:n]	I **meant** [ment]	I've **meant** [ment]	bedeuten, meinen
meet [mi:t]	I **met** [met]	I've **met** [met]	treffen (mit)
pay [peɪ]	I **paid** [peɪd]	I've **paid** [peɪd]	(be)zahlen
put [pʊt]	I **put** [pʊt]	I've **put** [pʊt]	setzen, stellen, legen
read [ri:d]	I **read** [red]	I've **read** [red]	lesen
ride [raɪd]	I **rode** [rəʊd]	I've **ridden** ['rɪdn]	reiten, fahren
ring [rɪŋ]	I **rang** [ræŋ]	I've **rung** [rʌŋ]	klingeln
run [rʌn]	I **ran** [ræn]	I've **run** [rʌn]	rennen, laufen
say [seɪ]	I **said** [sed]	I've **said** [sed]	sagen
see [si:]	I **saw** [sɔ:]	I've **seen** [si:n]	sehen
sell [sel]	I **sold** [səʊld]	I've **sold** [səʊld]	verkaufen
send [send]	I **sent** [sent]	I've **sent** [sent]	senden, schicken
shine [ʃaɪn]	I **shone** [ʃɒn]	I've **shone** [ʃɒn]	scheinen
show [ʃəʊ]	I **showed** [ʃəʊd]	I've **shown** [ʃəʊn]	zeigen
sing [sɪŋ]	I **sang** [sæŋ]	I've **sung** [sʌŋ]	singen
sit [sɪt]	I **sat** [sæt]	I've **sat** [sæt]	sitzen, sich setzen
sleep [sli:p]	I **slept** [slept]	I've **slept** [slept]	schlafen
speak [spi:k]	I **spoke** [spəʊk]	I've **spoken** ['spəʊkn]	sprechen
speed [spi:d]	I **sped** [sped]	I've **sped** [sped]	rasen, schnell fahren
spend [spend]	I **spent** [spent]	I've **spent** [spent]	(Zeit) verbringen, (Geld) ausgeben
stand [stænd]	I **stood** [stʊd]	I've **stood** [stʊd]	stehen
steal [sti:l]	I **stole** [stəʊl]	I've **stolen** ['stəʊlən]	stehlen
stick [stɪk]	I **stuck** [stʌk]	I've **stuck** [stʌk]	kleben
swim [swɪm]	I **swam** [swæm]	I've **swum** [swʌm]	schwimmen
take [teɪk]	I **took** [tʊk]	I've **taken** ['teɪkən]	nehmen, hinfahren, dauern
tell [tel]	I **told** [təʊld]	I've **told** [təʊld]	erzählen, berichten
think [θɪŋk]	I **thought** [θɔ:t]	I've **thought** [θɔ:t]	denken, glauben
understand [ʌndə'stænd]	I **understood** [ʌndə'stʊd]	I've **understood** [ʌndə'stʊd]	verstehen
wake [weɪk]	I **woke** [wəʊk]	I've **woken** ['wəʊkn]	wecken
wear [weə]	I **wore** [wɔ:]	I've **worn** [wɔ:n]	tragen, anhaben *(Kleidung)*
win [wɪn]	I **won** [wʌn]	I've **won** [wʌn]	gewinnen
write [raɪt]	I **wrote** [rəʊt]	I've **written** ['rɪtn]	schreiben

BILDQUELLEN

Inhalt **Alamy**, Abington, UK (S. 8 *Apartheid Museum*: Julius Lando; S. 20 Robert: Travelshots.com; S. 22 *Quebec*: Stock Connection Blue; S. 23 *Furtado*: Content Mine International; S. 23 *Reeves*: Allstar Picture Library; S. 25 o.: Megapress; S. 25 u.: Bryan & Cherry Alexander Photography; S. 26 *part three*: Danita Delimont; S. 29 *Drumheller* (4): Robert McGouey; S. 30 *Rodeo*: Bill Brooks; S. 30 *Inuk*: Bryan & Cherry Alexander Photography; S. 38 D: Reimar; S. 39 *snowboarding*: Dan Galic; S. 41 3.2 re.: Stockbyte; S. 41 3.3: Manor Photography; S. 41 3.6: LOOK Die Bildagentur der Fotografen GmbH; S. 52 *didgeridoo*: Photocritic.org; S. 54 M.: Mary Evans Picture Library; S. 55 o. li.: WorldFoto; S. 56 *didgeridoo*: music Alan King; S. 57 *painting*: Michel Friang; S. 71 M.: Bill Bachman; S. 71 u.: Edd Westmacott; S. 90 *Ella*: tbkmedia.de); **Alinari Archives**, Florenz (S. 54 o.); **Associated Press**, Frankfurt/M (S. 20 u.: Peter Magubane; S. 21 *Free South Africa*: Martin Cleaver; S. 21 u.: Jon Eeg; S. 37 li.: Aaron Harris); **The Arrogant Worms**, Kanada (S. 37 re.); **Backpacking South Africa** (S. 13 o.); **Bank of Canada/Banque du Canada** (S. 23: Gord Carter); **Barunga Statement 1988**, Australien (S. 67 u.: YUNUPINGU, Galarrwuy, RUBUNTJA, Wenten, JAMPIJINPA, Lindsay Turner, JAPANANGKA, Dennis Williams, MARAWILI, Bakulangay, MARAWILI, Djambawa, MARAWILI, Marrirra, NGURRUWUTHUN, Djewiny, reproduced with the permission of the Northern and Central Land Councils. Gifts Collection, courtesy of Parliament House Art Collection, Department of Parliamentary Services, Canberra A.C.T.); **Baz Bus**, Südafrika (S. 13 u.); **Jutta Brendemühl**, Toronto (S. 50, 51 u.); **BridgeClimb** (S. 55: OTTTO Holdings (Aust.) Pty Ltd trading as BridgeClimb); Courtesy of **The Cancer Council Australia** (S. 71); **Cinetext Bild- und Textarchiv**, Frankfurt/M (S. 92: Paramount Pictures); **Richard D. Comely** (S. 36 Captain Canuck ®. Used with permission); **Corbis**, Düsseldorf (S. 8 u. li.: Gideon Mendel; S. 20-21 o.: Andrew Lichtenstein; S. 20 M.: Bernard Bisson/Sygma; S. 21 *Mandela Supporters*: Peter Turnley; S. 22 *Inuit*: Staffan Widstrand; S. 26 M. + S. 38 E: Hulton-Deutsch Collection; S. 43 u.: Pallava Bagla; S. 52 *christmas*: Jenny Evans/epa; S. 54 u.: Paul A. Souders; S. 66 o. re.: Kit Kittle; S. 69 *Raoul*: Ken Redding; S. 71 o. + S. 74: Patrick Ward; S. 75 *Schlange*: Theo Allofs; S. 76: Vera Devai/epa); **F1 Online**, Frankfurt/M (S. 10 o.); **Getty Images**, München (S. 10 *Funani*: Image Source Pink; S. 10 *Soweto*: Mark Peters; S. 66 *railway*: Chris Sattlberger; S. 75 o.: Scott Stulberg); **Dick Hemingway Photographs**, Toronto (S. 23 o. re.); **Inmagine**, London (S. 8 M. li., S. 9 M., S. 9 u. re., S. 15: Bananastock; S. 9 u. li.: Polkadot; S. 39 o., S. 40 o., S. 40 M.: Radius-images; S. 40 u.: thinkstock; S. 42 C: Inspirestock); **iStockphoto** (S. 45 o.: Jesse Smith; S. 69 *Jan & Berta*: Duncan Walker; S. 69 *Irina*: Tavrov Konstantin); **laif**, Köln (S. 43 o. re.: Butzmann); Courtesy **Arthur Mafokate / Gallo Music Publishers**, Südafrika (S. 16 u.); Courtesy of **John Marsden** (S. 83); **Masterfile**, Düsseldorf (S. 70); **McArthur** (S. 52: © 1979); **Chris McCarthy** (S. 36 M.); **Métis Matters Foundation of Alberta** (S. 25 M.); **Mobile Hamish** (S. 67 o.); Courtesy **Newfoundland and Labrador Tourism** (S. 51 li.); **Newspix/News Ltd**, Australien (S. 73: Manuela Cifra); Courtesy **Mitch Nur** (S. 56 *bullroarer*); **picture alliance**, Frankfurt/M (S. 21 *prison*: Krista Kennell/maxppp, *Button*: KPA/HIP/The British Museum; S. 22 *Ice hockey*: Icon SMI; S. 23 *Dion*: Schroewig/Cyberimage); **Photolibrary**, London (S. 7 *speaking*: Allan Danahar/Digital Vision, *listening*: Jack Hollingsworth/Photodisc, *reading*: Doug Menuez / Photodisc, *writing*: Heather Monahan Photography / Uppercut Images; S. 10 *Delani*: Creatas; S. 38.F: Hans-Peter Merten/Mauritius Die Bildagentur GmbH; S. 39 u. re.: Design Pics Inc; S. 42 B, S. 42 D, S. 57 *Liam*: Radius Images; S. 44: Image Source Limited; S. 50 o.: Pixland / Jupiter Images; S. 52 *Sydney*: Digital Vision; S. 53 *Canberra:* David Messent; S. 59 o.: Jules Frazier Photography/ Uppercut Images RF; S. 64: Kerstin Layer/Mauritius Die Bildagentur GmbH; S. 66 o. li.: Peter J. Robinsons/Australian Only; S. 68 o.: Image Source; S. 68 u.: BlueMoon Images; S. 75 M.: David Messent; S. 90 o.: Terry Vine/Blend Images Llc); **Random House Canada** (S. 43 *Buchcover*); **Reuters** (S. 67 M.: Dan Chung); **Royal Flying Doctor Service of Australia** (S. 73 *Logo*); **Schapowalow**, Hamburg (S. 8 u. re.: Robert Harding); Courtesy **Scholastic**, New York (S. 80, *Foto für das Cover*: Tatiana Sperhacke); **Shutterstock Inc.** New York (S. 6/7 + 69 *Weltkarte*: coko; S. 8 *Planet*: Ali Ender Birer, *Löwe*: Jonathan Heger; S. 9 *Flaggen Kanada, Australien*: Andrew Chin, *Israel, Südafrika*: Kurt De Bruyn; S. 13 *Hintergrund*: Perov Stanislav, *Pin-Nadeln*: BruceParrott, *Löwe auf T-shirt*: Black Ink Designers, Corp, *T-shirt*: Ronald Sumners; S. 22 *Vancouver*: kwest, *Flagge*: alysta, *The Rockies*: Ulrike Hammerich, *Prärie*: Tyler Olson; S. 23 *Hintergrund*: bluliq; S. 24 *Megan*: Charles T. Bennett, *Jake*: Ulrike Hammerich, *Jassim*: Tracy Whiteside, *Jill*: Harry Hu, *Carmen*: János Gehring; S. 27 *Hintergrund*: Armin Rose; S. 29 o.: Sofos Design, *Drumheller* (2): Marek Slusarczyk, *Drumheller* (5): John Kirinic, *Drumheller* (6): Jim White; S. 30 M.: Gail Johnson, *Flaggen* 1: Kurt De Bruyn, 2: Joel Calheiros, 3: Neo Edmund, 4 + 5: R. Gino Santa Maria, 6 + 9: Andrew Chin, 7 + 8: Alexander Zavadsky; S. 31 u.: July Flower; S. 34 *Hintergrund*: Ecoasis; S. 36-37 *Hintergrund*: Bruce Amos; S. 38 A: Jostein Hauge, 38 C: Martine Oger; S. 39 u. li.: Pierdelune; S. 41 o.: Julien Tromeur, *cool dress*: @erics, Exerc. 3-1: Andresr, 3-2 li.: @erics, 3-4: Najin, 3-5: James Thew; S. 42 A: Yuri Arcurs; S. 45 *Hintergrund*: sabri deniz kizil; S. 46: Teze; S. 52 *kookaburra*: Lee Torrens, *crocodiles*: Bryan Michael Dirk, *emu*: Eric Isselée, *Australian Rules*: Nicholas Rjabow, *cricket*: Lance Bellers, *rugby*: artproem, *boomerang*: Vladislav Gurfinkel, *kangaroos*: WizData, inc., *surfing*: Daniel Gustavsson; S. 53 *cockatoo*: Eric Isselée, S. 56 *drum*: Scott Leman, *boomerang*: David Franklin; S. 57 o.: Ashley Whitworth, *Hintergrund* u.: Jenny Solomon; S. 59 *Handy*: Elnur; S. 60 *Herz*: Manfred Steinbach, *Fahne*: First Class Photos PTY LTD; S. 66-67 *Hintergrund*: Nigel Paul Monckton; S. 66 *Sonnenbrille*: Peter Guess; S. 69 *textiles Muster*: Joan Kerrigan; S. 69 *Silke*: Yuri Arcurs, *Faisal*: Kirk Peart Professional Imaging, *Jason*: Alistair Cotton; S. 72: Mechanik; S. 77 o. li.: Boguslaw Mazur, o. re.: Miguel Angel Salinas Salinas); Courtesy of **South Africa Tourism** (S. 13 o.); **Students on ice** (S. 27 o. und u.); **Three dead Trolls in a Baggie** (S. 37 *CD-Cover*); **Tourism Australia** (S. 52 *Koala*); **transit** (S. 16 *Safari*: Peter Hirth); **Ullstein Bild**, Berlin (S. 22 *Bären*: Still Pictures; S. 23 *Adams*: ddp; S. 34 u.: Granger Collection; S. 57 *Tina Grove + Touristen*: Imagebroker.net); Courtesy of **Uluru-Kata Tjuta National Park** (S. 57 *map*); **Christian Williams**, Edinburgh (S. 22 *mounties*; S. 29 *Drumheller* (3); S. 31 o. + M.); **Vera Wohlfarth** (S. 11); **Christopher Woo**, Toronto (S. 43 o. li.); Courtesy **YFM radio** (S. 10).

u.= unten, o. = oben, re. = rechts, li. = links, M. = Mitte

Cover Henry Georgi / Avenue Images

TEXTQUELLEN

S. 53 (Statistik, Juli 2008): https://www.cia.gov/library/publications/the-world-factbook

S. 81 und 82: Excerpt from: *Tomorrow, when the war began* by John Marsden. Reprinted by permission of John Marsden.

LIEDQUELLEN

S. 36: *Don't call me Eskimo.* © Christ McCarthy

S. 37: *Canada's really big.* K + T: The Arrogant Worms. © The Arrogant Worms 1997

S. 67: *Treaty.* K + T: Yothu Yindi (Kellaway, Stuart Adam; Kelly, Paul Maurice; Marika, Witiyana Philip; Mununggurr, Milkayngu; Williams, Cal Standley; Yunupingu, Gurrumul; Yunupingu, Mandawuy Bakamana). OV: Paul Kelly Music, Sony Tunes Inc, W B Music Corp, Yothu Yindi Music Pty; SV: Neue Welt Musikverlag GmbH Co KG, Hamburg, und Sony/ATV Music Publishing (Germany) GmbH, Berlin